Understanding Enterprise SOA

(Enterprise Services-Oriented Architecture)

ERIC PULIER
HUGH TAYLOR

MANNING

Published by:
dreamtech PRESS

This edition has been published by arrangement with the **Manning Publications Co., USA.** andpublishedinIndiaby **DreamtechPr ess,19-A, AnsariRoad,Daryaganj,NewDelhi-110002.**

Edition : 2006

Printed at : Himal Impressions, New Delhi

contents

foreword

Over the past decade we have seen big improvements in productivity: in most sectors of the economy, people are doing more for less. Factory workers produce widgets faster, service workers solve problems more quickly, banks even clear checks faster. The process of integrating business software applications, however, has resisted this productivity trend: it seems just as slow and unproductive as ever to make one piece of software talk to another. Any promises of a silver bullet to solve integration problems sound like one of those hand-waving vendor fantasies that promise the moon but deliver the marsh.

I have worked in the business process and technology areas for several large companies including KMart, Office Depot, Charles Schwab, and Staples. In roles as diverse as head of a large direct-marketing organization (with a significant web-based business), CIO of one of the world's largest specialty retailers, or head of a multi-billion dollar global supply chain, I have seen millions of dollars spent integrating between modern and legacy systems and between internal and external applications. Until recently, it was impossible to improve the return on those investments or the certainty with which those investments might pay off. I believe the technology for solving those problems is finally here. It is a broad and complex subject called Enterprise Services-Oriented Architecture (SOA). Until recently, the subject was accessible only to the high priests of technology. I am excited that Eric Pulier has set out in this book to make the concept accessible to the general business audience.

I've known Eric Pulier for many years and have watched him build companies that helped solve large systems integration problems; he is uniquely qualified to deliver the SOA message. We both believe in the power of SOA and have worked together to deploy it in a variety of business settings. Unlike many other technology promises, SOA is real, the result of decades of evolution toward more agile and cost-effective enterprises. It requires a number of pieces of new technology infrastructure and, thankfully, the software market is providing those tools. More importantly, it requires business people to change the way they think about interactions among business processes; this book helps business people understand how to change that thinking.

Enterprise SOA is a subject that, by its very nature, cuts across a variety of disciplines and functional specialties, both in IT and in business. Opening up enterprise systems using the new standards is both exciting and challenging—it can be difficult to know where to start. This book takes a generalized approach that makes this subject matter understandable to a broad range of readers. At the same time, it is technical enough to be relevant for those who have to work with technologists to get the job done.

I will use this book to help drive even more use of services to increase productivity. And I hope that you too will find this book useful in taking your applications and business processes to the next level of productivity.

PAUL GAFFNEY
Executive Vice President,
Supply Chain
Staples, Inc.

preface

Service-oriented architecture (SOA) is a remarkable evolutionary step in technology's march toward one of its greatest unfulfilled goals: the ability to connect a wide variety of systems without proprietary software in order to achieve truly open interoperability.

At its core, SOA is a simple affair. Imagine two software programs that were written in different languages running on different operating systems. It has always been possible to establish a connection between two such programs using custom or proprietary code, but this approach has proven to be both costly and inefficient. Web services, which form the underpinning of SOA, have made it possible to create an operating connection between two pieces of software using a new common language known as XML. This is the promise of SOA.

For some, SOA is a great advance in computing. For others, it is the latest come-on from an industry that has seen its share of dark moments in the last decade. Whichever you believe, the reality is that SOA *is* happening. If you work in any sizable business, government, or nonprofit entity, you can be sure that SOA planning is underway in your workplace.

This book gives you, the business professional, the tools to make sense of both the corporate and technology issues involved in realizing return on investment from an enterprise SOA. This is a challenging proposition but, if done correctly, entirely possible. The tech world is abuzz with SOA-related conjecture, overeager vendors, ambiguous alliances, overblown paradigms, and a lot of hype. Some of it, I must confess, I've spun myself over the years. I am a vendor. I'm here to evangelize, a little, but also to caution you about the sensible, businesslike way to approach SOA. My goal is to help you confidently assess the best SOA options for your organization. SOA requires you to orient yourself quickly amid a great deal of market noise. I ought to know: This is my second time in a similar situation.

In 1999, I traveled the world on an IPO road show with a message heralding the exponential curve of Internet technology adoption in corporations and governments. The global imagination was running wild with the many implications of network standards coming of age. Every major newspaper, magazine, and television show took notice—the world was changing and apparently for the better!

Within months of the IPO, the company I had founded had achieved a market cap of more than $1.5 billion. The age of "Internet standards"—the common *lingua franca* of instantaneous global communication—had arrived. With the universal adoption of TCP/IP, HTML, HTTP, and web browsers, a set of standards was embraced that laid the foundation for a new era in computing. The result could only be unprecedented efficiency for business, education, health care, and government. The prospects were dazzling, and we had only explored the tip of the iceberg.

One year later, the tide turned. Enthusiasm for the explosive power of network technology reversed with the same ferocity that had fueled it months before. The new common wisdom was: The Internet was a fad, the benefits illusory; the analysts, entrepreneurs, engineers, venture capitalists, and financial markets were insane! The NASDAQ collapsed and continued to sink over the next three years so precipitously that every tenet of the initial promise fell into question. The counter reaction of the market was so severe that the Internet technologies seemed not only to be forgotten, but suspect at the core. Rather than weed out overvalued stocks, poor business plans, inexperienced executives, or immature technologies, the market condemned everything.

Clearly, there was merit in bringing the market back to earth. Valuations were high and rounds of venture capital funding, rather than business models, were sustaining many poorly conceived companies. But had the "irrational exuberance" been wholly irrational? The answer will surprise many: the initial optimism was justified. In fact, the potential had been understated. As we will explore in this book, the fruition of the Internet's promise is coming and the resulting value creation will dwarf even the boldest estimates of the past.

The power of network technology manifests in three distinct forms of connectivity: person-to-person, person-to-computer, and computer-to-computer, and each of these carries a myriad of cultural and economic implications. It is the third form of communication, computer-to-computer, that I will explore in this book. It is not only the least developed so far, but also the most valuable and essential.

Enabling electronic person-to-person communication via e-mail has become a staple of our consumer and business world. It seems inconceivable that just a decade ago this capability was relegated to a select few. Seemingly second nature in our lives, e-mail is a recent innovation based entirely on network standards. It was not immediately obvious that it would be possible to get a message from one person to another, without a direct line between them, without knowing what kind of client software they might have, or what kind of computer they might be using. By building on the same standards, providers of e-mail software and services have thrived on the basis of full interoperability. You can e-mail anyone anywhere in the world without knowing the recipient's geographic location or computer platform, and your message will arrive and become available within seconds.

Similarly, Internet standards ushered in another great shift in computing capability—the transition from client/server to browser-based applications. This enabled the utilization of software over a network without specific code on the user's side of the conversation. Within a few years, the World Wide Web linked hundreds of millions of computers and applications via browser-based interfaces, providing hundreds of millions of remote transactions throughout the world, none of which involves a mandate for specialized software to enable interaction. Again, it was only a decade ago that this capability was nothing more than a novelty to a select group of early adopters, scientists, and inventors. Today, the world is fundamentally different as citizens of countries in every part of the globe are empowered by access to the collective knowledge base of the human race.

The staggering implications of these technologies can be traced to one core principle: network standards. E-mail can be sent and delivered to any e-mail recipient across providers, computers, devices, and so forth, because everyone has adopted the same language of communication. Websites can be viewed by anyone with any standard browser for the same reason. It would not be in any business's interest (be it IBM, Microsoft, or the U.S. government) to push their own standards into this mix, for in so doing they would only be harming their own capabilities to leverage the power of interoperability. If Acme E-mail Company generated e-mails that could only be read by other Acme E-mail Company users, this company would quickly become irrelevant. In a spectacular cycle of enlightened self-interest, every major company in the world has built on top of standards which have ushered a potentially exponential release of value from investments in information technology.

If we take this trend to the next level of execution, we soon arrive at the ultimate fruition of the promise of these standards: application-to-application interoperability. The value of software in a networked economy will grow in direct proportion to how well it interoperates with other software via standards. As we will see in this book, this same principle applies not just to how software is built but also to how companies and governments build efficient processes in order to compete.

Open interoperability is the mother lode of potential value in information technology. While e-mail and browser-based applications are significant, the view that these technologies would change the face of business was the most misunderstood concept of the bubble era, leaving confused executives and investors scrambling to understand how or when a website would affect their business in some mysterious, profound manner. The unrealized promise came not from falling short in these aspirations (they're delivering plenty) but from the immaturity of the standards in the area of computer-to-computer communication.

As "application" interoperability standards mature, the mystery is resolved—for it is in this equation that the heralded benefits are revealed. Organizations that take advantage of this evolution in computing will compete and those that do not will find themselves in the same position as the Acme E-mail Company: relegated to a stiflingly small world while competitors around them thrive in the next era of global, hyper-efficient networked computing. This is the power of the service-oriented architecture.

To understand enterprise SOA, you must get the full technological and political flavor of what can happen when a large organization makes a commitment to this exciting but challenging new technology. That is the goal of this book in presenting the case study of Titan Insurance, a large company grappling with many real-world issues that come up when open standards are introduced into a complex environment.

ERIC PULIER

acknowledgments

It takes the contributions and talents of many people to realize a book that covers an emerging, complex technology. I am deeply indebted to those who helped in this effort, especially my coauthor, Hugh Taylor, who worked closely with me and helped give form to many aspects of the book, in addition to creating all the graphics that you see in it.

This book would not have been possible without the input and guidance of my colleagues at SOA Software: Alistair Farquharson, Rasta Mansour, Pranav Parekh, Ramesh Sakala, David Weil, Michael Gibson, Ananth Arunachalam, Abongwa Ndumu, Michael Berkovich, Bill Knutson, and Mark Shvets.

At Manning Publications, I am very grateful for the professional guidance of publisher Marjan Bace and development editor Jackie Carter, as well as the expertise of everyone on the production team, especially technical editor, Jeff Cunningham. I would also like to thank the peer reviewers who gave valuable feedback at different stages of manuscript development: Nikhilesh Krishnamurthy, James McGovern, Jeff Machols, Henry Chiu, Tom Valesky, Keyur Shah, Jamiel Sheikh, Doug Warren, and Jason Bloomberg.

about this book

This book is for anyone in the business world or in the public sector who needs to make sense of the new emerging standards for virtually all major information technology decisions. For business professionals, this book is meant to explain and clarify—in business terms—the way web services and SOA work in a business setting. For IT professionals, the book provides a business-oriented overview of SOA.

HOW THE BOOK IS ORGANIZED

The book is organized around the two critical areas necessary in realizing an enterprise SOA: technology and people. The nature of SOA is integrative; by definition, SOA pushes boundaries. Enterprise SOA cuts across multiple lines of business and technological disciplines. In the book this is amply illustrated through the presentation of the Titan Insurance case study, an up-close look at an insurance company that is suffering from the IT aftermath of a troubled merger.

In addition to an Introduction that sets out the parameters of Titan Insurance, and provides the back story, the book consists of two parts:

Part 1 "Understanding the technology of enterprise SOA" delves into the technological aspects of web services, as well as other technological issues that underlie the enterprise SOA. Chapters 1, 2, and 3 provide a broad overview of web services, how they work, and what they can do for your business. Chapter 4 introduces the concept of the service-oriented architecture. Chapters 5, 6, 7, and 8 explore how the enterprise SOA changes the terrain of enterprise application integration, software development, business-to-business commerce, business process management, and real-time operations. Chapters 9 and 10 introduce the extremely important discussions of security and management of enterprise SOA. Chapters 11 and 12 look at SOA networks and utility computing, two deployment scenarios that are likely to be on your horizon if you are considering an SOA.

Part 2 "Understanding the people and process of enterprise SOA, returns to the Titan case in full depth and provides a thorough look at the political, personal, and technological factors that arise when implementing an enterprise SOA at a real company. Chapter 13 looks at realizing Titan's wish list for its SOA and begins to sort out how to deal with the individual players involved in the process. Chapter 14 continues with a description of how we achieved consensus among the players about how to pursue an effective SOA. Chapter 14 also introduces the "four P's"—people, pilot, plan, and proceed—my suggested four-stage process for best practices in enterprise SOA. Chapters 15 and 16 go into more depth on how the training and pilot planning process works. In addition, these chapters outline a best practices approach to identifying the applications in an enterprise that are best suited for exposure as web services, a process I call service discovery. Chapter 17 examines platform selection and establishment of project goals and measurements of success. Chapter 18 concludes the book with a look at how Titan Insurance has moved forward with its SOA plan.

ABOUT THE GRAPHICS

In the illustrations used in this book, several images appear repeatedly, representing typical situations that occur in corporate information technology. The following is meant to serve as a guide to the graphics and symbols you will find as you read on.

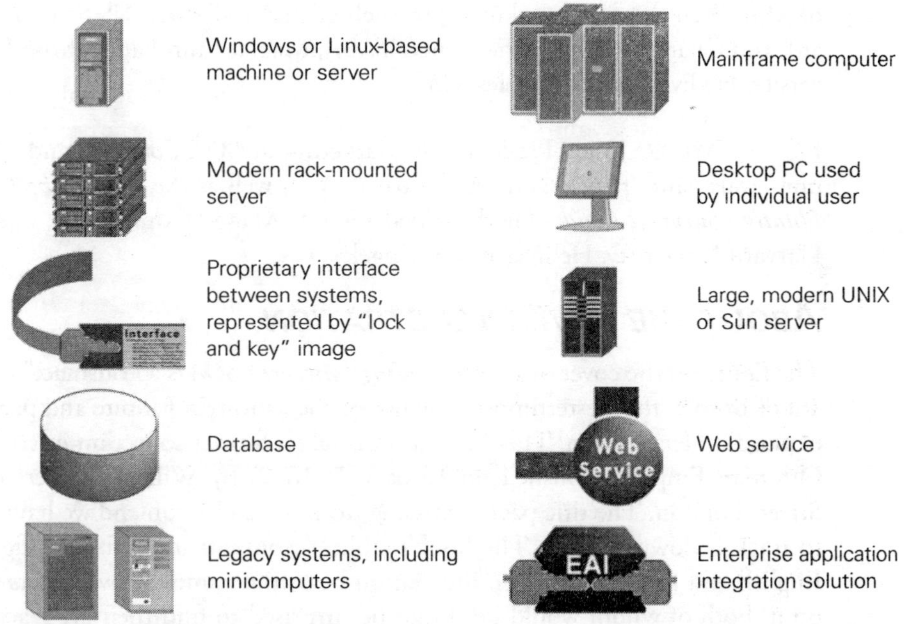

AUTHOR ONLINE

Purchase of *Understanding Enterprise SOA* includes free access to a private web forum run by Manning Publications where you can make comments about the book, ask technical questions, and receive help from the authors and from other users. To access the forum and subscribe to it, point your web browser to www.manning.com/pulier.

This page provides information on how to get on the forum once you are registered, what kind of help is available, and the rules of conduct on the forum.

Manning's commitment to our readers is to provide a venue where a meaningful dialog between individual readers and between readers and the authors can take place. It is not a commitment to any specific amount of participation on the part of the authors, whose contribution to the AO remains voluntary (and unpaid). We suggest you try asking the authors some challenging questions lest their interest stray!

The Author Online forum and the archives of previous discussions will be accessible from the publisher's website for as long as the book is in print.

ABOUT THE AUTHORS

ERIC PULIER Founder and Executive Chairman of SOA Software and a widely recognized pioneer and visionary in the world of information technology. Named one of 30 e-Visionaries by VAR Business, Eric is a featured speaker at industry conferences and events and a member of the IBM's UDDI Advisory Community. He leads SOA Software's trailblazing efforts to develop breakthrough solutions for the management of XML Web Services, working with such clients as Toyota, US Steel, Hewlett Packard, and Charles Schwab. Eric earned his BA, Magna Cum Laude, from Harvard University. He lives in Los Angeles, CA.

HUGH TAYLOR Vice President of Marketing at SOA Software and the author of numerous white papers and articles on SOA, as well as the book, *The Hollywood Job Hunter's Survival Guide*. Hugh earned his BA, Magna Cum Laude, and MBA from Harvard University. He lives in Los Angeles, CA.

ABOUT THE COVER ILLUSTRATION

The figure on the cover of *Understanding Enterprise SOA* is a "Bosniac," or an inhabitant of Bosnia, the westernmost province of the Ottoman Empire and part of the state of Bosnia-Herzegovina. The illustration is taken from a collection of costumes of the Ottoman Empire published on January 1, 1802, by William Miller of Old Bond Street, London. The title page is missing from the collection and we have been unable to track it down to date. The book's table of contents identifies the figures in both English and French, and each illustration bears the names of two artists who worked on it, both of whom would no doubt be surprised to find their art gracing the front cover of an information technology book...two hundred years later.

The collection was purchased by a Manning editor at an antiquarian flea market in the "Garage" on West 26th Street in Manhattan. The seller was an American based in Ankara, Turkey, and the transaction took place just as he was packing up his stand for the day. The Manning editor did not have on his person the substantial amount of cash that was required for the purchase and a credit card and check were both politely turned down. With the seller flying back to Ankara that evening the situation was getting hopeless. What was the solution? It turned out to be nothing more than an old-fashioned verbal agreement sealed with a handshake. The seller simply proposed that the money be transferred to him by wire and the editor walked out with the bank information on a piece of paper and the portfolio of images under his arm. Needless to say, we transferred the funds the next day, and we remain grateful and impressed by this unknown person's trust in one of us. It recalls something that might have happened a long time ago.

The pictures from the Ottoman collection, like the other illustrations that appear on our covers, bring to life the richness and variety of dress customs of two centuries ago. They recall the sense of isolation and distance of that period—and of every other historic period except our own hyperkinetic present.

Dress codes have changed since then and the diversity by region, so rich at the time, has faded away. It is now often hard to tell the inhabitant of one continent from another. Perhaps, trying to view it optimistically, we have traded a cultural and visual diversity for a more varied personal life. Or a more varied and interesting intellectual and technical life.

We at Manning celebrate the inventiveness, the initiative, and, yes, the fun of the computer business with book covers based on the rich diversity of regional life of two centuries ago, brought back to life by the pictures from this collection.

introduction

A TIGHT COUPLING CASE STUDY

For decades, IT departments have labored toward the goal of achieving efficiency for the benefit of the corporation, offering the flexibility to adapt to changing business needs rather than constraining them. For the most part, these aspirations have gone largely unrealized—the result of incompatible systems and architectures that harden business processes rather than free them to become agile and responsive to the market. This book seeks to shed light on an evolution in the way IT is approached and to offer hope that the goals of the industry may finally be in sight.

In writing a book of this kind, it is tempting to stay in the relative safety of the whiteboard. Colored arrows and paradigms are easy. Too easy, really. Actual IT is challenging. For this reason, we have decided to present the issue of making business sense of service-oriented architecture (SOA) through an in-depth case study.

What follows is an example of what an SOA project looks like at a real business. To this end, we are going to spend much of this book inside the walls of Titan Insurance, a large company that is grappling with the many real-world issues that come up when open standards are introduced into a complex environment. Titan Insurance is a case study based on our actual experiences, but the names have been changed to protect, well, us.

AUTHORS' NOTE Though the book is written together, for the sake of simplicity and style, the authors henceforth refer to themselves in a singular voice.

MERGING TWO INSURANCE COMPANIES

I first heard about Titan Insurance about a year ago when a former colleague, Jay Franklin, who had recently been hired as Titan's senior vice president of architecture, called me for advice. Jay was evaluating Titan's IT options as the company began to upgrade and integrate its legacy systems following a merger. The company was experiencing a number of serious operational and financial difficulties, many of which could be traced back to problems with IT. He confessed that he was a bit stumped about how to proceed, and he wanted my insights regarding how Titan could improve its situation. We agreed to meet for lunch, and over some outstanding sushi, he told the following story.

Titan is a medium-sized insurance company that came into being two years earlier as the result of the merger between Hermes Casualty and Apollo Insurance. Titan writes $1.5 billion a year in auto and homeowner policies to nearly a million policyholders in five different states. The company has three thousand employees spread out among headquarters and two regional offices.

Hermes had been the bigger of the two companies in the merger, and Apollo had experienced the fate of the smaller entity in these kinds of deals. The management of Hermes was in power at Titan, while the management team from Apollo was in second position. In the IT area, Dorothy "Dot" Bartlett, who had served as CIO of Apollo, was now CTO of Titan. Henri-Pierre ("H.P.") Wei had been CIO of Hermes and remained in that position with Titan. Of the two of them, Dot clearly had the superior command of actual IT issues, whereas H.P. was more of an executive management figure with experience in running large organizations. My colleague Jay reported to Dot.

Systemically speaking, the company was your average IT disaster. Disparate legacy operated semi-independently among divergent corporate cultures, with limited budgets and regulatory mandates further cramping everyone's style. Regulations mandated absolute process integrity and auditable data flows within and between processes. Each of the former businesses still operated in nearly complete IT autonomy. As figure 1 shows, each of the former Apollo and Hermes IT organizations operated separately and still reported to their old bosses. However, this split between the two organizations existed for a good reason. The two companies had approached system architecture completely differently. As a result, integration of applications and implementation of new requirements had not gone much further than a long series of frustrating meetings. In any event, there was only limited desire for the two groups to work together, but even if they had both wanted to get together and collaborate on IT, it would have been nearly impossible.

According to Jay, insurance companies usually have two major areas of operation, policy and claims, each of which is supported by a set of IT systems. The policy system manages the insurance policies for the insured customers of the company and keeps track of the type of policy that the customer has purchased, the date it was purchased, its premium, and so on. The claims systems deal with the filing, tracking, investigating, and paying of insurance claims. Both groups of systems have to interface with the insurance company's financial systems.

Hermes's legacy architecture

Hermes Insurance had built its IT infrastructure around a centralized, "monolithic" mainframe-based platform from InsurTech, a British software company that specializes in insurance industry solutions. The InsurTech solution, which the Hermes IT staff jokingly referred to as the "HAL 9000" after the infamous computer in *2001, A Space Odyssey*, handled all the policy, quoting, billing, underwriting, and claims work

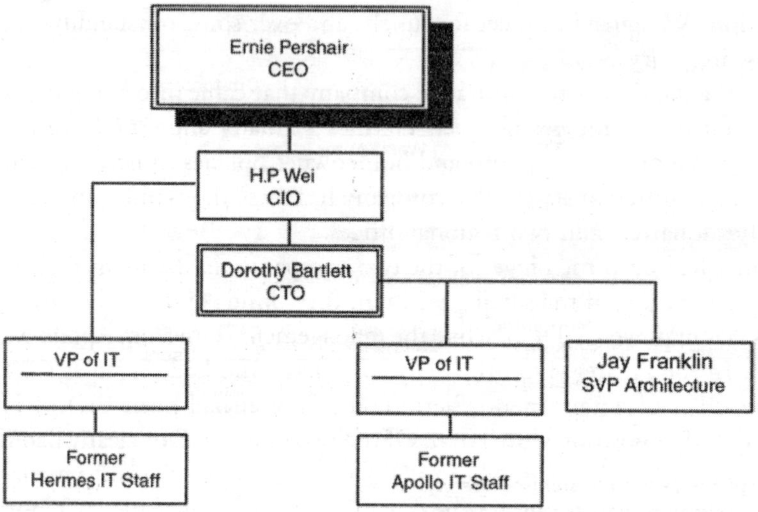

Figure 1 Titan's IT organization chart reflects the influence of Hermes insurance in the merger of Hermes and Apollo in the formation of Titan Insurance. Hermes's CIO, H.P. Wei, is now CIO of Titan, and his old team reports to him. The former Apollo IT team reports to Dot Bartlett, who is now CTO of Titan, and second-in-command in terms of IT decision making at Titan.

for the company. The system applications, which had been in use since 1979, were written in a language for which it was getting increasingly difficult to find developers. This is typical with many legacy systems; though the "guts" of the system functioned well, InsurTech had been hinting for several years that it was going to phase out support for the product in the near future.

Secondary systems connected with the InsurTech system through custom interfaces. As figure 2 shows, a series of interfaces connected the InsurTech system with Hermes's financial system and an interactive voice response (IVR) system for customers to find out the status of their policies. Hermes agents and customer service staff used a proprietary "fat client" terminal emulation application. The terminal emulation software was written for use on the Windows 95 operating system. At the time of the merger, Hermes had upgraded to more recent versions of Windows.

Hermes maintained a marketing-oriented website that was completely separate from the main systems of the business. There had been discussions about connecting the website to other systems, but the decision to do so had been postponed at the time of the merger.

Apollo's legacy architecture

Apollo had approached IT differently. Its legacy architecture was more distributed than that of Hermes. Apollo had separate systems, each from different vendors. Policy, claims, and finance were all connected by a proprietary enterprise application

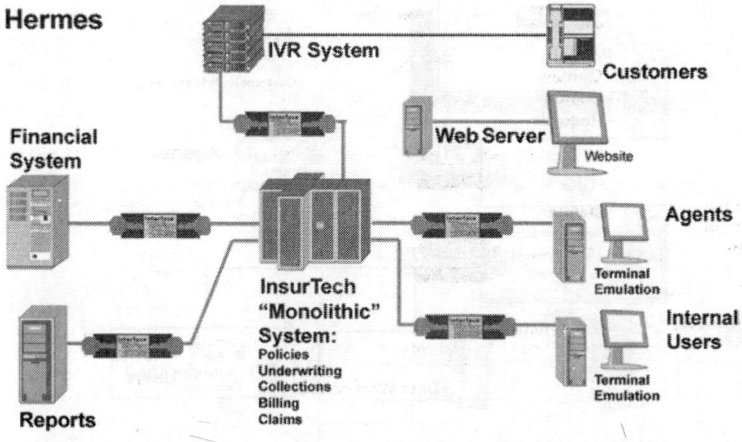

Figure 2 Hermes's legacy architecture was built around a 1979 monolithic insurance industry solution from InsurTech, a British software company that is planning to discontinue service on the installed version that Hermes is operating. All other systems connect to the InsurTech solution through custom interfaces.

integration (EAI) system, in which the company had made a significant investment. Internal users operated a fat client to access the three major systems. The fat client had been developed for Windows 2000, which is the operating system that Apollo staff used on their desktops. The company's agents had web access to the policy and quoting systems through a J2EE application running on an application server. The same application server also provided customers with a website for premium and billing information, though not online payment options. A proprietary electronic document system fed incoming documents into the claims system. All systems fed into a data warehouse, as shown in figure 3.

INTEGRATION OF PROCESSES AND OPERATIONS

Jay explained to me that the separate, parallel sets of IT systems from the companies that combined to create Titan caused numerous problems for Titan's overall IT situation. The company was facing trouble from system incompatibility, data "silos," and application incompatibility, among other issues.

The most basic problem for Titan stemmed from tight coupling. Because the former Hermes and Apollo insurance companies had pursued different approaches to enterprise architecture, the Titan IT department had to contend with parallel systems for each major area of business. In policy, claims, and finance, Titan was operating two separate systems, each running on a different operating system, hardware platform, and programming language. There was no simple or cost-effective way to break

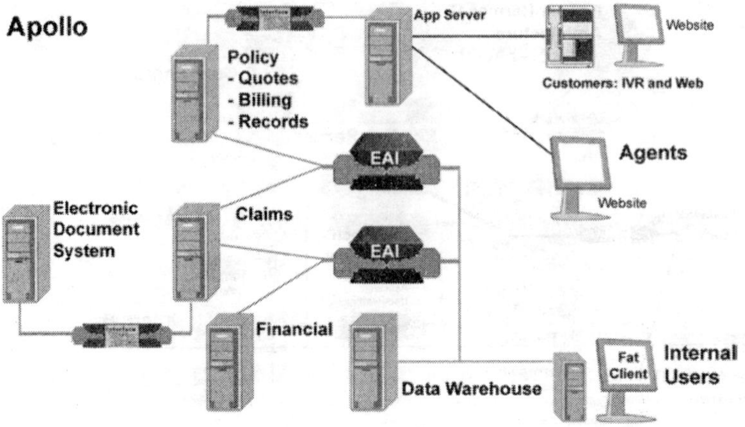

Figure 3 Apollo's legacy architecture relied on a set of distributed systems, connected mostly through proprietary EAI modules, to handle the core functions of policy, claims, and finance.

the tight couplings and establish seamless, real-time communication between these systems. The result was a pair of data silos for policy, claims, and finance.

In the case of policies, former Hermes policyholders' data was stored on the InsurTech "monolithic" mainframe system in the old Hermes infrastructure. The former Apollo policyholders' data was stored on Apollo's Windows-based policy database. For the first year of Titan's existence, the two databases had remained completely separate, with policy underwriting members checking each database separately to ensure that no policy was duplicated from one system to the other. In addition to being cumbersome, this approach did not guarantee good data integrity. Indeed, an audit of the two systems revealed hundreds of errors and duplications of policy information.

Finally, after a year of work and at the cost of nearly a million dollars, the former Hermes application development group wrote a custom patch in the mainframe language that performed a daily database update and reconciliation between the former Hermes and Apollo policy databases. As figure 4 shows, the two systems were now connected by yet another proprietary interface. The two systems continued to run separately and the policy underwriting staff still had to access each database separately.

Jay was confused about why the Hermes team was selected to write the patch in the old mainframe language. I explained that, in my opinion, although it was a mistake to create more proprietary interfaces in an essentially obsolete language, the act was a reflection of the political dominance of the Hermes group in Titan's organization. The Hermes people had close relationships with H.P. Wei, so when the issue of data integrity had come up, they had suggested right away a solution that they knew they could deliver. And, not so coincidentally, it was a solution that only they knew how to write and maintain. Jay was beginning to get what I was saying: "They're

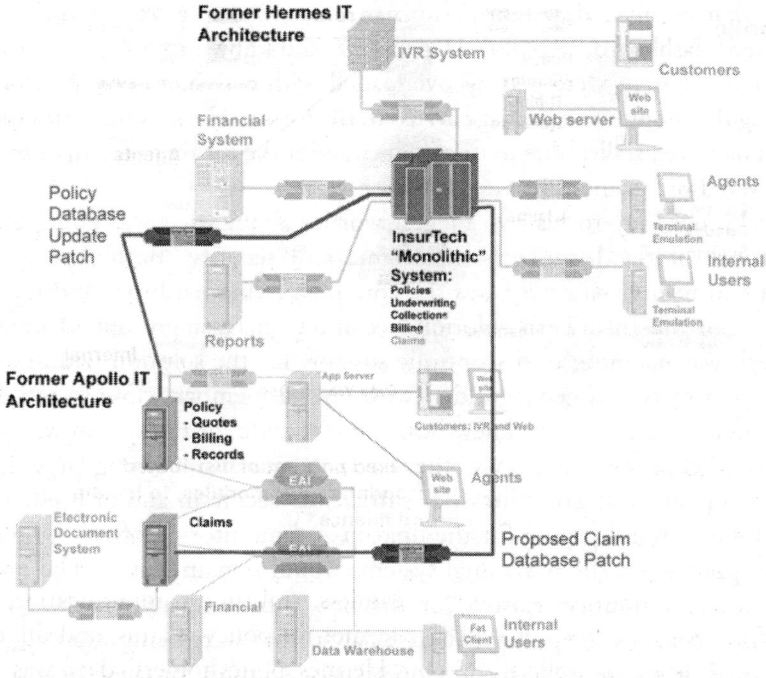

Figure 4 Because of disaggregation of databases, the former Hermes IT team developed a custom patch that updates and synchronizes the former Hermes and Apollo databases using a daily upload of new data and comparison between the two databases.

building job security with that patch as much as anything else." I told him that yes, companies are made up of people, and people often take self-interested action that may or may not be beneficial to the enterprise overall. Often these decisions are subtle and not even consciously motivated by self-interest, but the result is a deepening of the mess.

Jay's main concern was that the Hermes group was preparing to develop another patch to connect to connect Hermes's monolithic InsurTech legacy system with the old Apollo claims database. There was a clear need for a solution—the claims management staff was having trouble keeping track of claims using the two systems in parallel. Examples of the problem abounded. In more than one case, a claim had been paid twice.

"Don't get me started on change management," Jay said. "We have a long change request list for the claims system—among others—but we can't do anything until we resolve the patch issue. Then, even if they do the patch, it will still be extremely complicated and challenging to make changes to the two systems simultaneously."

Jay described further problems at Titan with regard to monitoring of the infrastructure management and operational monitoring. Apollo had invested in a software package that monitored system performance across the entire enterprise. With this centralized "dashboard," Apollo's IT people would know immediately if a server went down or if a system were getting overloaded with activity. There had been talk of extending the monitoring package across to the former Hermes infrastructure, but the decision had been stalled due to uncertainty about the future of the mainframe system that powered the former Hermes operation.

That brought Jay to his two biggest worries about what was going on at Titan: obsolescence of the InsurTech mainframe and security. Both worries were well grounded in reality. Not only was the core mainframe hardware and operating system that ran the InsurTech solution becoming increasingly out of date, but also InsurTech was planning to discontinue support for the solution within a few years. The Hermes team was getting older, with several members close to retirement age. Finding new developers who knew how to write code for the system was going to be a major challenge. Security, Jay's other concern, was also looming large. Each of the former company's infrastructures was sufficiently secure in and of itself, and as long as Titan didn't mind paying for the upkeep and monitoring of two wholly separate security apparatuses, the individual systems would remain secure. The problem was that no security solution existed for the new intracompany, machine-to-machine connections (such as the policy database patch) that were being exposed. Of course, as Jay noted, it was possible to develop security features for these new connections, but the challenge was to create a security infrastructure that was simple to manage, maintain, and change.

Managing Titan's operations

Jay told me that Titan's tight coupling–based IT problems were causing trouble outside of the IT department as well. Indeed, numerous operational aspects of the company were being negatively affected by the difficulties in integrating the systems of the two former companies. With the legacy systems still not integrated after two years, Titan was in effect operating as two separate companies united in name only. Management was seeing evidence of this problem in customer service, sales, and finance.

According to Jay, Titan's two customer service groups—the former Hermes and Apollo—each operated well on its own, but their lack of coordination caused many problems with Titan's customers. On a typical day, thousands of customers called the company to inquire about policy details, billing and accounting issues, and claims. The customer service representatives who answered the calls used desktop PCs to look up the customer information in order to respond to inquiries. When the companies had operated separately, each had had quite good customer service performance. Now, however, customer service performance was suffering.

Because Hermes and Apollo had each used its own proprietary fat client on customer service reps' desktops to access the policy and claims databases, it was not practical for a former Hermes customer service rep to look up a former Apollo customer's information. Nor was it practical to install both fat clients on the desktop of each of

Titan's customer service reps. The Hermes client was a mainframe "terminal emulation" program that ran on Windows 98. The Apollo client was developed for Windows 2000. It was not possible to install the Windows 2000 client on the old Hermes machines without upgrading all the machines to Windows 2000. Although it was possible to do the upgrade, H.P. Wei wanted to upgrade everyone to Windows XP at the same time. The costs and hassle involved in upgrading 1,500 desktops to Windows 2000 and then again to XP in a short period of time did not seem to be worth it.

While it was theoretically possible to install the Hermes terminal emulation client on the desktops of the Apollo customer service reps, it was not realistic or desirable to train all of the former Apollo customer service people to use the terminal emulation and have them toggle back and forth between the applications as they worked. Nor was it was desirable to set up a situation where the IT department would have to support twice as many terminal emulation clients on new desktops where they might create system conflicts.

There was a simple workaround for this problem: Upon hearing the policy number, which identified the customer as either being from Hermes or Apollo, the customer service rep would know immediately if he or she could look up the customer's record. If necessary, the customer service rep would transfer the customer call to the other customer service group and let them handle the customer.

This approach had several problems, though. It was costly to have the extra steps of looking up the policy and transferring the call built into each customer service inquiry. Customers grew irritable having to wait on hold longer because of the increased time required to process each call. And customer service management had no real sense of how well each customer service unit was performing.

Titan's agents were having a similar problem. Because the Apollo agents were able to access customer information through a website, it was relatively simple to extend access to Apollo customer, policy, and claim information to the former Hermes agents. And, again, while it was possible to install the Hermes terminal emulation application on the agents' desktops, it was not practical to train all of the agents to use the software. In addition, the terminal emulation software was not configured to work securely over HTTP outside of the enterprise domain. Fixing the security problem would have been costly and time consuming. As a result, Titan's agents were placing many more calls to customer service to get help with customer questions than in the past.

Overall, the increased agent call volume and higher rate of call transfers internally due to incompatible fat clients was creating a situation where Titan customers were experiencing longer wait times on hold. The vice president in charge of customer service was starting to complain that his phone bills were growing each month while customer complaints were increasing. It was possible to hire more customer service reps to handle the longer call queues, but that was specifically against the goals of the merged companies.

According to Jay, the two IT groups had met repeatedly to discuss a solution to the problem. The most expedient action was to quickly install a special EAI module from the vendor that had already connected most of Apollo's systems. The new EAI module would enable the developers to create a new fat client that would allow the former Apollo customer service reps to access Hermes's InsurTech mainframe without having to use the terminal emulation client. In turn, as shown in figure 5, the former Hermes customer service reps could access the Apollo systems using a separate fat client.

To connect the former Apollo agents to Hermes's InsurTech mainframe, the IT groups contemplated creating an interface between Apollo's application server and the InsurTech system. The former Apollo agents could then use their browsers to access the mainframe.

Though this was a possible solution, Jay told me, it was an expensive way to get to a fairly poor result. In the end, each agent and customer service rep would still have to use two clients to access two separate sets of systems. The project was estimated to take nine months to complete at a cost of over half a million dollars for outside consultants who would have to be brought in to develop some of the solution. Finally,

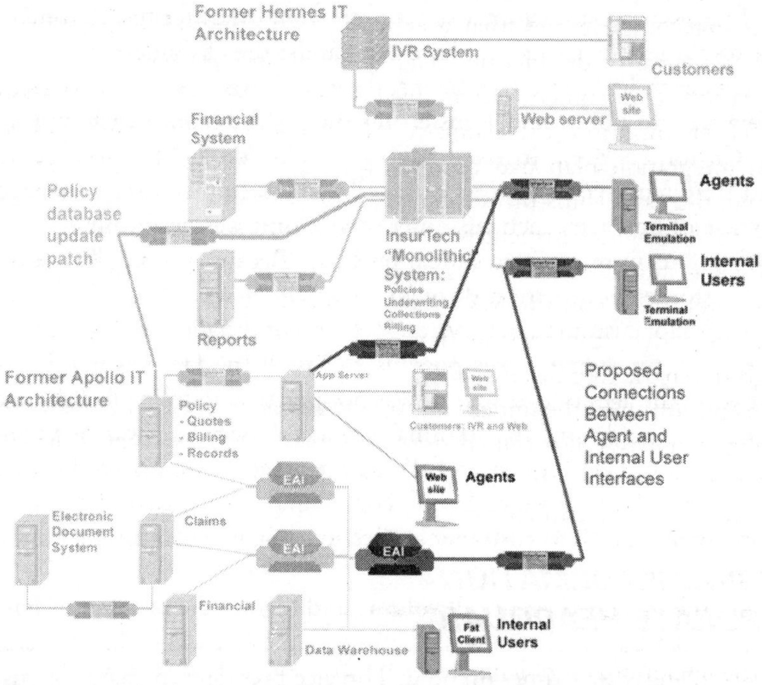

Figure 5 To correct a major set of problems in customer service and agency interactions, Titan was considering developing custom interfaces to connect the existing "fat client" applications used by both the former Apollo and Hermes customer service staff and agents to their respective counterparts within the IT infrastructure.

the solution would result in Titan buying another EAI module, with attendant maintenance fees, which the company had not originally planned to do.

Claims processing, Jay continued, was hampered by the various approaches taken by the two former companies. Apollo had invested in an electronic document management system that enabled a claims processing staffer to access any written document related to a claim using a proprietary electronic document client on his or her PC. The system worked quite well for Apollo, and helped the company save millions of dollars in the storage and retrieval of paper documents used in claims processing. The Apollo claims management cubicles were conspicuously free of paper, whereas the Hermes claims processors appeared to be buried in piles of paper and file folders.

The problem in claims processing was that the two claims-processing organizations could not be integrated because of the divergence in the methodologies. One suggested solution Jay related was to migrate all new claims onto the Apollo electronic document system and let the old Hermes claims atrophy away until they were all finished. This solution was not ideal because the Apollo claims staff was substantially smaller than the Hermes staff and could not possible handle the complete claim volume on its own. That, in combination with the political reality that it was Apollo, not Hermes, that was likely to trim its staff after the merger, would require that most of the Hermes claims-processing staff would have to be upgraded to the electronic document system and trained on its use. Like other issues pending in the IT organization, the claims-processing matter was deferred until a comprehensive integration plan had been developed and ratified by management. Until that time, the two claims-processing organizations operated in parallel.

The marketing department was suffering its share of IT-related problems as well. One problem was the Titan website. Unable to fully integrate the former Apollo and Hermes sites, the Titan site was a lesser version of each, lacking much in the way of useful interactive features that connected with the policy and claims systems. Though the marketing department had grand plans for the Titan website, its realization was put off until the underlying architectural issues could be solved. Overlaps in the policy databases also caused duplication in marketing efforts. Many customers were getting the same brochure or sales phone call twice, which was both a waste of money and a nuisance to customers.

MISSING INFORMATION AT CORPORATE HEADQUARTERS

All of the operational problems stemming from IT incompatibility were resulting in a far more serious problem for Titan. The reality was that the business was operating as two completely separate organizations that were joined in name only. That alone was a big problem, but the issue that was really causing heartburn for Ernie Pershair, the CEO of Titan Insurance, was the double whammy of poor visibility into operations combined with a nearly complete lack of synergy in the postmerger company. Pershair had sold the merger to Hermes's stockholders by promising them big reductions in operating expense from postmerger synergies and efficiencies. Now, two years after the merger, very few of these efficiencies had been realized.

Titan's finance department did not receive timely reports on the performance of the company overall. Instead, they got separate reports from each of the former companies in formats that were not compatible. The two companies had not set up reporting to track spending and revenue in the same way, so each set of financial reports needed to be manually reconciled before top management could view integrated financial data for the business. This caused a management problem—delayed and incomplete financial information did not allow effective corporate management. And, with the Sarbanes–Oxley corporate governance regulations coming into effect, there were serious issues relating to compliance coming up for Pershair and others on his team.

In pure financial terms, too, the IT-related problems at Titan were causing serious problems. Lagging performance in the customer service area and claims processing, as discussed earlier, were costly in terms of customer relationships as well as high overhead. The merger plan had called for the elimination of a certain percentage of redundant staff in customer service and claims processing, but none of these reductions had been carried out. In actuality, the company was considering hiring more staff to compensate for the operational problems caused by the lack of integration.

The IT budget, too, was looking pretty dismal to top management. At the time of the merger, IT had been neglected as a major topic of discussion. The lawyers and investment bankers who had driven the merger forward had taken the attitude "It'll all get worked out by the folks in white lab coats so we don't have to care." They just assumed that IT would sort itself out. It always did, didn't it? Jay rolled his eyes in exasperation as he recounted what he had heard about these deliberations. "They did the deal on the premise that two totally different IT architectures could be integrated just like that," he said with a snap of his fingers. "They didn't take the time to understand the enterprise architectures of the two companies."

The postmerger IT budget was, not surprisingly, just about exactly the sum of the two former companies' respective IT budgets. There had been no staff reductions at all. Even after retirements and resignations, each position had filled again because the workload was still high—indeed, it was higher than before because of the development of the new interfaces. Software license and maintenance fees were still exactly what they were before the merger.

After carefully considering his options, I recommended to Jay a potential solution that could sidestep many of these issues. Luckily, Jay had come to me in 2003 as opposed to 1996. Indeed, Jay's issues were tailor-made for the advances in computing standards that had matured in just the past few years.

Realizing the wish list

"Don't get me wrong," Jay wanted to explain. "The people I work with are not stupid. Far from it. They are some of the best in their field. They simply have never faced this kind of integration challenge before and the costs of following our typical path are just not acceptable."

"What are you hoping to accomplish in the next 12 months?" I asked.

"Well," he said, taking a folded piece of paper out of his pocket, "we have a wish list." He spread the paper out in front of me. It read:

1. Lower the IT budget.
2. Enable telephone and web access to all policy information for both agents and policyholders.
3. Develop a single application through which any employee or agent can access any claim or policy information from any location.
4. Implement a seamless, unified claims-processing system.
5. Develop a single claims payment check-printing system.
6. Implement a single bill-printing system.
7. Create a single payment and credit card processing system.
8. Develop a company portal.
9. Develop an agent portal.

And the final wish: Ensure that the systems are flexible for change in the future.

I studied the list. "What are you considering to make all of this happen?"

"Well," Jay said. "There are a number of options, but most of them are either too expensive or create more problems than they solve." He then proceeded to explain the proposals that Titan had received from outside vendors to solve their IT problems.

Mammoth migration

A handful of global IT giants had presented Titan with proposals that called for a wholesale migration of all of Titan's systems to new platforms based on the vendors' core technologies. This was, as Jay noted, a viable solution, but highly problematic. For one thing, the lowest bid of the group was in excess of $10 million, and some were a great deal higher than that. All of the proposals included years of intensive service and support contracts, which were also in the millions of dollars. And the migration project was estimated to take at least two years and would likely take longer. The translation of complex business logic between old and new systems was a subjective process and highly prone to error. Then, while the migration was going on, it was highly probable that requirements would change, and people would come and go from both Titan and the vendor. The end result, many people warned, would be a situation where Titan might spend $20 million or more over a five-year period, while contending with the existing problems during that time.

And then, Jay went on, Titan would be a prisoner of that vendor forever. It's very tempting to become "all IBM, or BEA, or Microsoft, or Oracle," he explained. "But they own you at that point. Anything you want to do later will require additional products and services from that vendor. I'm not putting myself in that position again."

In a comparable pitch, InsurTech had proposed migrating the old Hermes system to a newer version of the InsurTech solution and at the same time migrating all of the old Apollo systems over to InsurTech. This proposal had some appeal in that migration between platforms from the same software company was simpler than migration between different vendors. InsurTech had performed this migration upgrade many times, and Titan had confidence that it could handle this situation well. However, after having lived with a monolithic system for many years, the Hermes people were not eager to perpetuate such a situation. They preferred proposals that included a degree of flexibility and less dependence on a sole application and vendor to run everything, forever.

Massive EAI

Another approach being discussed was to extend the EAI package that Apollo had used to connect all of the disparate legacy systems in Titan. There were several reasons why this idea was getting serious attention. Apollo already had it, so the investment in expanding the EAI system was incremental and therefore far lower than a complete system migration. EAI provided a measure of flexibility as well. The legacy systems could remain in place, while access to them could be opened up. In addition, the former Apollo team also had experience with the EAI platform, and thus the learning curve would not be so steep as with other solutions.

On the downside, implementing a large-scale EAI project to connect Titan's systems would take a long time, with a complicated training process for new members of the team that could extend the project timeline, scope, and budget. Once complete, the system would require that dedicated, experienced EAI developers be kept on staff at significant expense. After the project has been completed, change management might be difficult, and the maintenance of many legacy systems would have to continue indefinitely after the installation of the EAI package. Even if the legacy systems were replaced one by one, the estimated budget for keeping the legacy systems online for many years was daunting. Finally, the EAI solution did not solve the problem that InsurTech was about to pull the plug on the solution that Hermes had used for so many years. No matter what happened, Titan was going to have to replace that system soon.

Custom code

One group of developers at Titan had suggested creating custom-coded interfaces and replacement applications that could accomplish the same goals as the massive migration concept but preserve Titan's ability to choose best-of-breed solutions for its various business processes. With a set of custom interfaces, the developers argued, Titan could selectively begin replacing components of the InsurTech solution and other systems that were no longer needed. Other custom interfaces and fat clients could integrate the customer service and agent desktop access to the multiple underlying systems that these people needed to access. The timeline to complete the interfaces was relatively short—about a year—and the budget was attractively low. Most of the developers needed to do the work were already on staff.

In an unusual display of cohesion, though, both H.P. Wei and Dot Bartlett refused to look into this option with any seriousness. The development staff was already overburdened with day-to-day assignments. A customer interface project of this scale would necessitate hiring additional developers, which both the CIO and the CTO wanted to avoid. Further, both executives doubted that the developers were good enough—both at software development and project management—to handle such a complex and important project. Perhaps most important of all, they had very little appetite for a set of custom interfaces that would soon become yet another bundle of poorly documented legacy applications that would be nearly impossible to update once their original creators retired or resigned.

"So, this is a mess, wouldn't you say?" asked Jay. At this point, I felt that I had enough information to help Jay see that his "mess" was similar to what faced most companies in the world and was in fact precisely the reason that the revolution in XML, web services, and open standards—the basis for "loose coupling" of systems—was coming to fruition.

"Have you considered creating an SOA?" I asked. "Loose coupling?"

"Loose coupling?" he asked. A glimmer of hope appeared on his face. "Sounds promising."

"It might be a good thing for you, though doing it right is not easy. Nothing is easy."

"Of course," he replied. "But I want to learn." And with that, we got started.

PART 1

Understanding the technology of enterprise SOA

Because enterprise SOA cuts across multiple lines of business and technological disciplines, I have divided this book into two parts. Part 1 deals primarily with the technological underpinning of an enterprise SOA. Specifically, it describes web services as the enabler of true interoperation between distributed systems. Though I will refer to the Titan Insurance case study periodically, the emphasis is on specific technological issues. For the most part, I have tried to illustrate my points using a variety of small case examples. Part 1 is cumulative; if you read it sequentially, you should arrive at a fairly complete understanding of the core technologies involved in SOAs and the critical factors inherent in their deployment.

CHAPTER 1

The goal of loose coupling

I invite Jay Franklin, Senior Vice President of Architecture at Titan Insurance, to spend an entire day at my office to go over service-oriented architecture (SOA) in detail. There is just no way to do it justice over a cup of coffee at the tail end of a lunch. We hole up in my conference room, armed with legal pads and wall-to-wall clean whiteboards.

"Web services," I tell Jay, "is the rallying cry of every major software company in the world. As if from nowhere, an entirely new system of computing has swept the industry with a promise so significant that even the most wide-eyed idealist is forced to doubt the reality of the trend. Yet certain facts are undeniable. Observe the public strategies of IBM, Microsoft, Hewlett-Packard, Oracle, BEA, Sun Microsystems, SAP, PeopleSoft, and any one of the ten thousand other significant companies that drive the IT economy. Explore the changing dynamics of how organizations—from telcos to chemical factories, automotive manufacturers to retailers—are planning to do business with one another. Examine the aspirations of the U.S. federal government to unlock the flow of critical information between agencies for intelligence, defense, and homeland security. You will find one thing in common: web services as the technology that enables a service-oriented architecture."

And so, we begin. To understand SOA, I explain, you need to go back to the beginning and see how loose coupling has been an elusive goal of the IT industry for a generation. Today, however, it is finally happening through the development of *web services*. Web services, the most promising technology for making a service-oriented architecture possible, are software components capable of communicating with each other over multiple networks using universally accepted, nonproprietary "open standards." The concept is based on Extensible Markup Language (XML), a method of "tagging" data to make it understandable from one system to the next. Web services enable disparate pieces of software to communicate and operate with each other regardless of the platform and the programming language being used. The vision of web services is a world where systems can discover and utilize each other's capabilities without human intervention. In this environment—known as SOA—software offers itself as a "service" to any other software that needs its functionality.

Before we go further, I try to make an important clarification on how to understand my descriptions of web services and the SOA. An SOA is a general principle of IT that has been around for many years. A number of technologies have attempted to realize the goal of an SOA, where each software function in an enterprise architecture is a "service" that is defined using a description language with invokable interfaces that are called to perform business processes. Web services, a recent development, are one effective way to create an SOA. However, they are not the *only* way to make an SOA, and you will no doubt hear of other quite valid approaches to this goal. In this book, though, I am working from the assumption that the best and most practical way to build an SOA is with web services.

Today's web services are a simple evolutionary concept, with their predecessors going back many years in the history of computing. As early as the 1960s, software engineers recognized the need to achieve distributed computing models, seeking easier integration and reusability. In fact, many of the basic concepts inherent in web services were invented, implemented in various forms, and utilized for decades.

Looking back on the history that has led inexorably toward the emergence of web service standards, it is clear that a number of promising ideas failed because a workable technology for universal interoperability had not yet appeared on the scene. In the last ten years, we have witnessed the development and maturation of several key enabling technologies that have provided the foundation for today's web services. The story of web services is in many ways the story of achieving spectacular heights on, as Sir Isaac Newton said, "the shoulders of giants."

The purpose of this chapter is not to wax nostalgic on the history of computing or to meander effusively on the great thinkers and pioneers who made web services possible. Rather, it is my belief that only by examining the precursors for this phenomenon can we fully understand the implications today for business and government worldwide. In other words, the answer to our future is in the journey we have just completed.

I need to make a somewhat obvious disclaimer right here at the start and say that the following account is far from comprehensive. One could easily write a substantial book about the history of web services. Instead, my intent here is an overview that traces the key events and breakthroughs that had to occur in order for web services to come into being. With this as a foundation, we can then explore the implications to the future of competitive and agile enterprise operations.

1.1 *In the Beginning, There Was Distributed Computing*

Let's look at how businesses and organizations use computers and how it has become necessary to utilize more than one computer to accomplish a given task. Within a corporation or government, specialized software applications are introduced through homegrown efforts, the introduction of third-party packaged software, or both. These applications rapidly become interdependent, needing one another to complete basic business processes, such as taking and fulfilling a customer order. Indeed, the optimization of business processes soon demand interaction not only between a company's systems, but between the systems of other companies and government agencies as well. While integration between these systems has long been desired, the costs and complications involved in integration have resulted in most organizations containing hundreds of "silos" of information. Each silo is a separate, insular collection of data. Often these silos can only be connected through enormous cost and effort. Approximately half of all IT spending in the world is related to building and then maintaining interfaces between disparate silos of information within and between companies. The inefficiencies are staggering.

1.1.1 What is distributed computing?

Distributed computing is a term that describes a hardware and software architecture where more than one computer participates in the completion of a given task. For example, let's say that an auto parts company uses a UNIX-based system to process incoming orders. The company's older mainframe computer holds the complete parts catalog. To process an incoming order, the UNIX computer needs to look up a part number. Figure 1.1 shows how the two computers need to function together to complete the order-entry task. One machine needs the part information and the other has that very information. The information needed to process the order is "distributed" across the two machines. To complete the order, the mainframe computer must help the UNIX computer by sharing information from its parts catalog.

At this point in our discussion, Jay asks, "What about my insurance company?"

"Let's use some smaller, simpler examples," I reply. "We'll circle back to Titan once we've achieved a grounding in the basics of web services and SOA."

Now, you might wonder why the auto parts company doesn't just load the entire parts catalog application onto the UNIX computer and eliminate the need for this distributed architecture. That is certainly possible, and in many cases it is actually done under the category of "consolidation." However, the migration of data is time consuming, error-prone, and expensive. Further, the business logic in legacy systems is Byzantine and elaborate, often having grown over decades and hundreds of human

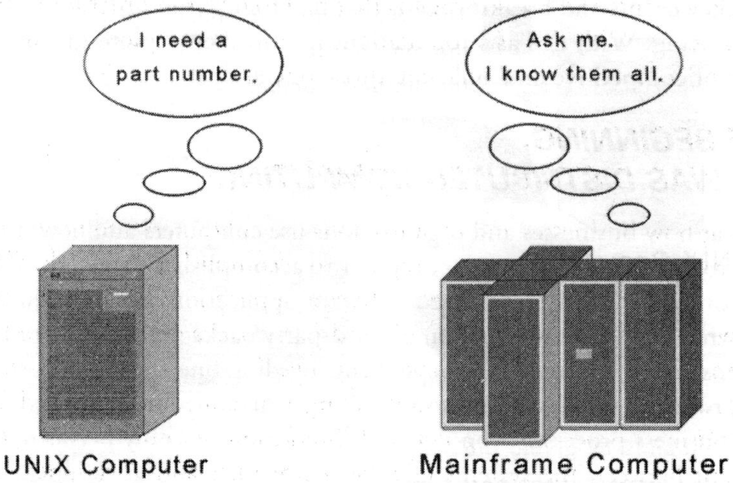

Figure 1.1 Distributed computing arose when it became necessary for multiple computers to share information and procedures, as illustrated by this hypothetical case of two computers that need to talk but can't.

hands. It is likely that under certain circumstances, for instance, the parts catalog application knows how and when to reject a request, or to respond with a certain answer based on the particular tax code, business practice, or regulatory rule. Often this logic has been created in outdated languages that demand rare skills—or worse, the actual people who wrote the code may be needed to interpret undocumented functions (and as a rule, these people are usually dead, extremely cranky, or both). To understand and reverse-engineer the legacy code (which, by the way, is often working just fine, thank you!) is likely a nightmare. In many situations, it is preferable from a budget and operating perspective to leave existing systems alone and arrange for them to operate in tandem in a distributed fashion. In addition, quite often the distributed transaction may involve systems outside your own company or control, rendering any consolidation out of the question. As a result, while consolidation efforts are common, integration projects abound.

Needing to exchange messages to make distributed computing work, each computer that is required to help complete a given task must be able to communicate with the other computer or computers involved in that task. In our auto parts company example, the UNIX computer and mainframe must be able to communicate with each other. The UNIX computer has to be able to "request" the mainframe for a part number, and the mainframe must be able to "respond" with the part number.

How do computers in a distributed environment communicate? Essentially, they send discrete messages to each other. As shown in figure 1.2, the UNIX computer sends a message to the mainframe requesting the part number. In response, the mainframe sends a message back with the appropriate information. The two machines can

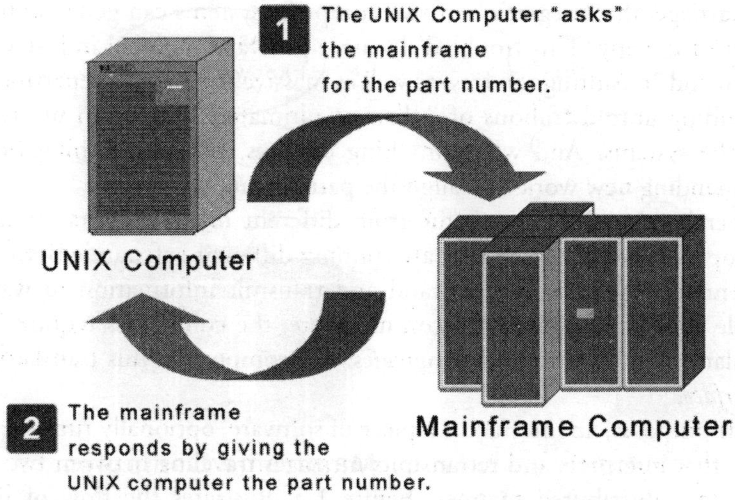

Figure 1.2 In this example of distributed computing, the UNIX computer sends a message to the mainframe to "request" a part number. In response, the mainframe sends the UNIX computer a message that contains the part number.

communicate through a variety of methods, ranging from the Internet to dedicated wide area networks (WANs) or local area networks (LANs).

Messaging is the wellspring of virtually every issue and solution related to managing distributed computing. Whether it is electronic data interchange (EDI), enterprise application integration (EAI), or any one of a dozen other ways in which IT vendors have attempted to address challenges in distributed computing, the core issue is almost always the same: transmission, receipt of, and response to messages between the computers involved. Web services are simply the evolution of the techniques for flowing messages between computers in distributed environments. At last, it appears that with web services the world has come to a standard path to accomplish these goals. As we will see, the implications of these standards are staggering.

1.2 THE TWO PROBLEMS OF INTEROPERABILITY

Distributed computing sounds pretty simple, right? A marriage between two systems: the computer that needs information sends a message to the computer that has it. The message recipient returns the required data and they live happily ever after. This works well in the storybooks, but in the complexities of real work the interactions between the two systems are more like those described in the book *Men Are from Mars, Women Are from Venus*. No matter how much the two sides want to communicate, something gets lost in the translation with disastrous results. Without open communication formats, information tends to flow very specifically, by hard-coded request and response interchanges, and often only after extreme coaxing. Like with a human marriage, the integration of two computer systems can generate the need for quite a bit of therapy. This troubled dynamic generates a global industry of systems integration and consulting services, as well as massive internal IT departments, collectively spending untold trillions of dollars to ultimately achieve an uneasy harmony between the systems. And when anything changes, the whole thing breaks down again, demanding new work to realign the participants.

In general, computers that come from different manufacturers, or that run on different operating systems, or that are running different software written differently by different teams, do not understand and transmit information in ways that are compatible with one another. To communicate, the computers require the services of a translator that "speaks both languages." In computing, this translator is known as an *interface*.

For our purposes, an interface is a piece of software, optionally running on its own hardware, that interprets and retransmits messages traveling between two computers operating in a distributed manner. Figure 1.3 illustrates the flow of information through such a system. The interface must process each request for information twice: once on its way from the requesting computer to the source of information and then again on its way back. If the interface were not available, the computers would not be able to communicate. They would be like people who could not speak the same language waving their hands wildly to no effect, such as in a presidential debate.

1.2.1 Proprietary standards

In figure 1.3, the access point on each side of the interface is represented as a lock and key. This metaphor is meant to illustrate a profound problem with interfaces: proprietary standards. Whether an interface is custom-coded or purchased off-the-shelf, most interfaces rely on proprietary messaging protocols and data management standards. In some cases, someone owns the interface and charges to use it; in other cases, the interface has been custom-coded and is unique to the project at hand, unsuitable for reuse by other systems in the future. If you only intend to connect two computers together, then your challenges are limited. The real problems occur when you want more than two computers to interoperate in a distributed environment. Imagine a company where tens of computers must communicate, or a supply chain where scores of computers seek to exchange information, or a world where billions of messages a second must be interchanged among computers across the world (see figure 1.4).

1.2.2 Tight coupling

The proprietary connection between computers shown in figure 1.4 creates a condition known as *tight coupling*. The computers are bound to each other through the strictures of the custom-made interface. Nothing is intrinsically wrong with tight coupling of computers in a distributed environment. However, when you want to make a change, it is time consuming and costly to connect additional computers to the interface or to change the computers that are currently connected.

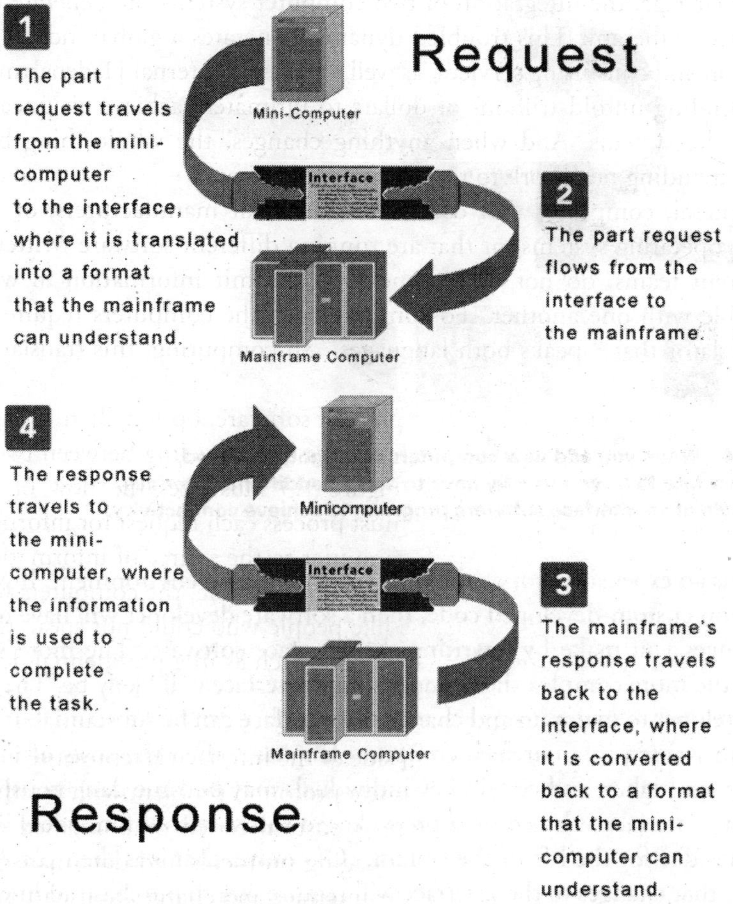

Figure 1.3 In a distributed computing, software interfaces serve as message-processing intermediaries between computers that must communicate.

If you want to allow more computers to communicate with each other in your distributed computing environment, then each machine will have to connect to the interface. As shown in figure 1.4, this means that each computer will require its own "lock and key" to transmit and receive messages. That is, each different type of computer has its own operating system, programming language, and communication protocol. As the number of machines in the configuration grows, so does the complexity of the interfaces. In figure 1.4, the hypothetical distributed environment includes a mainframe, two minicomputers, and a modern server. Each machine type has its own unique mode of communicating with the interface.

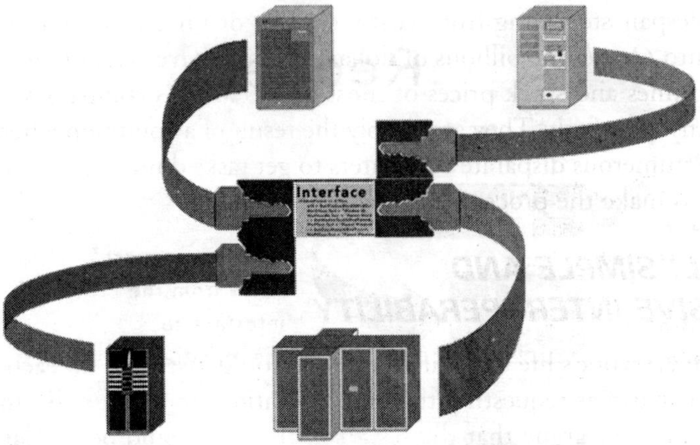

Figure 1.4 When you add new computers to a tightly coupled, proprietary interface, you usually have to add an additional interface, or a module of an interface software program, to achieve connectivity.

Change is an expensive proposition in a tightly coupled environment. If your interface is based on custom-developed code, then a software developer will have to implement any changes you make by rewriting the interface software. The more extensive the change, the more complex the changes to the interface will likely be. The cost of staffing a developer to maintain and change the interface can be substantial. If the interface is custom-written in an archaic computer language, then the costs of maintaining it may be even higher, and certain key individuals may become dangerously important

If your interface is based on a prepackaged software solution, you will be married to that vendor for the life of the system. (Of course, that was their plan!) It is highly probable that changes to the interface will require you to purchase additional modules of the software or develop custom patches to it. You will be saddled with license, maintenance, and development fees. If the vendor goes out of business, you may be stuck with a dead interface connecting two critical systems. The costs to replace the interface could be astronomical. Imagine if the television networks broadcast each show in a unique format and that anyone who wanted to watch had to design a new kind of reception mechanism for their television for each show that became available, and update it every time the network made a change to their delivery mechanism. The cost of owning and maintaining a functional television would be more than the cost of owning a house for even one family, and completely untenable in scale. Yet in the business world this is precisely what we face, wasting billions of dollars every year on "tuning and retuning" to make sure we can get the messages from our partners and even our own environments.

At this point, you may be nodding your head up and down: Yes, we've all been there. Or left and right: Why was I born before the advent of application interoperability standards, relegated to a horrible life of pain, misery, and monstrous IT budgets!

Though the despair stemming from costly custom or proprietary interfaces has not yet made it onto *Oprah*, the billions of dollars of waste have certainly made their way to the bottom lines and stock prices of most of the world's companies. These problems are not anyone's fault. They are simply the result of a condition where businesses needed to use numerous disparate computers to get tasks done and no common standards existed to make the process efficient.

1.3 THE GOAL: SIMPLE AND INEXPENSIVE INTEROPERABILITY

It would make everyone's life easier if computers could just "talk" to each other. That is, of course, as naive as requesting the United Nations to conduct business without translators. Some may argue that the results at the UN would be similar either way, but the negative impact of "silo"-based architectures is universally decried. The goals were apparent from the start: we must set standards for messaging between computers. If the various computers involved in a distributed environment can abide by uniform standards of communication, then a great deal of the complexity in interface development can be eliminated. That ideal, shown in figure 1.5, is one where any computer can send messages to any other computer through the use of an interface based on nonproprietary, open standards of intercomputer messaging.

Though the concept of standards is seemingly simple, it has taken decades for truly usable standards to emerge. The trouble came from the fact that each vendor would develop a set of technologies for their own platforms and then expect other vendors to accommodate their proprietary "standards." Rarely can a company (i.e., Microsoft with Windows) get away with dominating an industry by setting and controlling the

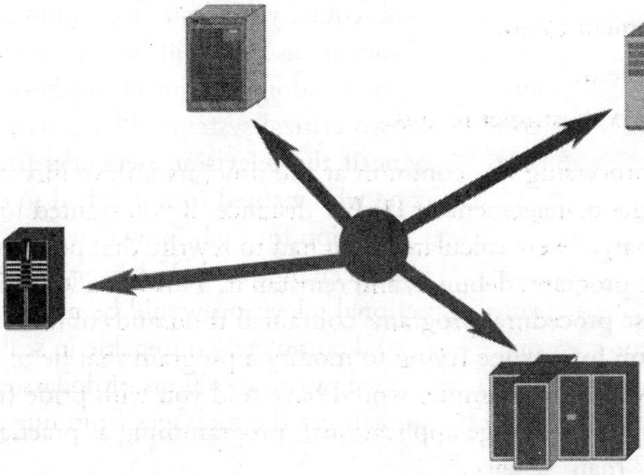

Figure 1.5 With an open standards–based interface for distributed computing, it is theoretically possible for every computer in the architecture to communicate with one another using open standards.

"standards" for the rest. Generally, to work effectively each of the major players (IBM, Microsoft, HP, Sun, Intel, Oracle, etc.) must participate and agree. This is a difficult, halting process. Often even when there was apparent agreement among parties about a standard, such as there was in the 1980s with the distributed computing environment (DCE), political issues and turf battles sabotaged the effort. The result was the same set of difficulties and costs that IT managers faced with proprietary interfaces.

1.3.1 The impact of object-oriented software

The advent of object-oriented software provided the basis for a strong step forward in the conceptual framework for interoperable distributed systems. In object-oriented software, the software developer converts a process into a discrete "object" that another piece of software can utilize. For example, you might develop an object that calculates mathematical equations and call it "the calculator object." Whenever you need to calculate something, instead of writing software code for the entire calculating process, you simply instruct the program to summon the calculator object. To understand the significance of object-oriented software, it is necessary to appreciate what computing is like in its absence.

In the first few decades of computing, software programs processed data sequentially through a series of instructions known as *procedural code*. For example, a computer operator at the phone company would command the computer to "run" the software program that printed the monthly customer statements. The computer would then follow a series of steps that were coded into the software:

- Retrieve the record of the customer name and address from the customer database.
- Retrieve the record of customer call details from the call detail database.
- Calculate customer charges using a set table of toll charges.
- Calculate statement totals.
- Print the statement.
- Go on to the next customer record.

While this type of processing was common at the time, its inflexibility caused many costly problems in the management of IT. For instance, if you wanted to modify the way in which toll charges were calculated, you had to rewrite that portion of the program, test the whole program, debug it, and reinstall it. This was a lot easier said than done. In reality, these procedural programs contained thousands of lines of code that could cause confusion for anyone trying to modify a program that he or she had not originally written. As any programmer would have told you with pride (much to the dismay of those paying to manage applications), programming as practiced that way was often more "art" than "science."

If the program required a distributed operation—that is, if the call details were on a different computer from the one calculating the statements—then the instructions for the interface that connected to that remote computer were hard-coded into the

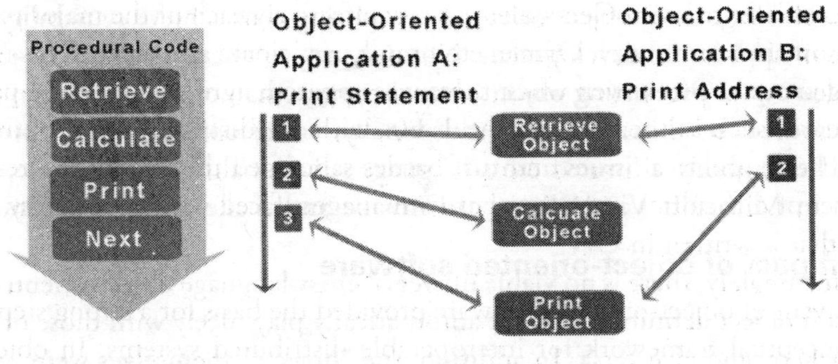

Figure 1.6 Procedural versus object-oriented software

program. Old-time programmers labeled procedural code "spaghetti code," though in more common parlance it was also known as a "nightmare." Changing and modifying code like this is similar to a crime investigation where the investigators need to decipher evidence, gather clues, and chase leads to eventually, with luck, figure out what happened. Overall, this method of software programming was incompatible with the modern requirement of an IT organization: flexibility and adaptability to change.

The object-oriented approach to the phone bill program would look like this:

- Call the "Customer name and address" object (which retrieves the customer name and address).
- Call the "Customer call details" object (which retrieves the call detail).
- Call the "Calculate customer charges" object, which in turn calls the "Toll charges" object and the "Calculation" object.
- Call the "Calculate statement totals" object.
- Call the "Print the statement" object.

The beauty of the object-oriented approach—assuming it is executed properly—is that, theoretically, each object used in the execution of the task is a separate component that can be modified or replaced without affecting the other objects. More important, the theory was that if another application was built for a completely different purpose and yet needed, say, the ability to perform the same "calculation" as the example above, then this same object could be reused in a completely different context. Objects abstract the functionality of a piece of software from its actual underlying code, greatly simplifying the use and management of the software in the process. Change and adaptation of data processing becomes easier with object-oriented computing.

Figure 1.6 shows the contrast between the traditional, procedural approach to programming and the object-oriented approach. In an object-oriented program, you can activate the functionality of any object in any order. In example A, you can run the retrieve-calculate-print routine of the statement-printing program. In example B, you can retrieve the customer information and then print it, skipping the calculation step if you wanted to.

One of the goals of object-oriented computing is to achieve reusability and lower the cost of application development. Not only can software programs be theoretically assembled out of preexisting objects, but also more than one program can share common resources of those objects. Additionally, some object-oriented programming approaches embody a limited cross-language functionality. For example, a program written in Microsoft Visual Basic can invoke and make use of the function of an object that is written in C++.

Unfortunately, there is no viable universal cross-language object-oriented software. Microsoft object definitions do not automatically play nicely with those of other software makers, and vice versa. In addition, the "objects" themselves were typically relegated to fairly small subroutine functions and fail to entice programmers to reuse them over rewriting the same functionality themselves. Pulier's rule of reuse states that a programmer will look at another programmer's output, no matter how brilliant, and declare it garbage. For this reason, many attempts at using object-oriented computing to enable interoperation of heterogeneous, distributed systems have largely been unsuccessful, as they were not universally adopted and ultimately their usefulness was stunted. As you will see a little later on, though, web services make more coarse-grained functionality available as reusable software components that can interoperate across programming languages. As a result, web services take the reuse concept to new heights, potentially eliminating the expensive hassles of custom or proprietary interfaces that connect one system with another.

1.3.2 Client-server

The IT field advanced again with the rise of *client-server* computing. Client-server describes a software architecture wherein one computer program, the *client*, requests data or functionality from another piece of software, usually on a remote computer, which is known as the *server*. The World Wide Web, for example, is a client-server architecture. Your browser is a client and the computers that contain the websites you visit are the servers. Another great example of client-server architecture is a bank automated teller machine (ATM). The ATM is the client; the bank's central computer is the server. When you make a request for cash at the ATM, the ATM client invokes a piece of "server" software sitting on the bank's computer called "Approve transaction. " If you have enough funds, the server sends a message back to the ATM client that says, in effect, "pay up."

From the perspective of open interoperability, the significance of rise of client-server architecture was its "call and response" design, which is the essence of web services and the SOA. The emergence of client-server and its subsequent rise to prevalence taught a generation of system architects and software developers the advantages of creating distributed systems based on messaging. The rise of the Internet, as a logical next step, showed the power of open standards when applied to a client-server architecture, thus setting the stage for the development of Web service standards.

1.3.3 Setting the standards

We've talked a little already about standards, but it is important to make sure we explore the meaning of the term. What is a standard? A *standard* is a rule that everyone can agree on. A foot is 12 inches. Everyone can agree on that, so it is therefore a standard of measurement. Who gets to determine the precise definition of how long a foot really is? In the United States, the National Institute of Standards and Technology (NIST) will tell you that a foot is exactly 0.3048 meters. (They also tell you how long a second is.) The most important thing about the standard is that everyone can agree on it. If you were to make rulers with foot markings every 0.4 meters, you would be out of business pretty quickly because you would not be adhering to the standard. Once a standard has reached a tipping point—the point at which enough people have adopted a standard that has sufficient momentum to virtually nullify any competing standard—a flood of innovation occurs because you can now count on certain facts to exist as a foundation on which you can build.

Ted Schadler of Forrester Research described a great example of this phenomenon to me in 2001 during a discussion on the implications of web services technology. He pointed out that the 2 by 4 wooden beam gradually became a standard after many years of inconsistent, unpredictable building materials. Once the standard was in place, an explosive housing boom occurred, as homes could be built with far greater precision and less cost than in the past. The reason? With the advent of the 2 by 4, design and construction could occur with greater efficiency. Everyone involved in the process could assume that a standard would be employed.

How do standards work in IT? In IT, *standards bodies* perform a function similar to that of the NIST. The standards bodies are collaborative, nonprofit industry groups that develop and publish the standards that are used to develop technology. For example, the World Wide Web Consortium (W3C) publishes the Hypertext Markup Language (HTML) specifications used to ensure that all web browsers can read the HTML documents that are found on the Web. If browser developers did not adhere to the W3C specifications for HTML, there would be the risk that websites might begin to offer content that only certain "clients" could understand, a situation that would result in the failure of the Web. In fact, this was typically the case in the early years of the Web where we had to develop three or four versions of a site just to be sure that the different browsers could interpret our content. For our purposes, the important standards bodies make up the W3C, the web services Interoperability Organization (WS-I), and the Organization for the Advancement of Structured Information Standards (OASIS).

The most crucial aspect of standards is that they are *open*. An open standard is one that is not owned by any company or organization that charges for or restricts its use. Again, on occasion a company such as Microsoft can become so pervasive that a "closed" standard can dominate a sector and an industry can be built on top. More often, standards are powerful because they are free and universal. The rapid rise of the Internet was due, in part, to the fact that it was based on a set of free technologies built on open standards. If someone had tried to license TCP/IP, HTTP, and HTML for a fee, the Web might never have grown into the global network it is today. The advance of web services parallels the fits and starts in the advance of web services standards, a constant battle to reign in rebel, competing technologies and achieve some basic agreements between the major technology providers.

Of course, just because a group of companies or people agree that a standard exists does not automatically guarantee its broad acceptance. Conversely, you can have highly effective standards that are not officially sanctioned by a standards body. People just agreed over time to use them and they became de facto standards. To work, a standard has to be accepted and put it into use by a large enough number of users that it becomes an everyday fact of life for the technologists who use it. If standards are in place, a new conflicting standard, official or not, would in all likelihood fail.

1.3.4 Early loose coupling

It should not come as a surprise that the most significant advances in distributed computing came after the rise of object-oriented software programming. In the 1990s, the Object Management Group, another standards body, developed a specification for interoperation of distributed computers known as Common Object Request Broker Architecture (CORBA). With CORBA, one computer in a distributed environment could request the services of an object through the "broker," which served as a common interface among all the computers involved. In theory, CORBA was a great idea. However, it failed to live up to its promise—chiefly, in my opinion, not because of the shortcomings of the technology (and there are many) but because of the discord among many companies in deciding which object model to adopt.

Microsoft's answer to CORBA was the Distributed Component Object Model (DCOM), which simplified the process of using objects in a Microsoft environment. However, as you might guess, DCOM was only a limited success because its use was restricted to Microsoft platforms. If you were on UNIX or Linux using Java or a mainframe language, then you could not use DCOM.

Around the same time, IBM came out with the Distributed System Object Model (DSOM), which had many of the same features of CORBA and DCOM. DSOM did not succeed because its fortunes were tied to the ill-fated IBM OS/2 operating system. The failure of DSOM provides an excellent example of the problems faced by the initial round of standards development in distributed computing. DSOM could have been the "magic bullet" of distributed computing. All that would have needed to happen for that to take place would have been the dissolution of Microsoft, the abandonment of Windows as an operating system, and the decision on the part of every computer owner in the world to switch to OS/2. Not too big an order, right?

As the 1990s drew to a close, it became clear that the ideal of open interoperability would have to depend on open standards for messaging that were owned by everyone and no one at the same time. The opinion leaders who would take on the challenge of making this happen had the good fortune of having just witnessed the most remarkable adoption of open technology standards in history: the Internet.

1.4 REAL LOOSE COUPLING

The Internet set the stage for the emergence of true open standards for interoperability of computers in distributed environments. As a massive network of computers that connect to each other using common communication and data transmission protocols, the Internet showed that it was possible to achieve global interoperation of computers, albeit with a very limited range of functionality in these early stage years. To truly understand the potential of the Internet, it is key to recognize this fundamental quality (i.e., standards-based networking). You can then begin to surmise that the explosive value of the Internet is not behind us, but in fact only now just beginning.

1.4.1 Hardware, software, and network transparency

From the perspective of web services, perhaps the most important achievement of the Internet is its ability to render all of its hardware, software, and network infrastructure "invisible." It makes no difference whatsoever on the Internet if the content you are requesting comes from a Sun machine, an IBM mainframe, or a Windows box. Your browser can be running on a Windows PC, a Macintosh, or a UNIX machine. The content appears on your screen just the same. And, on the Internet, the physical location of a computer means nothing. As long as a computer has an address on the Internet—a universal resource locater (URL) such as www.digev.com—any computer can access its Internet-formatted content from anywhere in the world.

Figure 1.7 shows the openness of the Internet's network. The hexagons and thick bars represent the universal Transmission Control Protocol/Internet Protocol (TCP/IP) network that the Internet uses to move messages around. TCP enables two computers

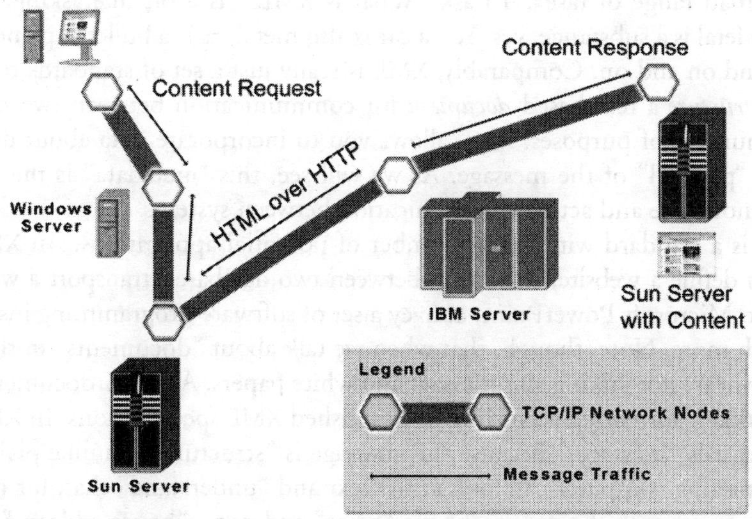

Figure 1.7 The open standards network of the Internet allows packets of data to travel from point to point without regard for compatibility at the destination.

on the Internet to connect and exchange packets of data. A packet is a discrete piece of a larger data stream that travels across the Internet. Any given Internet message, whether it is an e-mail or a webpage, may consist of a number of separate packets that arrive separately at the receiving computer. The Internet Protocol gives each packet in a stream a position—first, second, third, and so on—so the complete stream can be assembled and understood at the receiving end when all the packets arrive. TCP guarantees delivery of data (that the entire message eventually gets to its destination) and also guarantees that packets will be reassembled in the same order as they were sent. Regardless of the underlying hardware or operating system, the open standards of TCP/IP, HTTP, and HTML make it possible for any computer on the Internet to share a certain type of content with any other computer, so long as it employs those open standards. This content is known as "unstructured data," that is, content that can be received and displayed by a standards compliant client but that cannot actually be "understood" by the receiving computer. Next we examine the difference between structured and unstructured data—the key to unlocking the value of the Internet.

1.4.2 XML

XML is the standard that would begin to realize the long sought-after ideal of open interoperability. XML is one of those technological touchstones that many people discuss and few people understand comprehensively. I am reminded of the parable of the three blind men and the elephant, where each man's interpretation of the beast will depend on where he is standing when he explores the topic. Though this parable is apt for describing most discussions of new technology, it is perhaps most appropriate here because XML is a set of standards that enable software developers to accomplish such a broad range of tasks. To ask "What is XML?" is a bit like asking, "What is metal?" Metal is a substance, yes. Yet, a car is also metal, as is a bullet, a plane, a girder, a ruler, and on and on. Comparably, XML is really just a set of standards that specify how to *structure* a text-based *document* for communication between two computers for any number of purposes. XML allows you to incorporate data about data, along with the "payload" of the message. As we will see, this "metadata" is the difference between nonsense and actual communication between systems.

XML is a standard with a vast number of potential applications. An XML document can define a website, share data between two databases, transport a word document into Microsoft PowerPoint, convey a set of software programming instructions, and much more. Note, though, that when we talk about "documents" in the context of XML, we are not talking about essays and white papers. An XML document is a text message that is formatted according to established XML specifications. In XML, "document" equals "message." Because this message is "structured," unlike plain HTML, the interpreting computer can look at the text and "understand" that, for instance, a particular number in the document is a "price" and not a "house address," etc. XML is the marriage facilitator of the Internet, offering a path to communication where data can be transmitted *and* understood by the receiving party.

The key to understanding XML is to understand metadata, the data that describes another, more primary set of data. More dynamic metadata *tagging* differentiates XML from HTML. *Metadata tagging* is a term used to denote data that describes subsequent data. XML tags offer a way to know what the data "means" and therefore how to use it. Imagine if you had ten seemingly identical pills sent to you from your doctor in a single bottle with these instructions: "If you take the ten pills in the right order, you will live. If you take the ten pills in the wrong order, you will die." How could you search through them, sort them, and ensure your survival? To your eyes, they all look the same! However, if the pills came in a mutually agreed and understood sequence, tagged with appropriate labels so you could identify them, then you could remove each in the prescribed manner and live to see another day. Without metadata tags, data is "dumb."

As HTML's rigidity and lack of extensibility became problematic for robust business applications, XML began to rapidly mature. As demand grew for greater web content flexibility and dynamic functioning, the W3C oversaw the development of XML in addition to the HTML standard that is the foundation of the Web. To create a standard that would easily enable a website developer to build webpages that offered greater functionality and flexibility, the W3C adapted the grandfather of all markup languages, the ISO's Standard Generalized Markup Language (SGML), for Web use. The result was XML.

To illustrate the contrast between HTML and XML, let's say you wanted to place the words "Customer Name" on a website in the heading font. You would write HTML that looked like this: `<h1>Customer Name</h1>`. The `<h1>` is a *tag* that instructs the browser to create the words "Customer Name" in a specific font. `<h1>` is a fixed tag. Its definition was set years ago by the W3C. In contrast, XML gives you the ability to create your own tags and define them in any way that suits your purposes. If you were to create the same webpage in XML, you could create a tag called `<name>` and write it as `<name>Customer Name</name>`. The definition of the tag `<name>` is up to you. The XML *Schema*, the part of the XML document that explains your tags, working in tandem with the XML *processor* in the computer, gives you the ability to take advantage of a huge selection of functions that you can perform on your XML document based on your customized tags. XML allows you to create your own customized data tags that enable the definition, transmission, validation, and interpretation of data between applications and between organizations.

In many ways, XML is the new universal data format. A data format is a convention for storing or transmitting data. There are numerous data formats, including comma-delimited, which separates each element in a collection of data with a comma; Symbolic Link Format (SYLK); and Data Interchange Format (DIF). Figure 1.8 contrasts the ways in which a simple set of data, shown in table 1.1, is rendered in XML versus SYLK and DIF, for instance. Note the tags that delineate the data content in the XML. The difference between XML and SYLK and DIF is that XML, as a data format, describes the data that it contains. SYLK and DIF—and any

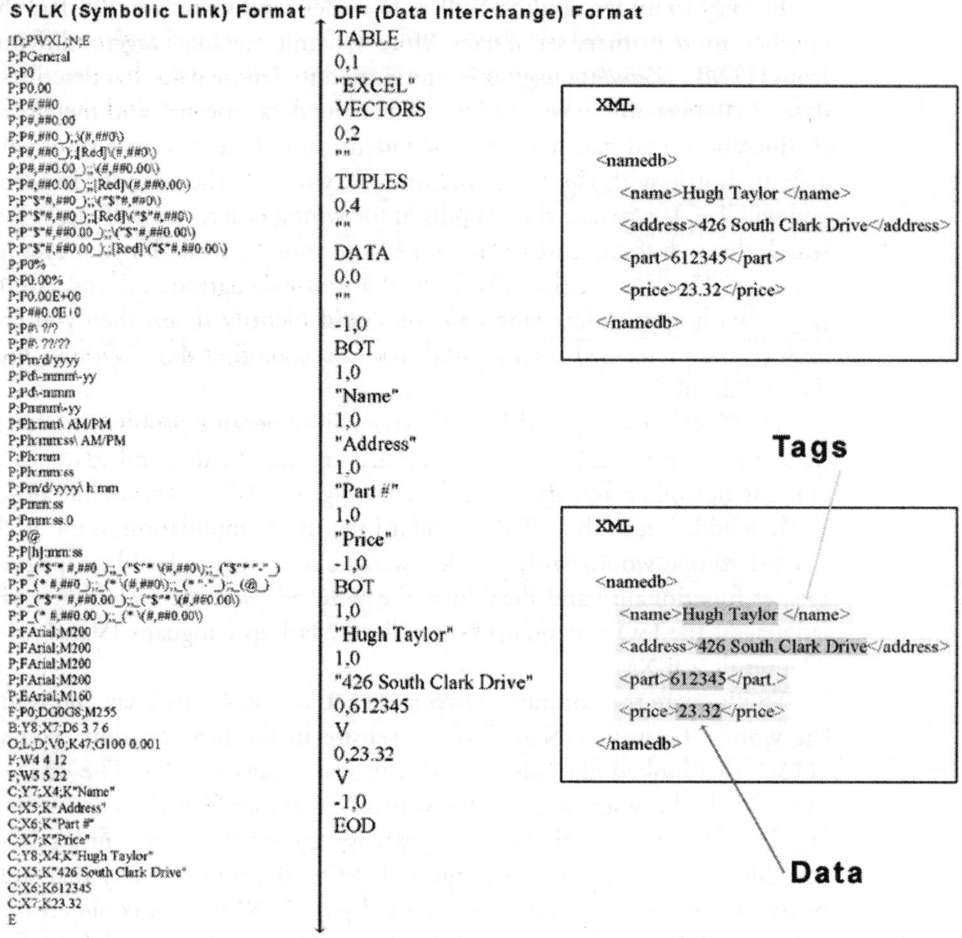

Figure 1.8 Comparison of XML with other data formats

number of other data formats—merely transmit the data set in a way that enables the user to assemble it into a tabular form.

XML is a global convention, accepted by virtually every IT person and software developer in the world, for describing data in a document. The significance is enormous: if you want everyone in the world to be able to share that document and interpret the data the same way, XML is the solution. But even XML is of limited use if everyone uses the flexible metadata tagging capabilities of XML in different, incom-

Table 1.1 Example Data Set

Name	Address	Part #	Price
Hugh Taylor	426 South Clark Drive	612345	23.32

patible ways. This is where web services come into the picture. Web services specify a precise set of XML standards that are to be used in interoperation of computers and data exchange. In the coming years, web service standards will be joined by XML tagging schemas for every industry in the world, and will usher in the next generation of computing.

1.4.3 The coalescing of key enabling factors

By the late 1990s, all of the elements that would comprise web services were in place. The network that would form the backbone of that interoperability—the Internet—was in place and its open communication protocols had established a global standard for networking. Furthermore, object-oriented software and client-server architectures provided a conceptual foundation for the use of remote modular software components, each with its own unique addresses. Lastly, with XML, we had the makings of a method to communicate information between computers globally. What was needed next was a seemingly small step—that the IT industry agree on basic XML standards—and the world could at last make a giant leap to distributed computing interoperability. This small step took about six years to come to fruition.

Around this time, someone at Microsoft coined the phrase "web services" to describe software components that could power interoperation of computers globally using HTTP and the Web as the communication network and XML as the messaging format. Like many others, I wonder if there might not have been a more descriptive term for what web services do (Internet objects? network services?), but the name stuck and here we are. I think the rationale for the name "web services" was to contrast dynamic, functioning software that can transact via the Internet to static "webpages" that are merely viewed over the network like so much HTML cargo. The delivery of software "as a service," that is, like electricity or gas to your home, has long been an ideal of the industry. With web services, the promise of the Internet is at hand.

In 2000, the W3C canonized a number of emerging web services standards that they along with other groups had begun to develop. The result was the ratification of a set of specifications for using XML and web communication protocols for universal computer interoperation. The standards, Simple Object Access Protocol (SOAP), Universal Description Discovery and Integration (UDDI), and Web Services Description Language (WSDL), which we will explore in great detail in the next chapter, are the foundation of web services.

While attempts in the past have addressed many of the same issues, none have tipped the scales from "fad" to "next stage in computing." Why? Because the power of web services is not in the idea itself but in the fundamental adoption of these standards by every major software vendor in the world. In 2001, IBM, Microsoft, Hewlett-Packard, Sun, Oracle, and others formed their own standards body, WS-I, for the purpose of ratifying the W3C's standards that they would each use in the development of their own web services technologies. The agreement by these major companies, many of them bitter rivals, to use the same open standards was a revolutionary breakthrough in the history of IT. The stage was set for the emergence of web services as the enabler of the long expected value of the Internet to business.

1.5 SUMMARY

Web services are software components capable of communicating with each other over multiple networks using universally accepted, nonproprietary "open standards" based on XML. Web services enable disparate pieces of software to communicate and operate with each other regardless of the platform and the programming language being used. As such, they enable the realization of an SOA. An SOA is an approach to enterprise architecture in which each software function in an enterprise architecture is a "service" that is defined using a description language with invokable interfaces that are called to perform business processes.

Though web services are a breakthrough in IT because of their almost universal adoption, their predecessors go back many years in the history of computing. The need for web services grew out of the need for, and the difficulties in managing, distributed computing environments.

In a distributed process, computers send messages to each other to retrieve data or invoke procedures. Traditionally, these messages have had to pass through proprietary or custom-coded software interfaces to reach their destinations and be understood. In the typical heterogeneous IT environment of today, where many different operating systems and computer languages may be in use, it is often necessary for IT managers to purchase or create a different interface for each pair of systems that they need to connect—a costly and complex proposition.

A number of attempts were made to solve problems in distributed and object-oriented computing through the 1990s, but they failed due to lack of support among industry players and the preponderance of proprietary standards that permeated these efforts. The open network of the Internet, as well as the universal data description capabilities of XML, comprised the key enabling factors that made web services possible and then inevitable. The agreement of the major industry players to adopt the emerging web services standards set the stage for a revolution in computing.

CHAPTER 2

Web services overview

I say to Jay, "Now that we know where web services came from we can take a closer look at what they actually are and what they do. Too much of the time, reading about web services in magazines and industry publications is an experience akin to hearing about the latest diet craze: 'Eat French fries, sit on the couch all day, and look and feel great!' Or, worse, the discussions sink you into a highly technical, jargon-filled swamp that you cannot readily relate to your business. What I want to accomplish here is to provide a solid overview of what web services are, what they do, and where reality separates from the hype."

2.1 WHEN YOU LOOK UP MY AUTO POLICY

Jay asks, "Could Titan have a web service that enabled a customer service rep [CSR] to look up the premium balance due on an auto policy?"

"Yes, of course," I respond. "Let's take a look at how it would work. A web service is a piece of software that conforms to a set of open interoperability standards. These standards enable global interoperation of computers regardless of hardware platform, operating system, network infrastructure, or programming language. The web service's extraordinary utility is based on the fact that it uses open Internet communications protocols and XML to transact its business. A web service is, therefore, a piece of software that can act upon a request from any network-connected computer in the world that communicates using web services XML standards."

2.1.1 Call and response

Many web services follow the classic request/response design of most distributed architectures, including the World Wide Web and client-server systems. Though other forms of web service messaging, such as "Send and Forget," are available, in this book we focus on the "Request and Response" form. It is quite common, and it illustrates the interoperability issues involved in the SOA extremely well. In our example, Computer A requests information or an operation from Computer B by sending a message over a network. Computer B responds by sending a message back over the network. As we discussed in chapter 1, and as illustrated in figure 2.1, this process has typically been troubled by issues regarding proprietary interfaces, incompatible network transmission standards, operating systems, and programming languages.

Web services, in contrast to the traditional distributed computing mode of messaging through proprietary interfaces, employ an interface that is universally accepted: a specific type of XML known as Simple Object Access Protocol (SOAP). As shown in figure 2.2, the requesting computer sends a SOAP message to the responding computer using any number of message transportation protocols, often HTTP. Because both the requesting computer and the responding computer understand SOAP as a "common language," the responding computer is able to receive the message, process it, and respond in a SOAP message that it knows will be accepted by the requesting computer. When a piece of software is ready to interoperate using web services, as the mainframe is in figure 2.2, it is said to be *exposed* as a web service.

To put it in human terms, imagine that you have two friends—one on an island in the Pacific and another in a one-runway village in Africa—neither of whom

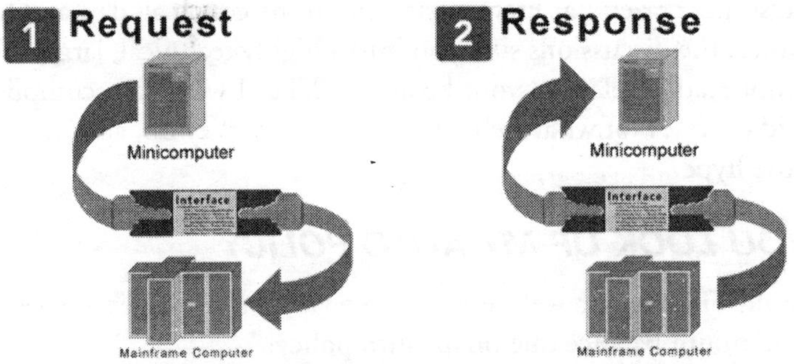

Figure 2.1 In an architecture that connects two systems through a proprietary interface, a request for data or procedure must travel from the requesting computer through the interface to the responding computer. The responding computer processes the request and sends back the response through the interface to the requesting computer.

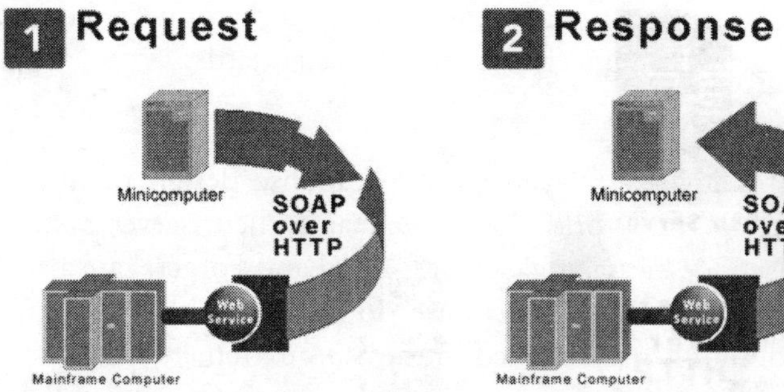

Figure 2.2 In this SOA, requests and responses in the SOAP XML format travel between two computers over HTTP. (Note: SOAP can also travel through JMS, FTP, SMTP, and other protocols.)

understands English. Over the years, you have successfully communicated with your friends by writing letters in English, chartering two private jets—one to land on the water near the island and one to make it through the bush to deliver the letters—and then employing translators to interpret your letters once they arrived. Oh, and of course, the jets are not initially equipped to land in these airports so they need to be retrofitted with special landing gear—different for each location—before embarking on the first trip. And, of course, every time the airports change, the airplanes need to be changed as well to ensure they can land properly.

In this scenario you would be communicating with your friends the way computers in traditional distributed environments have done for years. The system works, but it is cumbersome, and after a while, you tire of the hassle and expense.

One of the many advantages of using web services in the deployment of distributed computing environments is the universality of the interface. Since a web service can send and receive SOAP messages over Internet protocols, you can interoperate with that service using virtually any kind of computer. As shown in figure 2.3, a web service exposed on a mainframe can interoperate with a UNIX, Windows, or Sun Solaris computer without any modifications to its interface.

Contrast this with the traditional model of proprietary interfaces in distributed computing and you will see certain advantages right away. Instead of the proprietary "lock and key" design, with web services you have an open, universally accepted interface, illustrated in figure 2.3 as a sphere with rounded connectors. A web service is like an electrical socket. Every plug fits every socket in the United States. When you buy an appliance, you don't have to ask if it will fit the plug in your house. Why? The electrical industry agreed years ago upon standards for electrical outlets and all manufacturers have abided by them ever since. Web services are the distributed computing equivalent of the electrical socket.

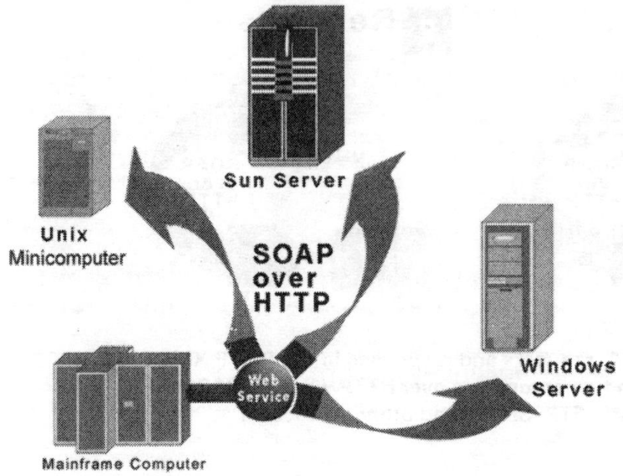

Figure 2.3 Because it uses open standards-based SOAP XML messaging, a web service can interoperate with multiple computers requesting the service.

2.1.2 How the CSR would consume web services

"Okay," Jay says excitedly, "the customer service rep types an auto policy number into a browser and hits Send. He's using the web service, right?"

"Almost," I reply. "In a Request and Response type of web service, the piece of software that needs the data or functionality offered by the web services is often referred to as the *consumer* of that web service. The consumer invokes the web service by sending it a request message. That would be the application your CSR is using. It may or may not be based on a browser. It could be any kind of software. As long as it invokes a web service, it is known as a web service consumer. The web service itself is frequently called the *provider* as a result. Keeping this concept of request and response and consumer and provider in mind will help you as you navigate web services marketing hype that can obscure essential facts. Web service operations typically involve a request and a response, although other scenarios (such as one-way) are also available. There is at least one consumer and one provider for each transaction, and these individual transactions are often part of larger processes. One provider may service a hundred consumers, each on different machines, invoking the web service for any number of different purposes. A complex distributed computing operation, such as processing a loan application, might require that dozens of web services be *orchestrated* in a process. However, the underlying operation of request and response still remains the same."

2.2 THE TECHNOLOGY IT'S BASED ON

A web service depends on three interrelated, XML-based software standards to function properly:

- **Simple Object Access Protocol** (SOAP)—The message format
- **Web Services Description Language** (WSDL)—The document that describes exactly what the web service does and how to invoke it
- **Universal Discovery, Description, and Integration** (UDDI)—The directory of web services that are available for use

Together, the three standards combine to give a web service the ability to function, describe itself, and be found within a network. While theoretically a web service could function fully using SOAP alone, figure 2.4 shows how a web service needs WSDL and UDDI to be effective.

2.2.1 SOAP

SOAP is the lingua franca of web services, the XML structure on which all web services messages are built. When we say that web services are based on XML, we actually mean that web services are based on SOAP messages, which are written in XML. What makes SOAP special and distinct from plain-vanilla XML is that every SOAP message follows a pattern that has been specified by the W3C standards.

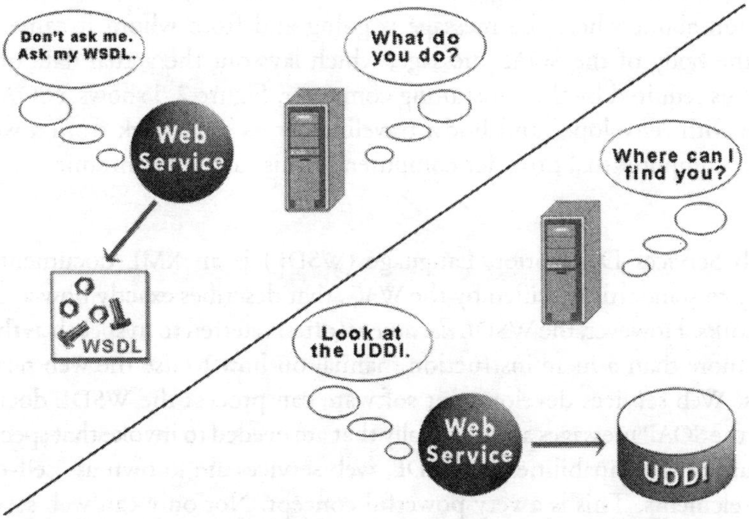

Figure 2.4 When it comes to describing its functionality and location, a web service is in and of itself essentially "dumb." To describe itself to potential requestors, the web service relies on its WSDL document, which provides a detailed explanation of the web service's functionality and how to access it. For location, the web service relies on its listing in a UDDI registry to enable potential requestors to find it.

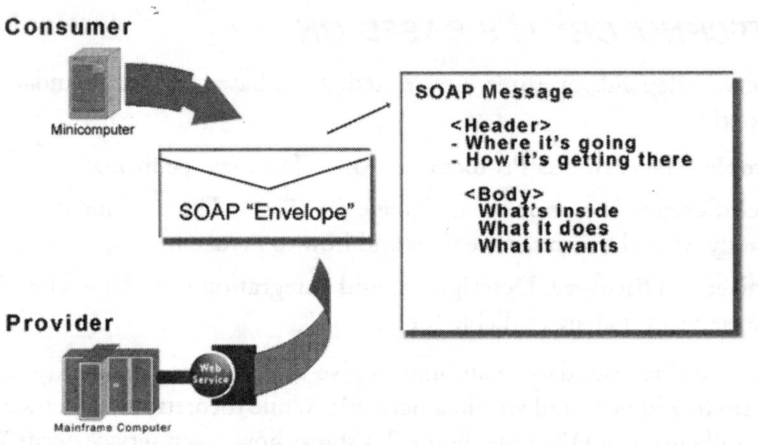

Figure 2.5 A SOAP message is formatted as an "envelope" of XML code that defines its beginning and end. The "header" describes where the message came from, where it's going, and how it is going to get there. The "body" of the SOAP message contains the relevant data or procedural instructions of the SOAP request of response.

SOAP is sometimes referred to as a "data wrapper" or "data envelope." Here's what those apt descriptions mean: Every SOAP message begins with a tag that reads `<SOAP-ENV:envelope>`. The envelope tag signals the message recipient that it is about to receive a SOAP message. What follows is a header, which contains the critical information about where the message is going and from whom it came. And then there is the body of the SOAP message, which lays out the actual data or operating instructions required by the consuming computer. Figure 2.5 shows a SOAP message, complete with "envelope" and body, traveling across a network from a web services consumer computer to a provider computer, in this case, a mainframe.

2.2.2 WSDL

The Web Services Description Language (WSDL) is an XML document, designed according to standards specified by the W3C, that describes exactly how a specific web service works. However, the WSDL *document* (often referred to in speech as the "wizdil") is much more than a mere instruction manual on how to use the web service that it describes. Web services development software can process the WSDL document and generate the SOAP messages automatically that are needed to invoke that specific service.

Because of the capabilities of WSDL, web services are known as "self-describing" software elements. This is a very powerful concept. Not only can web services interoperate universally through SOAP, they can also be described universally using WSDL. A software developer in Borneo can create a piece of software to invoke a web service in Trinidad just by reading and processing the WSDL document. He does not need to speak to anyone, read any particular manuals, or buy any special software—theoretically he need only conform to the standards. I say *theoretically* because clearly the developer in Borneo still would need to be properly authorized, and the transaction should be properly monitored to be safe, but the mechanism itself of achieving a request and a response between these parties has now been drastically simplified.

2.2.3 UDDI

Though several types of web service registries are available for use, we identify the Universal Discovery, Description, and Integration (UDDI) directory as the general standard used as a registry of web services that are available for use in a particular network. Think of the UDDI as a sort of "yellow pages" of web services. If you wanted to find a web service in your enterprise, you would look in the UDDI. The UDDI would tell you where to find that service, and it would link you to the WSDL document so you could examine the web service and make sure it was the one you wanted. This has many ramifications for using web services as components of software applications, a subject we explore in greater depth in chapter 7.

A UDDI registry is a central concept as one shifts to a model that assumes a distributed, loosely coupled set of web services. The services your process may want to consume could be anywhere at any given moment, and in fact the same function may be performed by a different service depending on changing criteria, such as availability or price. In this environment, operating without a directory of sorts to find the services would mandate "hard-coding" the location of the service into the consuming application, undermining a key reason for having adopted web services in the first place. Imagine depending on a person for a key task and then finding that individual has moved without leaving a forwarding address.

Web services have Uniform Resource Locator (URL) Internet addresses. To the requesting computer, a web service is simply a URL. As we noted in the previous chapter, a URL is the "address" of a program or a website like Amazon or Yahoo. Because web services utilize Internet protocols, they can be invoked by sending the requesting SOAP message to the web service "address." (Note that most web service URLs are not as simple as http://www.amazon.com; they might be more like http://qams1:8080/8f3af62e=11d7-a378.) This may not seem like such a big deal, but in fact it is at the core of how the entire system functions. The magic of web services is that they are located at addresses to which any computer can connect. The web service's URL is the basis for its universality and network transparency. Universality comes from the standard way to describe it, and the transparency comes from the ability to use a "logical name" in your consuming application that the UDDI can "resolve" for you into the appropriate URL. For instance, if I want to use a credit card authorization service in my application, rather than "hard-code" a location of the service, I can invoke a logical name (say, "CreditAuth") and allow the UDDI to resolve the name into a URL. That way, if the location of a service changes (and things always change), my program can stay the same—CreditAuth is still CreditAuth anywhere the service might be. Masking these kinds of changes from the consuming application is key to achieving the agility that web services technology promises.

2.3 CHARACTERISTICS OF WEB SERVICES

Web services behave differently from traditional software. As we have discussed, they are based on open standards, whereas most software in use today connects through proprietary technologies. In addition, web services are "loosely coupled" when compared to traditional distributed computer systems. And, like the Internet, web services offer total *network transparency* in their implementation and use.

2.3.1 Loose coupling

In chapter 1, we examined the ways in which computers operating in a traditional distributed environment are "tightly coupled." That is, each computer connects with others in the distributed environment through a combination of proprietary interfaces and network protocols. It is difficult, time consuming, and expensive to "un-couple" and "re-couple" computers in the system because such movement of computers necessitates some modification of the interface.

Web services, in contrast, are "loosely coupled." Once a piece of software has been exposed as a web service, it is relatively simple to move it to another computer. Why is that? It is simple to "un-couple" and "de-couple" web services because such services abstract the software functionality from the interface. Once a software program is available as a web service it can be accessed through SOAP in a variety of ways, including Internet protocols.

Figure 2.6 illustrates the web service's quality of loose coupling. In part 1 of the drawing, a minicomputer accesses a web service that has been exposed on a mainframe. Let's say, however, that the owner of the mainframe wants to replace the older machine with a new Sun server. As we see in part 2, the Sun machine replaces the mainframe, but the minicomputer, which is the consumer of the web service, doesn't "know" this. The minicomputer is still talking to a SOAP interface. It makes no difference whether the SOAP interface is sitting in front of a mainframe, a Windows machine, or anything else. Once the mainframe has been replaced by the Sun machine, the minicomputer continues to access the web service without being any the wiser.

In parts 3 and 4 of the figure, the process of replacing computers continues. The owner of the minicomputer replaces it with a PC. The PC, outfitted with its own SOAP interface, can easily access the web service on the Sun machine. Then, for whatever reason, the owner decides to replace the Windows machine with another Sun box. No problem—the new computer once again can access the web service without any special modifications.

2.3.2 Network transparency

Because the coupling between web services is "loose" and because web services consumers and providers send messages to each other using open Internet protocols, web services offer total *network transparency* to those that employ them. Network transparency refers to a web service's capacity to be active anywhere on a network, or group of networks, without having any impact on its ability to function. Because

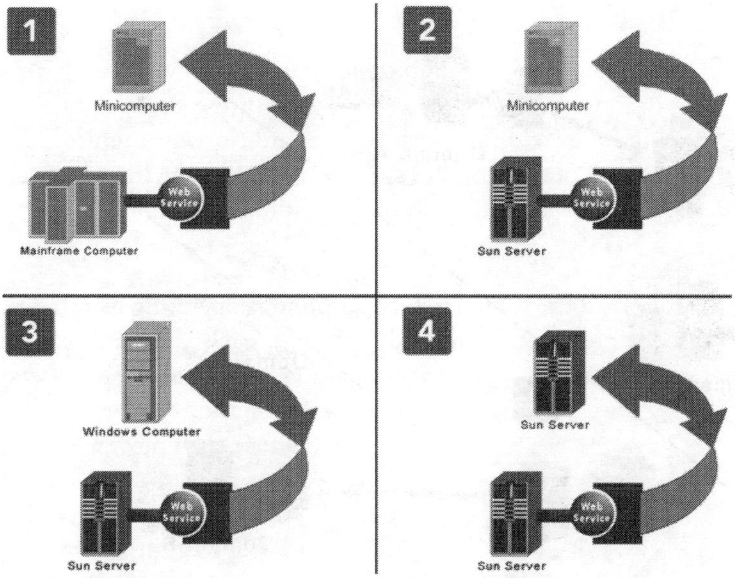

Figure 2.6 Web services do not rely on the "tight coupling" that is the side effect of proprietary interfaces. Because web services are "loosely coupled" software components that are comparatively simple (and inexpensive) to connect, any number or variety of requesting computers can invoke the same web service as long as those requesting computers adhere to the standards-based SOAP request format.

each web service has its own URL, web services have similar flexibility to websites on the Internet. In the same way that it makes no difference where in the world a website is hosted—you can still see it on your browser—a web service can be located on any computer that is connected to the network and communicates using Internet protocols. When you go to Amazon.com, for instance, to buy a book, you really have no idea, nor any need to know, where the applications reside that you are accessing with your browser—all you need to know is the address.

As shown in figure 2.7, the same web service may be located in two different domains. If for some reason Domain A becomes unavailable, then the consuming computer can access the web service from Domain B without requiring any major work to be done. Literally, all that needs to happen is the modification of the web service's URL in the WSDL document and the *binding* of the consuming computer to the web service's new address in Domain B.

Given our extensive experience with the Internet in recent years, the quality of network transparency may not seem so important, but in fact this is a core aspect of the future of computing. The combination of loose coupling and network transparency presents nothing less than a revolution in enterprise computing, not because the idea is new but because the infrastructure and standards have finally arrived to make

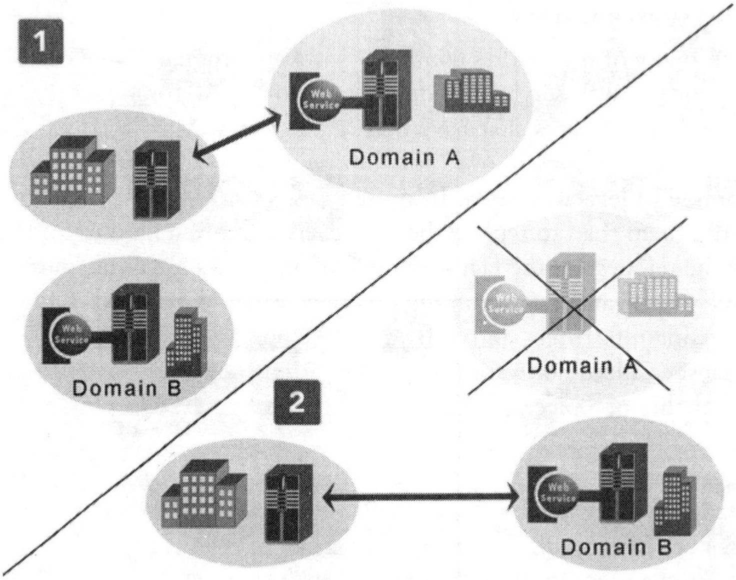

Figure 2.7 Network transparency allows web services to be located anywhere on a network or group of networks.

it a reality. Businesses have spent fortunes over the years managing interfaces that control the interoperation of computers in distributed environments. American businesses spend hundreds of billions of dollars per year on information technology. Gartner estimates that up to 40 percent of these funds are spent on system integration. The fact that web services will soon enable you to switch from one provider to another with relative ease is a development that promises to save billions of dollars in reduced fees and costs associated with developing and maintaining propriety interfaces in the coming years.

2.4 BIRTHING A WEB SERVICE

"Dad, where do web services come from?" Well, if two computers love each other very much... Actually, like so many other issues in this new field, the answer is at once simple and complex. Similar to bringing a baby into the world, creating the web service is the fun and easy part—securing and managing it for the next few decades is the real challenge. Other than having web services arrive as part of a packaged software purchase (PeopleSoft, SAP, etc.), there are essentially two ways in which web services come into existence: 1) exposing existing software as web services, or 2) developing new web services from scratch.

2.4.1 Exposing web services

Because so many of the world's computer software programs were developed prior to the emergence of web service standards, most of the web services that we see today come from *legacy* systems that have been *exposed* as web services. A legacy system is something that you already own and cannot replace right away. Mainframes are a great example of legacy systems. In most cases, it is far simpler and cheaper to continue to use them than to replace them. Indeed, it is often hard to find anything that will work better, despite the fact that many mainframes use older, more cumbersome operating systems and programming languages. The good news is that most of the mainframe manufacturers and software developers—companies such as IBM and HP—offer specialized software programs that enable software engineers to dig into the functionality of a piece of mainframe software and expose it as a web service.

Exposing a web service involves enabling the older software to receive and respond to SOAP message requests for its functionality. For example, an insurance company may have a mainframe computer that contains the premium balance due for each policyholder. Let's suppose that a customer relationship management (CRM) application needs a person's premium information to help handle a phone inquiry. As shown in figure 2.8, the CRM application sends a SOAP message to the mainframe requesting Nancy Smith's premium. A web service that has been exposed on the mainframe receives the SOAP request and responds by retrieving Nancy Smith's information, translating it into SOAP, putting it into a SOAP "envelope" and sending it back to the CRM application, which can, of course, understand SOAP and make use of it.

How does the mainframe web service know how to retrieve the data and translate it? From a business point of view, the specifics of how a web service "works" internally are less important than the concept that the application can now be thought of as a

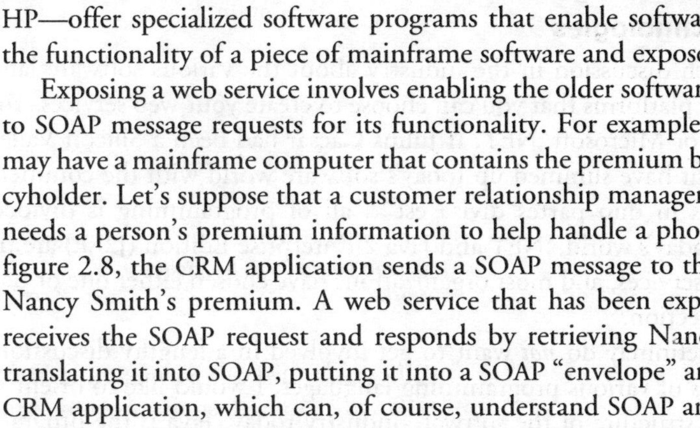

Figure 2.8 If a web service exposes a database that resides on a mainframe computer, the service will translate the data from the database into a standards-based XML message before sending it to the requesting computer.

"black box," effectively rendering the underlying platform irrelevant—the legacy application now "looks" the same as every other, accessed through standards.

2.4.2 New web services

The other way that web services come into the world is through new software development. Today, if you are developing software using development tools such as IBM WebSphere Studio Application Developer, Borland's JBuilder, or Microsoft's Visual Studio .NET, among many others, you will find that you have the ability to expose your program's functionality as a web service quite easily. These new software development tools have been created with web services in mind.

2.4.3 Specific technologies

There is much discussion in the industry about the various software languages and technological platforms that you can choose to create your web services. You have two choices: Java or Microsoft .NET. If Julius Caesar had been a Silicon Valley entrepreneur, he might have summed up today's software world with the comment, "Omnia programmatis in duo partes divisa est" ("all of programming is divided into two pieces"). In today's world, .NET and Java 2 Enterprise Edition (J2EE) are the two "flavors" of web services, and most organizations have chosen either one or both for their enterprise direction.

While I definitely do *not* want to get involved in a lengthy discussion about the pros and cons of various programming languages, I would like to orient you regarding the basic structure of the software industry today. Java is the programming language developed by Sun Microsystems that has subsequently been adopted as the primary development vehicle for thousands of other companies, including IBM and Oracle. .NET is Microsoft's web services–ready programming construct that promotes a new language called C# (C Sharp). Both languages provide extensive functionality for the development of web services. Java is the more open of the two, meaning that it can run on a wider variety of operating systems and platforms than can .NET. .NET requires the use of Microsoft servers and the Windows operating system on the web service provider. In addition, there is Mono, an open source implementation of .NET designed to run on non-Windows platforms such as Linux.

Java and .NET can interoperate, though some issues have arisen related to integrating the two in complex arrangements that are being resolved through a variety of standards-based solutions. One is not necessarily better than the other, yet if you are in the enterprise computing arena, you may find yourself working with Java for a number of reasons: Java is the language used by the popular IBM WebSphere Studio and BEA WebLogic application servers. As a result, Java is the preferred development language for web services that will have to sit on those platforms.

Ultimately, despite a huge amount of discussion on this subject and virtually endless comparisons between Java and .NET in the trade media, the debate is less important than the fact that both are driving forward together, ensuring interoperability and the power of web services. If we continue to refine the standards and then adhere to them, we will begin to move into a world where it truly doesn't matter what platform you used to create your software. In a network of web services, business processes will be created and optimized based on business priorities, unconstrained by the technologies underlying the distributed set of systems that are being orchestrated.

2.5 THE SAVVY MANAGER CAUTIONS: STANDARDS

This section, which will recur throughout the book, is meant to give you some caution on how to evaluate the way these technologies are presented in the marketplace. When it comes to standards, the savvy manager cautions you to differentiate between the potential of web service technology and the actual implementation. Standards are incredible in that they enable far-flung developers to create software that can interoperate without the need for proprietary technology. At the same time, that does not mean that every standards-based piece of software is going to work properly or even interoperate adequately on its own. Even within standards, there is room for discrepancies and subtle differences in interpretations of what each standard might actually require of a developer. Furthermore, certain standards are still immature. In other words, you might be presented with an expensive piece of standards-based software that uses a set of rules that have not been fully ratified by the standards bodies. Finally, some software makers have an annoying habit of seeding their standards-based products with little bits and pieces of proprietary functionality. We need to pity them. They can't help themselves…

2.6 SUMMARY

Web services consist of the exchange of SOAP messages over a variety of protocols, often HTTP. SOAP is a specific type of XML message format determined by the W3C standards.

Web services are based on a software architecture of request and response. A web services "consumer" computer invokes a web service by sending a SOAP request to the web service. The web service, in turn, performs the operation requested and responds with a SOAP message of its own. Each web service has a consumer and a provider.

Because of the open nature of web services, it is possible for many web service consumers to access the same service regardless of operating system or programming language. As long as a consumer invokes the web service using a SOAP request in standardized format, it makes no difference what kind of computer, operating system, or programming language the consumer is running.

To describe itself to the outside world, each web service has a Web Service Description Language (WSDL) document that provides the potential consumer of the service with an explanation of how the service works and how to access it. The WSDL describes how to create a SOAP request that will invoke that specific web service. If a software developer wants to create a web service consumer software program, all he or she needs is this descriptive document. The WSDL provides all the information the developer needs to create a program that invokes the web service. This means that developers can create web services consumers without ever meeting or speaking with the developer who created the actual web service.

Universal Discovery, Description, and Integration (UDDI) is a listing of web services available within a particular network. The UDDI functions like a "yellow pages" of web services. Potential web service consumers can look up web services that are available for use through the UDDI.

Though hundreds of standards will eventually be ratified, the core three web services standards are SOAP, WSDL, and UDDI.

In contrast to computers whose interoperation is "tightly coupled" through proprietary interfaces, web services are "loosely coupled." This quality enables system administrators to replace or move the computers that contain the web service with relative ease. Loose coupling also means that changes to the provider do not necessarily lead to changes for the consumer of the web service. For these reasons, and others, loose coupling has the potential to save time and money in creating interoperation between computers, and to dramatically increase an organization's productivity by enabling more agile business processes.

Web services function in a mode of "network transparency." Like websites on the Internet, web services can be located anywhere on a network, or group of connected networks. As a result, web services can be moved around the network with no impact on accessibility.

Web services can come into existence in two basic ways. Software developers can "expose" existing legacy software through the use of specialized web services programming tools. Alternatively, developers can create wholly new web services using the new generation of software development tools available from Microsoft and others.

CHAPTER 3

What web services can do

As Jay and I continue our exploration of web services, we begin to take a look at what they can and cannot do. Because of the agreement on basic web services standards among all the major IT players, web services have the power to enable dramatic changes in the way enterprise IT is designed and managed. However, it is important to keep in mind that web services cannot address every challenge. There are limits to their use, to be sure. My goal in this chapter is to give you an overview of the various ways in which web services can change how you approach information technology—and also to temper that view with an understanding of realistic expectations.

3.1 TECHNOLOGY WITH POTENTIAL

The interoperation of distributed computers that web services enable falls into two primary categories: 1) remote procedure calls, and 2) data exchange. Any implementation of web services in the real world involves one or both of these activities. Neither of these processes is new. Yet, because of their open nature, web services make remote procedure calls and data exchange far more versatile than they have been in the past. The result is an opportunity to interoperate on a much broader scale. Even more important, the ability to coordinate these web services into larger processes and then rapidly swap out the components for others creates an entirely new competitive opportunity—business agility.

3.2 INVOKING REMOTE PROCEDURES

Whenever one computer in a distributed environment asks another computer to perform a function, that is known as a remote procedure call (RPC). A currency exchange calculator is a good example of a software feature that might lend itself to an RPC. Let's say you have an international business that runs an order-processing computer. Every time you process an incoming order from a foreign country, you need to know the exchange rate for that currency. Assuming that the cheapest and most accurate exchange rate calculator is available on a computer other than the one that runs your order-processing software, you need to arrange for that order-processing software to ask the currency-calculating software on the other machine to figure out exchange rates.

So, if you need to know what $100 is worth in yen, then your order-processing software can send that information to the currency calculator. Figure 3.1 illustrates the request and response involved. The system making an RPC effectively says, "What is the yen equivalent for $100?" The currency system responds by saying, "¥200".

It has been possible to perform this kind of currency conversion using an RPC for many years using a client-server architecture. RPCs are a staple of client-server architectures. However, web services make RPCs dramatically simpler to carry out because they eliminate the need for the RPC to travel through any kind of proprietary interface that sits between the computers. And web services make it possible—easily—for computers to engage in RPCs even if they are running different operating systems and programming languages.

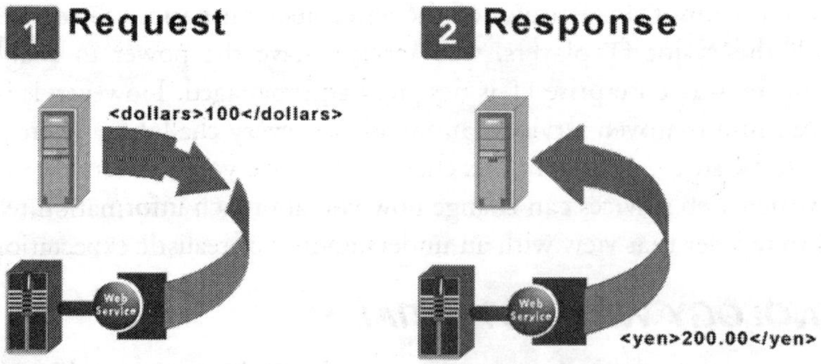

Figure 3.1 A currency calculator provides an example of a remote procedure call. The "consumer" sends a request asking another system to perform a procedure of converting dollars to yen. The system answers the remote procedure call by executing the currency conversion and sending the yen figure as the answer.

3.3 EXCHANGING DATA

Web services, because they use the universally accepted XML format for the transfer of data, are very good at helping distributed computers share data. Continuing with our currency exchange example, let's assume now that the order-processing software has the ability to calculate foreign currency totals using a table of exchange rates. Each day, the order-processing software needs to get an updated table of exchange rates in order to function properly. To accomplish this, you set up a web service that communicates the exchange rate data to the order-processing software in the form of a SOAP message. Figure 3.2 shows what this would look like. For every transaction, the order-processing software—now itself a consumer of a separate service—sends a SOAP request asking for the exchange rates. In response, the provider computer sends back the exchange rates as another SOAP message.

3.4 IMPACT ON EDI

One area of large-scale data exchange where web services have the potential to make major inroads is electronic data interchange (EDI). EDI, which has been around for many years, is a standard for sharing large amounts of data between business partners. For instance, many large manufacturers use EDI to transmit orders to their suppliers.

Web services have the potential to transform or even replace EDI in many cases—not that there is anything necessarily wrong with EDI. It served its purpose quite well, and certainly was a dramatic improvement over the hodgepodge of unmanageable formats that businesses used to employ to communicate to one another. However, EDI is rigid and expensive. To send information using EDI, one has to set up and maintain a value-added network (VAN). This kind of private network is costly to operate. With web services, you can achieve the same results as EDI without the cost

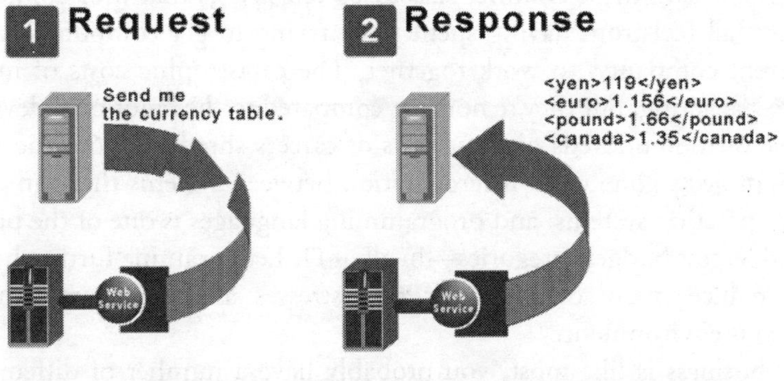

Figure 3.2 In this data exchange example of web services, the web service consumer sends a SOAP request to the web service asking for a table of currency conversion figures. The web service answers by executing the request and sending back the currency table formatted as a SOAP response.

of the VAN. And you get more inherent flexibility in the ways the data is composed and shaped. This is important because the complexity of conducting business with multiple partners often causes a great deal of frustration and costly workarounds, as companies struggle to force EDI to handle an ever-changing and expanding set of business-to-business rules and processes.

The reality is, of course, that many major enterprises rely on EDI and will continue to do so in the future. Though EDI is expensive, the costs and uncertainty of switching to web services will naturally cause a gradual shift to this more efficient computing model. It should be noted, therefore, that it is possible in this environment to combine the best of both EDI and web services by "wrapping" the EDI message in a SOAP envelope and allowing the EDI message to travel easily through Internet protocols and be readable by a wider range of consuming computers.

There has also been a movement to expand on the goals of EDI with a novel XML format of its own. Running parallel to the development of web services, a number of standards bodies have derived a standard known as Enterprise Business XML, or ebXML, to help transition EDI into the XML age. At this time, it is not known if web services or ebXML will win the battle to move business-to-business commerce into the realm of open standards. The debate is likely to be moot, however, because the ebXML and web services standards are rapidly converging. It is likely in the coming years that ebXML will become a simple variant in the way web services standards are deployed, and that ebXML will be supported in the web services development, management, and security tools of the major suppliers.

3.5 COMMUNICATING BETWEEN MULTIVENDOR SYSTEMS

Have you seen the commercials that say, "And then it hits you. You are so ready for IBM…"? The reason those commercials are so effective is that they connect with the pain that we all feel from having spent years trying to get computers and software from different companies to work together. The catastrophic costs of incompatible systems are staggering, but they're nothing compared to the emotional devastation left in the wave of the hundreds of thousands of careers shredded from the untold millions of IT projects gone wild. Interoperation between systems that run on different platforms, operating systems, and programming languages is one of the biggest headaches—and largest budget categories—in all of IT. Let's examine further how web services can reduce many of the costs and stresses associated with this kind of heterogeneous environment.

If your business is like most, you probably have a number of different software packages running on multiple platforms. Your IT environment might resemble the one shown in figure 3.3. In this illustration, SAP runs on an IBM AS/400, Oracle runs on Sun Solaris, Siebel on Windows, and a custom COBOL application from the 1970s on an IBM mainframe. When it's time to get any visibility across these systems,

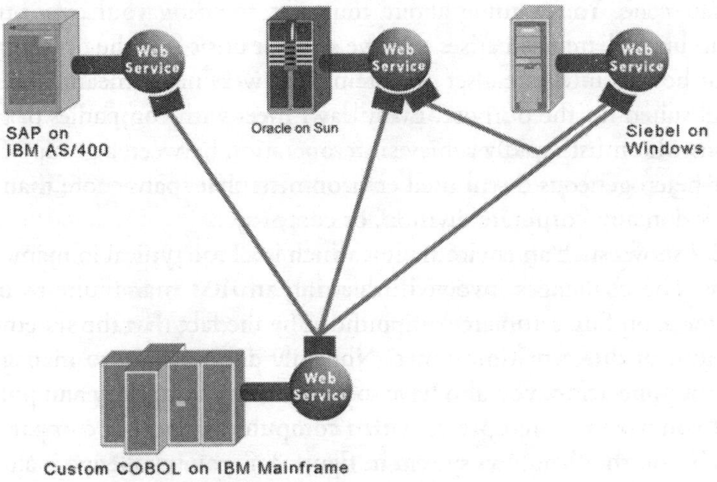

Figure 3.3 Because they are based on universally understood, standards-based protocols, web services enable interoperation in a heterogeneous vendor environment.

there seems to be no other choice other than to start spending big bucks. It's such a hassle that you may indeed be "so ready" for IBM to come in and replace all of your non-IBM hardware and software with IBM products and let them worry about consolidating or integrating it all. And there's nothing wrong with that choice—other than the extraordinary cost and a "vendor lock-in" that can leave you at the mercy of one powerful external organization forever.

As an alternative, you can let your systems run where they are and expose key functionality and data sources as web services. Then, with the universal interface of SOAP and the universal network function of Internet protocols, you can enable your mixed-vendor systems to interoperate with relative ease. In this model, you also gain the ability to take these exposed services and orchestrate them into business processes, and swap out in a modular fashion any specific service for another (from another vendor perhaps) as you see fit. The promise is clear: a modular set of loosely coupled services can free a business from the shackles of the old IT infrastructure. With a vendor-neutral approach, business processes can now be designed around business priorities—not technology or vendor mandates.

3.6 INTERACTING INTERDEPARTMENTALLY AND BEYOND

There's a great scene in the film *Apollo 13* where a bag of parts is dumped on the table in front of a group of scientists, who are then told they've got an hour to figure out how to come up with a solution to save the Apollo using only these components—none of them originally designed for the task at hand. I think any IT professional can relate to that scene. You're going about your day, minding your own business, and invariably an immediate need arises to solve a major crisis and the only way to do it is to figure out how to integrate a set of systems that were never meant to be integrated with tools ill suited for the purpose. Every day I meet with companies or government organizations who must rapidly achieve interoperation between a group of computers in a vendor-heterogeneous distributed environment that spans more than one building, network domain, corporate division, or company.

Figure 3.4 shows such an environment, which is all too typical in many large enterprises today. The challenges involved in getting an IBM mainframe to interoperate with that Oracle on Sun setup are compounded by the fact that the systems are in different divisions in different time zones. Not only do you have to manage the complexities of interoperation, you also have to navigate the budgetary and political issues involved. If you have to interoperate with a computer at another company, as we see with the Siebel on the Windows system in figure 3.4, your challenge is all the greater.

Web services give you a way to streamline many of the challenges inherent in achieving this kind of interoperation across corporate boundaries. By agreeing on a universally accepted mode of interoperation—one that costs nothing and requires no proprietary software to implement—you have gone a long way toward succeeding in this endeavor.

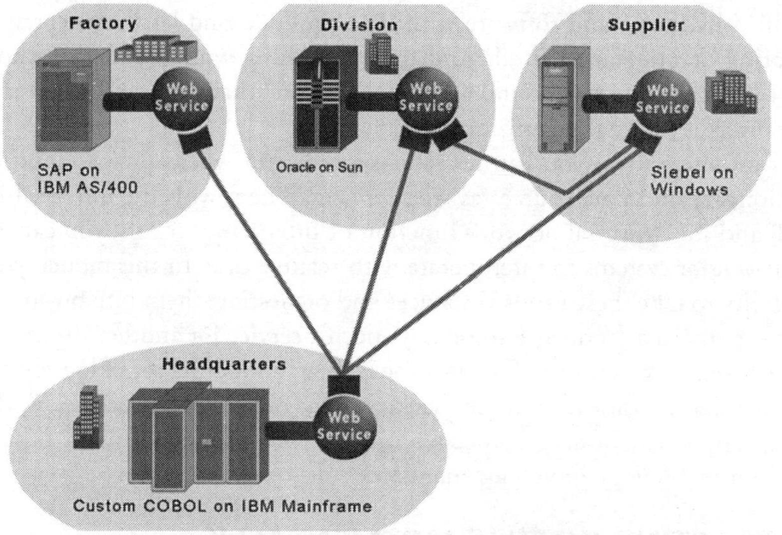

Figure 3.4 The need to achieve interoperation between divisions and separate companies is a process that normally taxes IT operations. Web services, with the universal, standards-based approach, make such cross-organizational interoperation comparatively simpler and cheaper.

3.7 INTEGRATING APPLICATIONS (EAI)

The field that has grown up around reliable interoperation among distributed computers in large companies is called enterprise application integration (EAI). EAI is a both a concept and a group of products. EAI refers to the process of linking large systems together. It is also a label that applies to a number of different software products, such as Tibco and webMethods, which provide interfaces between the distributed computers. EAI software products comprise many of those very same "proprietary interfaces" that we have been discussing in the previous chapters.

Web services stand to make a significant impact on EAI. As we have noted, web services simplify RPCs and data exchange, including EDI. As a result, web services can greatly simplify EAI and reduce or even eliminate the need for proprietary EAI interfaces. That is not to say EAI platforms themselves cannot still provide useful services, from security to business process modeling, but certainly aspects of the proprietary formats for interface exposure will be commoditized in light of these new XML standards.

Figure 3.5 shows a web services EAI situation. In this case, a series of web services are orchestrated to achieve a single result: a complete product order. To process an order, each computer must interoperate with the others in a specific, preset way that accomplishes the goal.

How is this different from simple RPCs and data exchange functions? The process must be reliable and auditable. EAI is about achieving a predictably high level of performance in interoperation. Proprietary EAI platforms can offer this today. Web

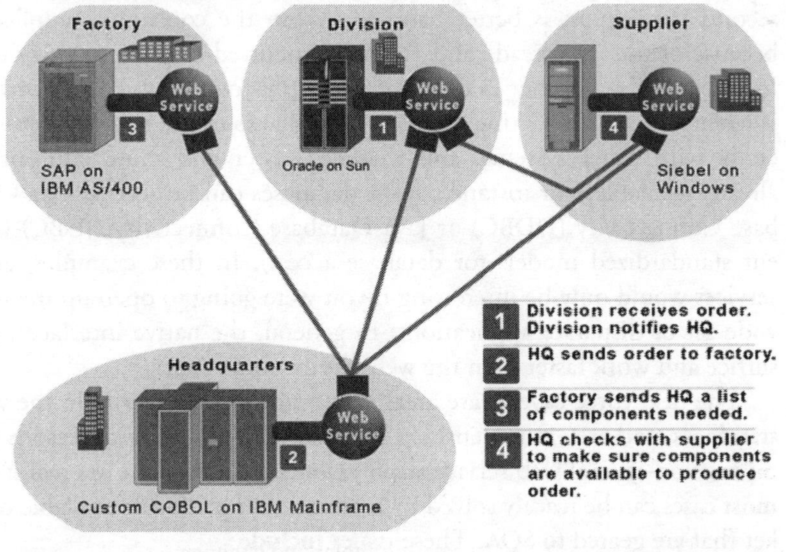

Figure 3.5 In this example of four enterprise applications interoperating to execute a factory order, web services provide a standards-based way to execute the necessary EAI.

services alone—without an EAI platform—can also make this happen, though it is first necessary to overcome a number of limitations in web services technology. Let's take a look at those limitations next.

3.8 THE SAVVY MANAGER CAUTIONS: THE LIMITS OF WEB SERVICES

Impressive as they are, web services certainly have limitations as well. These limitations are important to remember because technology is like politics—the claims and promises invariably diverge from what is delivered once the vote is cast. My goal in this book is to provide the ability to judge for yourself the strengths and weaknesses of web services. While the strengths clearly outweigh the downside, by understanding the pitfalls we can plan around them and also ensure we are applying the technology only where it is suited and not as a wholesale remedy to our ills.

Several key issues are often raised when considering web services:

- **Latency**—XML is considerably slower than communication formats that are more compressed. For this reason, web services are better suited for "coarse-grain" functions—that is, transactions that offer considerable value, rather than "subroutine"-level calculations. For instance, a good example of an appropriate web service is to offer the weather in a location (send me a zip code request in SOAP and I'll respond with a SOAP message with the climate in your region of choice); an inappropriate web service would be adding two numbers together. In the first example, a major set of algorithms and processes are invoked; in the second the request is better handled within the consuming application itself because of the "overhead" and "latency" incurred in going outside to a service for the answer. Another example of where this overhead is not worth incurring is when you are interacting with a system that is not meant to interoperate generally with other systems, and that has faster and more efficient interfaces already available. For instance, most databases can be accessed via Open Database Connectivity (ODBC) or Java Database Connectivity (JDBC) (two different standardized models for database access). In these examples, adding web services would only be interesting if you were going to open up the queries to a wide set of disparate applications; in general, the native interface options will suffice and work faster than the web service equivalent.

  The next three caveats are areas that point to immaturity in the web service standards, and are often identified by existing EAI vendors as reasons to hold off on mission-critical web service deployments. In fact, these are real issues but in most cases can be readily solved by management platforms available on the market that are geared to SOA. These issues include

- **Security**—Exposing sensitive data via "standards" that anyone can understand is a doubled-edged sword—efficient on one side, deadly on the other. Without protecting your services from unauthorized access, all the efficiency in the world is not worth the corollary risks. To deploy web services in an enterprise, one must therefore address issues of user and system authorization and authentication, and encryption of messages in flight.

- **Management**—Allowing "web service consumers" to directly interact with web services creates a peer-to-peer relationship that brings with it an inherent management challenge. How can one monitor performance and ensure reliability, audit results, or enforce service-level agreements without actually knowing anything about the interaction with the services? Enterprise class web service therefore necessarily means entering "the conversation" between your web services and those who consume them. This is a cornerstone of web services management, and will be addressed later in this text.
- **Transparency**—The reason transparency is important as you set up your web services network is simple: there's no reason to use web services in the first place if you fail to achieve transparency. In other words, all the benefits of shifting to this hyper-efficient computing model fall away if the model isn't able to handle change in the configuration of the "services fabric" without causing major upheaval and cost in your enterprise. Transparency lets you shield your enterprise from change and create an adaptive infrastructure that dynamically handles change without human intervention, allowing your dependent systems and processes to function unaffected.

In the case of latency, the key to web services usage is to apply the technology where appropriate and not willy-nilly. We will further explore where web services are most effectively applied in this book. In the case of the other often-heralded limitations, the objections are handily overcome with proper planning and education as to the standards and technologies available to assist. These standards and technologies will also be addressed in detail in this book as we demonstrate their enormous power even in these early years of the maturity cycle.

3.8.1 Replacing legacy systems

A confusing marketing message you may hear today is that web services can replace all of your old legacy systems. This is a misunderstanding of the purpose of the XML standards and where they are best applied. First of all, web services should not be confused with programming languages; web services are a mechanism for interoperability between applications regardless of the platform (mainframe, Linux, etc.) or language (Java, C++, etc.). The purpose of web services is quite the opposite of a "rewrite," but in fact enables organizations to leverage their existing assets by exposing them through standards.

In terms of cost, exposing key legacy system functionality as web services is usually a cost-effective, positive return on investment (ROI)-producing evolutionary step. Ripping legacy systems out and replacing them with more modern equivalents is an order of magnitude more expensive, and often not any more effective. Depending on the circumstances, it is usually more prudent to "expose" existing systems with standards rather than rewrite them from scratch.

The sensitivity of the applications running on mainframes is such that organizations were previously suspect of using web services technology to expose interfaces because of security fears. These fears are largely subsiding now in relation to the many success stories of secure mainframe web service exposure, and the enormous cost benefits that have resulted. In fact, based on clear adoption rates in 2004, I can easily predict that the majority of mainframe integration projects will be web service–driven within a few short years.

3.8.2 Operating securely or reliably on their own

At this time, web services standards do not specify any consistent methods to ensure security or manageability. You can buy a package, such as Microsoft Visual Studio .NET, that enables you to create web services. However, that package does not give you the ability to ensure that the SOAP message you send to a third party will arrive securely. A web service as defined by the standards cannot tell you that the consuming computer is legitimately who it says it is. Nor can you really be sure that your SOAP message arrived at all. I'm not singling out Microsoft for criticism here; any web services development package will give you the same problem. When you create software that can be used by anyone, anywhere, over virtually any network, you are in effect abandoning much of the control you normally have over enterprise systems. There are solutions to this issue, to be sure, but web services do not have any innate functionality to cope with security and manageability challenges. We will explore these solutions in great depth in later chapters.

3.8.3 Performance

And then, there is performance. Web services today tend to be a little slow when compared with other modes of interoperation. There are many reasons for this, and teams of technologists worldwide are solving, or attempting to solve, quite a few of them even as you read this page. However, overall web services and XML require more processing firepower to move through networks due to the nature of XML and existing computers' ability to process the messages. As a result of this performance deficit, you should consider system performance as a criterion when selecting which of your applications you want to expose as a web service.

3.8.4 It's not always SOAP, either

You may be wondering if it is possible to achieve the interoperability of web services without actually using web service standards. If this concept has occurred to you, then you are definitely paying close attention to the material presented in this book so far, or you are a bona fide genius and should stop reading here and call me for a job. Yes, using XML without SOAP, you can actually accomplish quite a bit that web services can do, although it is important to be using the same kind of XML on both sides of the transaction. These industry-specific XML standards are popping up in virtually every sector of the economy, and will eventually merge with web service standards.

A number of non-SOAP XML approaches to web services are in use today. I mention them here because there is some confusion in the marketplace today over what the "real" web services are—SOAP or non-SOAP.

RosettaNet was an early attempt to achieve standards using XML for the interoperation of computers used in supply-chain management. The Association for Cooperative Operations Research and Development (ACORD) is another set of XML standards used by the insurance industry. Enterprise Business XML (ebXML) is a set of standards that emerged from attempts to transition EDI to XML. All three of these standards groups are currently in use and enjoying some rate of success. As we move forward with web services, it is likely that overarching interoperability standards will merge with all of these different approaches.

3.9 SUMMARY

Web services enable two basic types of interoperation between distributed computers: remote procedure calls (RPCs) and data exchange. Both of these processes existed prior to the invention of web services. However, web services have the potential to simplify the cost and difficulty of their execution. In an RPC, the web service consumer sends a SOAP request to the web service asking that a specific procedure be carried out. The web service performs the procedure that has been requested and transmits the result back to the consumer in a SOAP response. A dollars-to-yen currency conversion would be an example of an RPC. In a data exchange, the web service consumer sends a SOAP request to the web service asking for a specific set of data. The web service answers by sending the requested data back to the consumer in a SOAP response.

Electronic data interchange (EDI), the standard of data exchange among corporate partners for many years, is now changing as a result of web services standards. Because many large businesses have an existing investment in EDI, it is probable that many will gradually convert their EDI systems to a web services basis rather than wholly replace them. For this reason, the web services community has paid a great deal of attention to EDI.

Web services enable interoperation between disparate systems with a heterogeneous mix of vendors, platforms, operating systems, and programming languages, such as Oracle on Sun interoperating with SAP on IBM. As a result, web services enable a greater degree of "vendor neutrality" than has traditionally been possible in corporate IT. This neutrality brings with it a new sense of modularity that, in effect, frees organizations from being locked into a specific company and liberates them to assemble their enterprise with a best-of-breed mind-set.

Web services make it possible for computers distributed throughout different divisions of a company, or even in different companies, to interoperate with relative ease.

As the pace of business quickens and more and more businesses rely on partnerships and alliances, web services stand to play an important role in connecting companies with one another. In a related vein, because of their ability to enable simple RPCs and data exchange among disparate and heterogeneous computers, web services are making a huge impact on the field of enterprise application integration (EAI).

Web services do have limitations, though. They expose legacy systems, but do not replace them. They cannot operate reliably or securely on their own, as they are merely a set of standards, not a comprehensive software package. In many cases, web services' performance is slower when compared with other modes of interoperation, and this latency makes them unsuitable for many tasks. Yet, there are many promising solutions to these problems coming onto the market. For virtually every limitation, there is an extant or emerging solution.

It is possible to achieve the same universal interoperation of web services using XML alone without SOAP, WSDL, or UDDI—as long as the communicating parties have adopted the same XML standards. There are several types of non-SOAP XML, including RosettaNet, which have been adopted in quite a few supply-chain management situations, particularly in the electronics industry. Other examples of non-SOAP XML are ACORD, which was developed for the insurance industry, and ebXML, which is an attempt to transition EDI to XML.

CHAPTER 4

What is SOA?

"Let's start mapping out web services for Titan," Jay says. "I'm ready."

"Not yet," I respond, omitting the term "Grasshopper," which is on the tip of my tongue. "We need to keep adding context and learn what an SOA actually is. In recent years, the vision of what IT can and should do for the enterprise, as well as the role of the IT professional within the organization, has become increasingly sophisticated and ambitious. IT has grown impressively from its humble roots as MIS [management information systems] in the 1960s. Top management's expectations for and investments in IT are far higher than they were in earlier times, even after the so-called 'tech wreck' of 2000. One of the highest-ranking and most influential executives at any major company today is the CIO [chief information officer]."

One fascinating result of IT's ascendance in corporate prominence has been the rise of a discipline known as enterprise architecture planning (EAP). EAP is the process of designing and implementing IT in a way that meets the goals and expectations of management while at the same time assuring the continuity and effectiveness of the IT systems themselves.

Web services are now making a major impact on the field of EAP. Their breakthroughs in interoperation, as well as their ability to improve alignment between technology and business processes, promise to usher in a new phase in EAP: the standards-based SOA. Because of its open nature, the SOA has the potential to deliver vast improvements in IT cost control, business agility, and business process efficiency.

4.1 ENTERPRISE ARCHITECTURE: THE BIG PICTURE

Before we begin, let's clear up any confusion on some terminology we'll be introducing in this chapter. Some define enterprise architecture (EA) as the total organizational design, a corporate blueprint that includes corporate culture, markets, geography, technology, and human capital. This may be referred to as "business architecture." To advocates of business architecture, what IT professionals do is called "technology architecture." For our purposes, however, EA will mean the design, planning, and execution of the overall IT systems of an enterprise.

To see how EA affects the role and circumstances of IT in business, we should first examine the concept of "architecture" itself. Architecture is the process of designing buildings so that they serve their intended purpose. If an architect designs a house, it is meant to be lived in; if he or she designs an office, it is meant for work; and so on. Similarly, EA is the process of designing IT systems in order to "build" an IT structure that fulfills the needs of the business. Unlike much physical architecture that can be admired for its aesthetics beyond pure functional success, EA has no higher purpose than to enable the business goals of the company involved. In fact, anything done beyond that in EA is not only extraneous but a dangerous self-indulgence that can detract from the success of the company it seeks to optimize.

Like the brick-and-mortar architect who designs buildings, the enterprise architect is constrained by several factors. Gravity and the laws of physics, for example, restrict all architectural decisions. It is impossible, for example, to construct a building that is not rooted in the ground at some point with a foundation. Almost all buildings have a foundation, a frame, and a workspace.

The IT equivalents of the law of gravity rein in the design characteristics of EA as well. Figure 4.1 compares the architecture of a building with an enterprise architecture. Like any office building, an EA is built on a foundation: the network. The steel

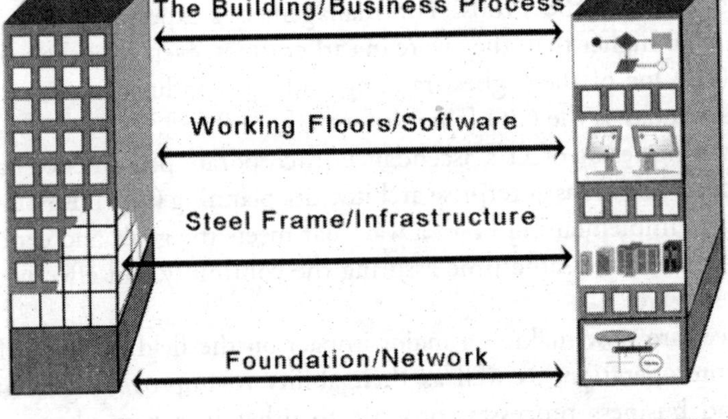

Figure 4.1 Comparing the architecture of a building and an EA in corporate IT

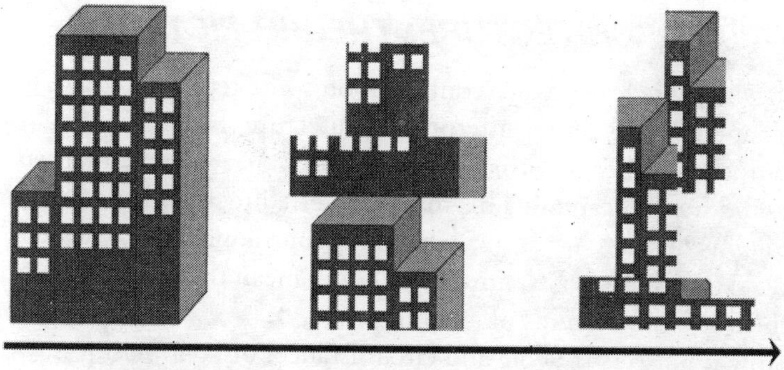

Figure 4.2 This illustration shows what a building would look like if building architects had to contend with the kind of disruptions that changes in business process models create in the IT world.

frame infrastructure of the building is analogous to the hardware infrastructure of the business. The building's workspace is like software; it's where the work gets done.

The laws of gravity and physics are relentless. It would be crazy, or even impossible, to design and build a set of buildings that resemble those on the right side of figure 4.2. And it would be even more impossible to take a building apart and put it back together again in whatever kind of layout you needed on a particular day.

Yet, in IT, that is exactly what is needed and expected. You may design an incredible set of systems with a brilliant enterprise architecture and six weeks after you've finished your CEO says, "We're going to be selling off the Asian subsidiary and buying a life insurance company. That doesn't make too much trouble for you, does it?" She or he is asking you to perform the equivalent magic trick to the one shown in figure 4.2. Somehow, you are supposed to be able to pull apart your "building" and put it back together again in whatever configuration is demanded. And then, you are supposed to do it again and again. How can you do that without having your whole "structure" come crashing down?

This has long been an intractable problem in light of tightly coupled, incompatible, and inflexible IT systems. The culprit: proprietary standards; heterogeneous vendor mix; heterogeneous operating systems; changing and disparate network protocols; changing programming languages... and on and on. The advent of SOA brings with it the promise of more flexible, adaptive enterprise architecture.

4.2 THE SERVICE-ORIENTED ARCHITECTURE

What if you could change the elements of your EA in relation to changes in your business without enormous expenditures of time and money? Suddenly enormous value would be created as processes are continually updated and optimized and as IT constraints give way to business strategies as the driving force in the company.

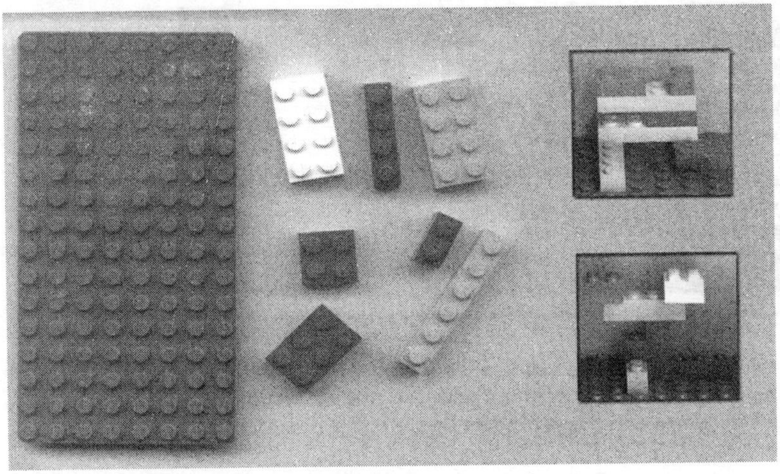

Figure 4.3 Lego blocks in changing configurations

This is the promise of the new service-oriented architectures. Because each element of an SOAcan be moved around, replaced, and modified. Because each of the services exists in a loosely coupled fashion, they can be assembled and reassembled in different forms for different purposes as circumstances warrant. The ability to create processes and composite applications from these services, combined with reusability and standards-based interoperability, creates what is finally the long sought-after goal of enterprise architecture—flexibility for change.

As technology commentator Rich Kuzyk aptly remarked, "…wrapping an application function as a Web service turns it into a Lego piece; now it can be plugged interchangeably into your other Lego pieces or a friend's Lego pieces, so it can be used whenever and wherever it's needed."[1]

The SOA turns your systems into the IT equivalent of Lego blocks. You can move and reconfigure at will. Figure 4.3 shows how a set of Lego blocks can be formed and reformed into a number of "gravity-defying" configurations. With an SOA, you are freed from building in the "bricks and stone" of traditional enterprise architecture.

4.2.1 Struggling to adapt in today's enterprise architecture

To see how the SOA can make a positive impact on IT, let's take a look at a hypothetical business that has a traditional EA plan. Figure 4.4 shows the enterprise architecture of a large business.

Like so many enterprise architectures I have encountered, this one is the result of an "accidental" EA process. The chief technology officer (CTO) inherited this

---

[1] Kuzyk, Richard, "Messaging Software Boosts Web Services," ZDNet, January 14, 2002. http://news.zdnet.com/2100-9595_22-813160.html.

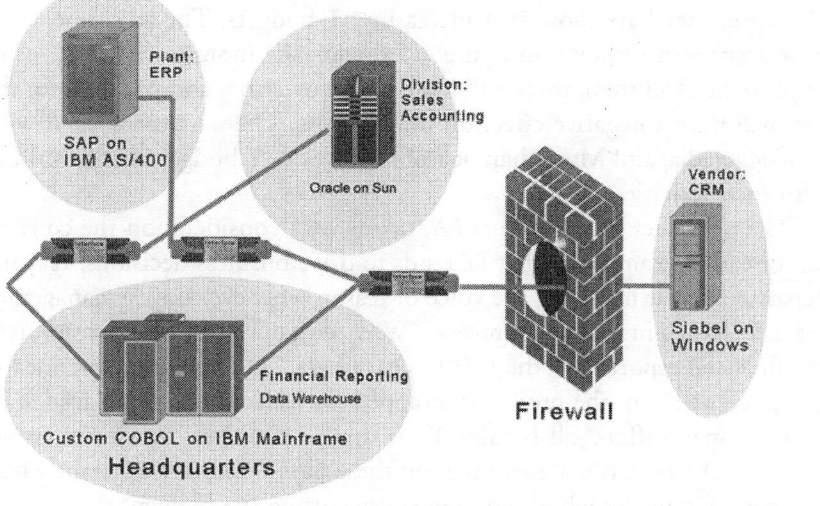

Figure 4.4 This traditional enterprise architecture, which consists of a set of legacy systems tightly coupled to each other with proprietary interfaces, is largely inflexible and costly to modify, in terms of both time and money.

patchwork of systems from her or his predecessor, who had probably also scrambled to make do with a complex legacy environment.

But, in the same way that "A stopped clock is correct twice a day," the fact that something is partially broken is not enough to cause a panic—after all, if it *kind* of works (despite enormous complexity and cost) it's not going to get the highest priority. For instance, a customer I assisted last year has a mainframe at headquarters that houses a data warehouse and corporate financial reporting software. The business receives information from a division, which runs Oracle on Sun, and a plant, which runs SAP on an IBM minicomputer. The plant, which is managed by headquarters, connects to an outside vendor, which runs Siebel on Windows, through an interface that spans the firm's firewall.

Though it is a little cumbersome and reliant on proprietary interfaces, absolutely nothing is wrong with this architecture. It runs well and serves the needs of the business. However… what happens when something has to change, as so often happens in business? What happens if, as we see in figure 4.5, the vendor changes to a custom Java application on Sun, the plant changes to SAP on Sun, and headquarters replaces the mainframe with a cluster of Windows machines? And the division is now responsible for financial reporting and management of the plant?

Oops. This kind of shift is a constant fact of life in large corporations, especially when new projects, partnerships, and mergers and acquisitions can occur at any time. Many CTOs find themselves in a never-ending game of catch-up as management works to make effective changes in the way the business is run. Those top managers, in turn, are frequently frustrated by the IT department's inability to "keep up," and of course, they hate those ever-increasing IT budgets. The adjustments to the enterprise architecture shown in figure 4.5 might take months and millions of dollars to implement. And then, there will likely be many errors and problems in the transition that will have a negative effect on the business. Then, a year later, it will all have to be rejiggered again! More than half of the typical IT budget in the world is consumed with such activities.

The net effect of traditional EA, taking into consideration the constraints shown in our earlier example, is that IT tends to drive business decisions. It is the "slow" IT department that has to be the voice of reason whenever upper management wants to make a change in business process. "What do you mean, the division is going to do the financial reporting?" the CTO says, aghast. "Do you have any idea what that is going to cost?" So, the project is scrapped, or scaled back, or delayed and the overall business may suffer—all because IT is driving the decision. It's no wonder that so many CTOs and CIOs are stressed out these days—they are constantly being asked to perform IT miracles while simultaneously cutting the budget.

Ideally, business goals ought to reign supreme in a business. The chief operating officer (COO) of a company should be able to dictate that the division is going to do financial reporting without having to worry about IT's financial and pragmatic concerns, as well as the likely delays and hassles involved. The CEO should be able to make a deal with a new partner and swap out a poorly performing part of the

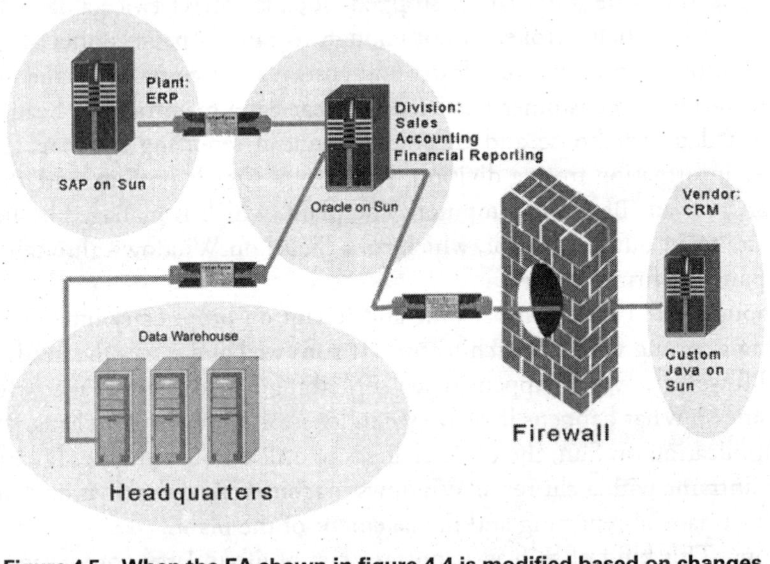

Figure 4.5 When the EA shown in figure 4.4 is modified based on changes in the business process, the result is another inflexible EA with new systems just as tightly coupled by proprietary interfaces as they were before. This EA will again be costly and difficult to modify.

supply chain without IT constraints. The board of directors should be able to approve a strategic acquisition without worrying that the cost of integrating the systems will overshadow the financial gains of the transaction. The manager should not be constrained by IT, as he or she is today. With the SOA, that vision takes a big step closer to being realized.

4.2.2 SOA solutions: theory and practice

Let's see how the company portrayed in figure 4.5 would look if it had an SOA. Figure 4.6 shows the SOA configuration. Now, each software application in the architecture is exposed as a web service. As a result, it can be accessed from anywhere on the network regardless of the makeup of the requesting computer.

There are several distinct advantages to this SOA model over the traditional model. At the very least, the company will save money by reducing the number of proprietary interfaces it must maintain. Change management becomes far simpler, too. If the vendor changes its Java implementation from the current Sun system to an IBM system, for example, the consumers of the CRM web service will not be affected. They need not even "know" that the computer behind the web service has been changed; it should make no difference.

Assume, for example, that in our hypothetical company, upper management decides to change its divisional structure and eliminate the division that had previously been responsible for accounting, sales, and financial reporting. Instead, management assigns responsibility for all those functions, as well as ERP, to the plant. And they decide to drop Oracle and put everything onto SAP. As figure 4.7 shows,

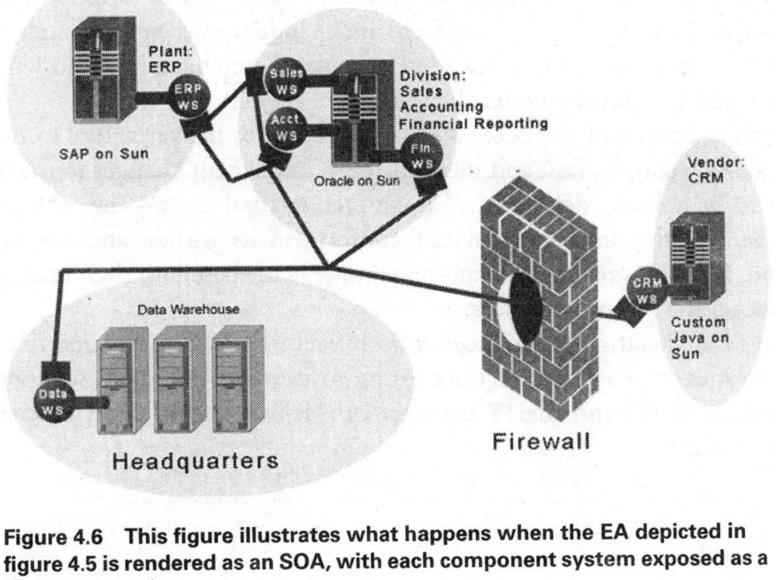

Figure 4.6 This figure illustrates what happens when the EA depicted in figure 4.5 is rendered as an SOA, with each component system exposed as a web service.

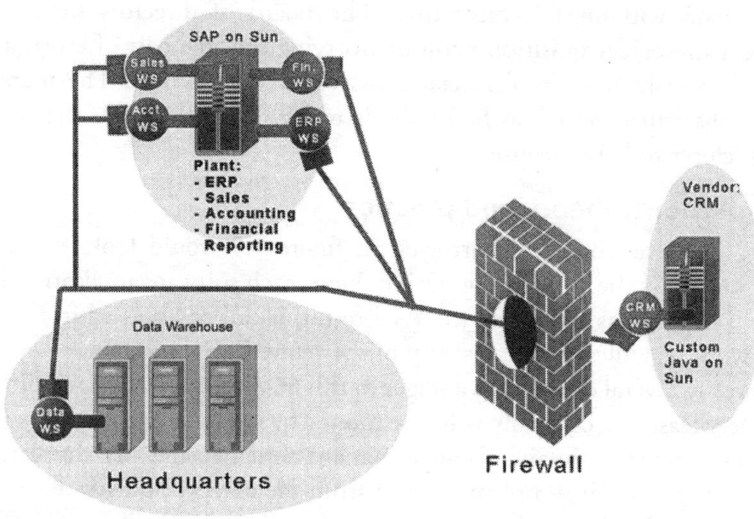

Figure 4.7 Implementing a change in an SOA is simpler than it is in a traditional, tightly coupled EA. All systems still communicate with SOAP; there is no need to acquire proprietary interfaces.

these sweeping changes do not necessitate the purchase of any custom or proprietary interfaces. All the systems are still communicating using SOAP, so the modification of the EA is simple compared to the kind of extensive code-writing that would be brought about by comparable change in a tightly coupled traditional EA.

How will this affect the enterprise architecture? With an SOA, the answer is "not much." Despite such a drastic set of moves, the web services can still easily work with each other because they are platform independent and network transparent. The amount of time and money required to make these changes would be a fraction of what would be required under the traditional model.

A main benefit of the SOA, then, is its ability to deliver agility to the enterprise. By making it simple, fast, and inexpensive to implement changes to the business process—to be able to "defy gravity" in an architectural sense—the SOA gives business management the power to make IT conform to its wishes, and not the other way around. Decisions related to management get made based on their management merits, not on the IT consequences.

This is a liberating experience for both the business manager and the IT manager. The business manager can act according to strategic mandates without the typical constraints of IT, and the IT manager can deliver results in an efficient and cost-effective manner.

4.3 THE SAVVY MANAGER CAUTIONS: EA IS A PROCESS, NOT A DOGMA

Enterprise architecture is an area where you need to be an especially critical consumer. For one thing, the term "architect" can mean many of things. There is no institute providing credentials for enterprise architects. Some are developers. Others have done architecture work. Others are administrators who manage architects and developers. When you listen to an architect, it pays to understand his or her background and objectives.

Also, I suggest you approach EA as a process rather than a dogma. Unfortunately, you may encounter some pretty dogmatic architects out there working either for your company or vendor firms. Enterprise architecture is typically an evolving set of design parameters. A good EA is flexible enough to embrace change but rigid enough to avoid the deployment of incompatible systems or costly system conflicts. An effective EA takes the business process into account, and the business process is always changing. As you move into SOA, you would do well to be circumspect about phrases like "We don't do that" or "That can't be done." Conversely, be careful with "That's easy" when it comes from an architect.

4.4 SUMMARY

Enterprise architecture (EA) is the total picture of an organization's IT systems, how they relate to each other and to the business processes that they drive. The discipline of creating EAs is known as enterprise architecture planning (EAP).

Traditionally, EAs have been inflexible, confined by the strictures of network protocols, hardware platforms, and programming languages—much the same way the remodeling of a building is constrained by the physical constraints of the original structures. This tight coupling of systems in traditional EAs has rendered them costly and time-consuming to modify. As a result, enterprise architects have difficulty keeping pace with changing business processes.

The service-oriented architecture (SOA) is an approach to EA where each major element is exposed as a "service." The result is a distributed computing environment with a high level of interoperability between systems. The SOA enables the enterprise architect to "defy the laws of gravity" and combine and recombine software elements without the necessity of spending substantial amounts of time or money, assuming it has been implemented intelligently.

Because of its flexible, easy-to-change, and economical nature, the SOA gives business managers the ability to modify their business processes without the kind of IT strictures that have hampered such changes in the past. By making it a relatively simple matter to change hardware and software, as well as the location of systems, business managers can pursue their goals with fewer constraints. For this reason, the early adopters of an SOA approach will have a competitive advantage in their sectors.

CHAPTER 5

SOA for enterprise application integration

I explain to Jay that web services and the service-oriented architecture (SOA) have the potential to facilitate real change in enterprise application integration (EAI). In addition, the new technology can have a major impact on two related areas: portals and software development. All three of these endeavors currently suffer from difficulties caused by proprietary standards. In this chapter, we look in detail at the way the open nature of web services may offer some welcome relief.

5.1 Is Titan happy with its EAI?

Using the Atticus Finch technique, I ask Jay a question to which I already know the answer. "Is Titan happy with its EAI?" Groan. "Yes and no," he admits. "Obviously, we like what it can do for us. We just don't like the cost, inflexibility, personnel demands, and—"

"The tight coupling," I say, cutting him off.

"Right," he agrees with a laugh. "The tight coupling." Titan uses a proprietary EAI technology on the legacy architecture from Apollo Insurance. As shown in figure 5.1,

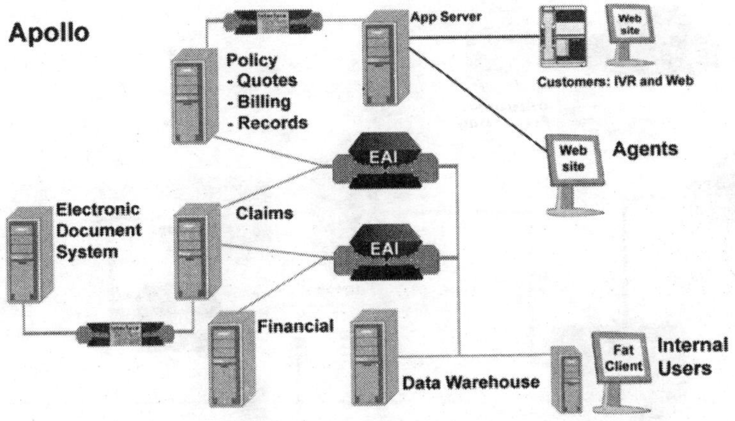

Figure 5.1 Titan uses an EAI solution to enable interoperation between its claims, policy, and financial systems.

the EAI solution provides a connection between the policy, claims, and financial systems. As is, it works fine. The problem is expansion and change management. Titan will need to buy more modules of the solution if it wants to connect the Apollo systems with the old Hermes architecture. That has indeed been considered, but temporarily rejected because the company wants to avoid buying more proprietary software that will further lock them into that one vendor and create permanent positions for software engineers who will be needed to maintain the system.

"What's more," I say, "you're lucky it works as well as it does."

5.1.1 First, the truth: EAI is broken

The unfortunate truth about EAI is that it often doesn't work. A recent Forrester report indicated that almost 65 percent of EAI projects are late or over budget. Yet, they cost on average over $6.4 million to complete—those that get completed, that is. EAI is generally a far longer and more expensive proposition than the final outcome would justify.

5.1.2 Islands of integration

Why do EAI projects go so badly wrong? Among the primary reasons that we will explore, perhaps the most problematic issue is simply the unstructured way EAI often just takes shape in an enterprise. Figure 5.2 depicts a typical EAI architecture early in its life cycle. Your company has three systems, but for any number of reasons—cost, management preference, politics, and so on—different parts of your company have elected to use two different EAI packages. Package A integrates accounting with the customer service department's customer resource management (CRM) while Package B integrates accounting with the mainframe. At this point, your company has to maintain (and pay maintenance fees) for one module each from two EAI packages. A third vendor may provide yet another proprietary EAI package.

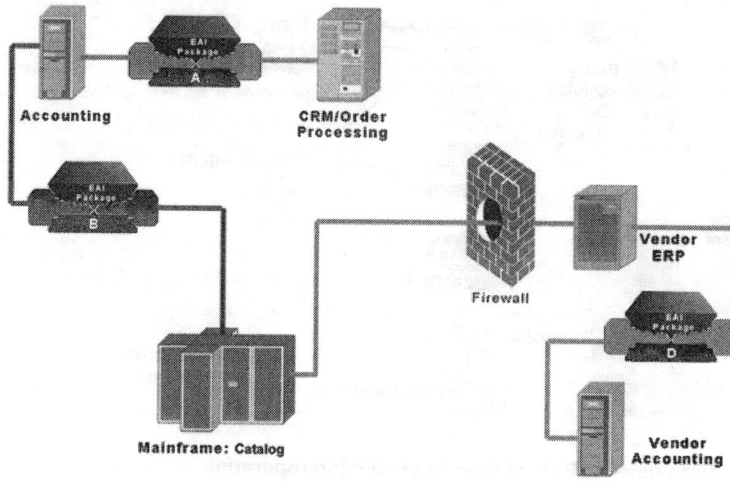

Figure 5.2 In a typical EAI architecture, as shown here, five applications might be linked by three different EAI platforms.

As time goes on, your company adds such new systems as enterprise resource planning (ERP) and a website. What happens if you need to connect CRM with ERP? In the majority of cases, you will have to buy additional modules of the EAI package to accomplish this task. You will require the "ERP to mainframe" and "ERP to CRM" modules, a situation shown in figures 5.3 and 5.4. Of course, each module brings with it annual maintenance fees. Adding EAI modules not only increases your IT management complexity, it also raises your budget permanently.

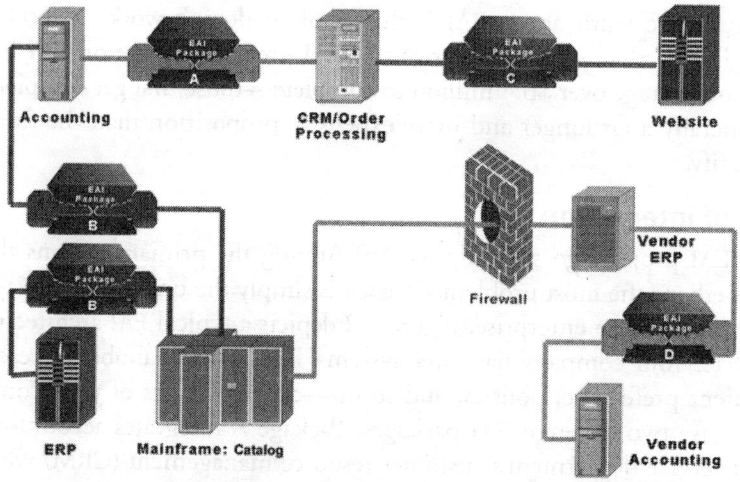

Figure 5.3 When a website and ERP application are added to the EA shown in figure 5.2, the company purchases a second module for EAI Package B and a whole new package, C, to achieve integration.

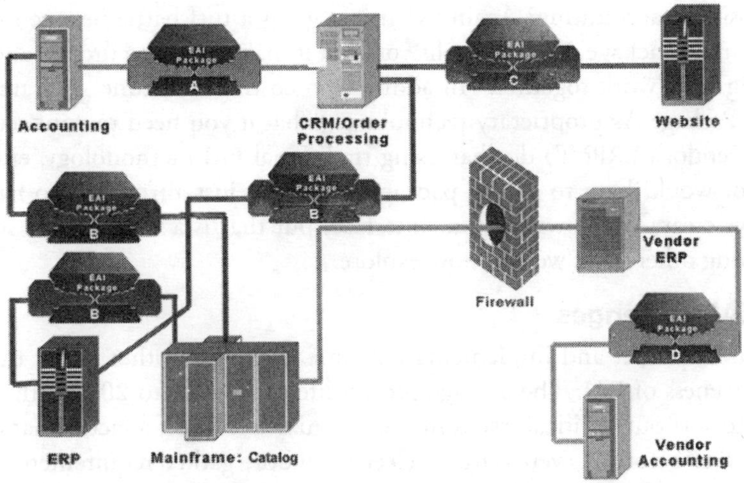

Figure 5.4 When the company wants to connect its CRM system with ERP, it now must buy another module of EAI Package B.

Whether the integration is done by a proprietary EAI package or through a custom development program, the result is usually a set of "islands of integration" in the enterprise. When integration is then extended beyond the firewall, the issues become even more complex. Figure 5.5 illustrates this dilemma. What if you need to connect

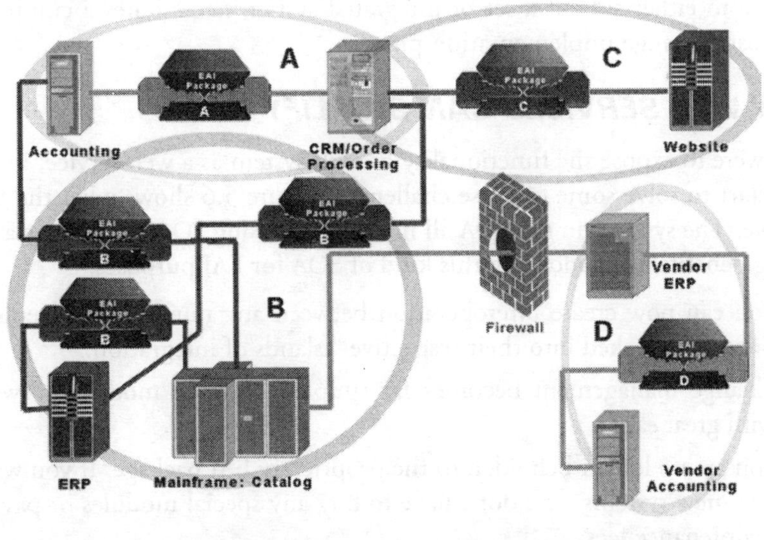

Figure 5.5 The reliance on four separate, proprietary EAI packages to achieve integration between the systems in this company and its vendor creates four "Islands of integration" that are complicated and costly to connect with one another.

your website to accounting? Again, what you get is a turf battle between the various EAI platforms. Package A's maker tells you that it makes sense to drop B and C so that everything will "work together." In addition to costing a fortune, you are still hampered by Package A's proprietary technology. What if you need to connect your ERP with the vendor's ERP? To do that using traditional EAI methodology, either you or the vendor would have to switch packages, and that just ain't going to happen. You can always create your own custom interface, but that is a whole other set of problems, among others that we will now explore.

5.1.3 Other EAI challenges

A long development and implementation time frame is another factor that impacts the effectiveness of EAI. The average project life cycle is 10 to 20 months. The time required to sort out political issues in the organization (itself a factor that can potentially kill EAI before it even starts), select a vendor, gather requirements, and then implement the solution may be so long that the early goals of the project are obsolete by the time it is completed.

The unintended result of EAI is often the creation of a high overhead "job for life" for a developer with specialized EAI package skills. When combined with the obligation to pay recurring maintenance fees on proprietary packages and buy add-on EAI components as systems grow and change, an EAI project can create a long-term maintenance overhead that is untenable.

Change management is perhaps the greatest cause of problems in EAI initiatives. With conflicts in data message definitions or mismatches in proprietary components, a change to either side of a set of integrated system necessitates a cumbersome and often costly change implementation process.

5.2 How web services can simplify EAI

If you were to expose the functionality of each system as a web service, in theory you could start to solve some of these challenges. Figure 5.6 shows what the SOA would look like. The systems in the SOA all interoperate using SOAP. There are a number of striking benefits from adopting this kind of SOA for EAI purposes:

- You can now create interoperation between any number of systems that were previously locked into their respective "islands of integration."
- Change management becomes far simpler. You can modify or swap systems with great ease.
- You are no longer beholden to the proprietary EAI package. If you want to connect new systems, you don't have to buy any special modules or pay additional maintenance fees.
- The EAI expert with the "job for life" is not needed.

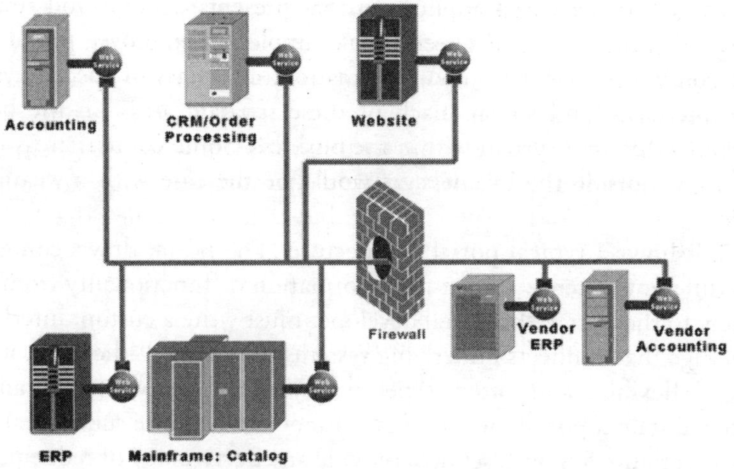

Figure 5.6 By opening all integration messaging up to the universally understood, standards-based protocols of web services, it is possible to break down the "Islands of integration" depicted in figure 5.4.

Comparing EAI and SOA side by side shows several differences between the two approaches to creative interoperation of systems. Table 5.1 presents a high-level comparison of EAI and an SOA based on web services. In each category, the SOA is more open and provides greater enabling of interoperation without reliance on proprietary vendor platforms. However, as we see in the next section, achieving integration of systems and applications using a web services–based SOA is not without challenges and limitations.

Table 5.1 High-Level Comparison between EAI and SOA Based on Web Services

EAI	SOA Based on Web Services
Based on proprietary technology	Based on open standards
Relatively tight coupling between systems	Loosely coupled systems
Minimal vendor interoperability	Standards-driver vendor interoperability
Restricted reusability of EAI broker interfaces	Highly reusable service interfaces by any SOA-enabled application

5.3 WEB SERVICES IN PORTALS

Portals, which can provide unified access to multiple applications, are in many ways comparable to EAI. As portals gain in importance with corporate users, the IT departments that develop and support those portals have come under increasing pressure to be more flexible in content delivery while continuing to trim the budget. Web services can deliver both of these desired objectives to portal management.

A portal is a browser-based application that presents content and functionality from a range of sources on one screen. For example, an employee portal at a business might contain human resources information, calendars of special events, sales forecasting interfaces, and so on. Each of these separate areas on the portal may originate from a different system within the business. Some content areas in a portal may come from outside the business, as would be the case with a weather report, for example.

Figure 5.7 shows a typical portal architecture. The portal draws content from a number of different systems. To get the information or functionality from the originating system to the portal, the portal developer must write a custom interface or buy a portal package that connects underlying systems to portals. Either way, it is a time-consuming, inflexible, and often expensive system. The workload and budget required to maintain a portal built in this manner can be quite substantial.

As shown in figure 5.8, web services provide an effective way of reducing the complexity and overhead that comes with custom-coded portal interfaces. With each supporting system exposed as a service, the portal can draw its content and functionality from each system without the need for any custom-coded connectors. The result is a simpler, lower-cost portal.

Change management in the portal environment is also greatly improved by web services. With a web service architecture, a portal can flexibly change its content sources. Figure 5.9 shows how a portal developer can "swap out" content sources by plugging in new web services.

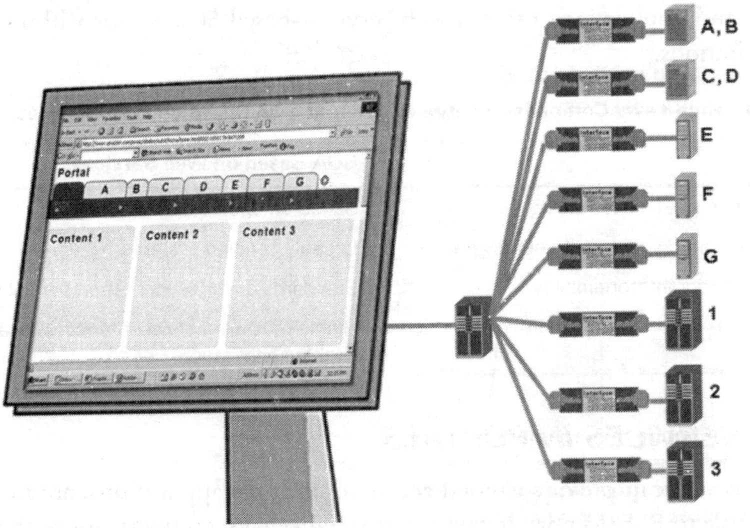

Figure 5.7 A typical portal architecture, shown here, might use a separate custom interface to connect with each underlying source of data.

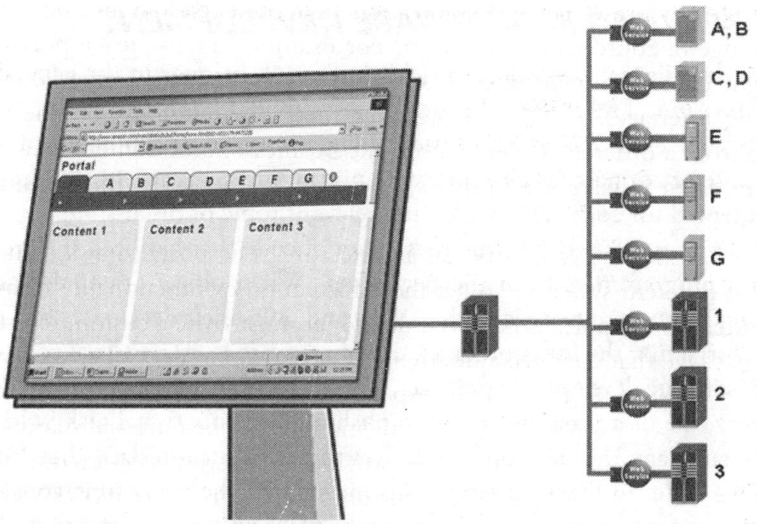

Figure 5.8 A portal based on web services acts as a web services consumer for each underlying data source that has been exposed as a web service.

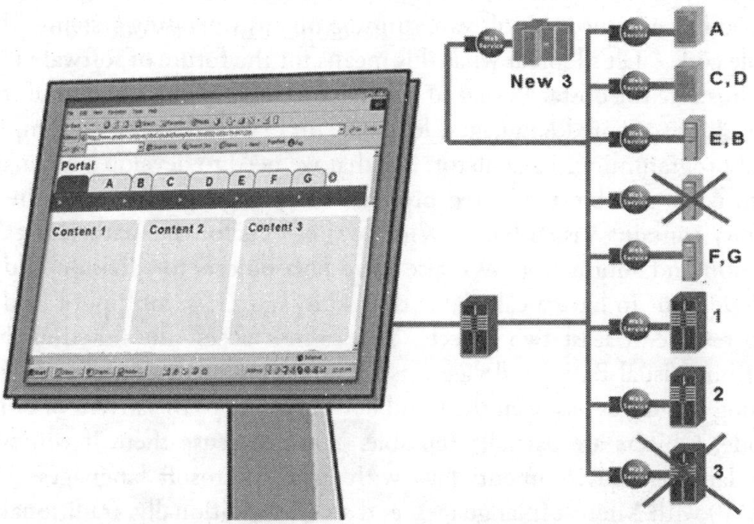

Figure 5.9 Change management is simplified in the portal architecture that is based on web services. The universal nature of SOAP makes it possible to add or drop data sources without having to rewrite custom-coded interfaces or buy new proprietary ones.

5.4 WEB SERVICES IN SOFTWARE DEVELOPMENT

Software development, although a field unto itself, belongs in the general discussion of EAI and SOA. The reason: the area of software development that touches on SOA and web services is that of application integration, the development of software for the purpose of connecting two software applications together. In this arena, web services' potential for code reuse makes it a relevant topic of discussion.

Web services embody the true reusability of code that has been the great dream of computer programmers from the beginning. When object-oriented computer programming languages emerged in the 1970s and '80s, their developers had in mind the goal of abstracting the function of a piece of software from its actual code. In contrast to earlier software development practices, where a software developer would have to hard-code every line of a program to accomplish a given functional task, with an object-oriented language the developer only has to access an interface that fronts for the underlying code. In practical terms, this means that the really time-consuming work of coding a piece of software will have to take place only once. After that, the code will then become an object that can be invoked without the necessity of coding it all in again.

Though it is far from simple, object-oriented programming has streamlined software development in many ways. Web services take object-oriented programming to the next level. Web services are, in effect, "universal objects" or components that can be understood by any piece of software running on any operating system—they are truly "reusable code." Let's look at what this means for the future of software development.

To illustrate the obstacles that to date have hampered the creation of truly reusable code in object-oriented languages, let's take an extremely simple example of object-oriented programming: a calculator. Say that we need to develop a calculator software program using an object-oriented programming language. As shown in figure 5.10, our library contains Visual Basic (Windows) objects for the mathematical operations of addition and subtraction. We also have Java objects for division and multiplication. If we want to have a calculator that adds, subtracts, multiplies, and divides, we have to rewrite at least two objects. You cannot access the functionality of a Java object from Visual Basic, and vice versa. The requirement that objects "match" programming languages has been the number one barrier to the advent of objects as reusable code. Objects are partially reusable. You can reuse them if you stay within a specific language environment: Java with Java; Microsoft languages (Visual Basic, C++, ASP) with Microsoft languages, and so on. Additionally, traditional objects had to communicate with each other over compatible message transport protocols. Incompatibility between message transport protocols was another barrier to the potential for objects to become universally reusable code.

Putting web services to work in our calculator example, we can expose each of the four existing objects as web services. (Note: This example is hypothetical and not meant to indicate an actual recommended use of web services in the real world.) Figure 5.11 presents this new object-oriented programming paradigm. Using SOAP and Internet

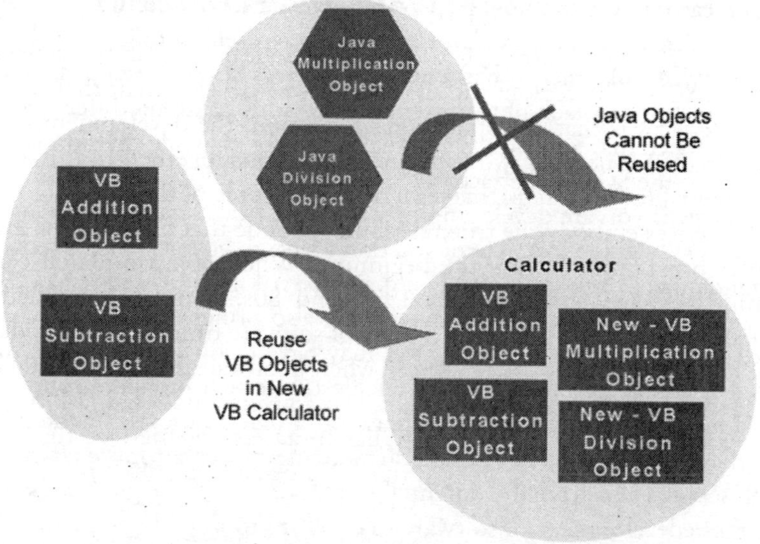

Figure 5.10 If you were developing a calculator software program using Visual Basic (VB), for example, and had objects for the addition and subtraction math operations in VB, but multiplication and division objects written in Java, you would have to create or find those operations in VB because Java and VB objects are not compatible with each other.

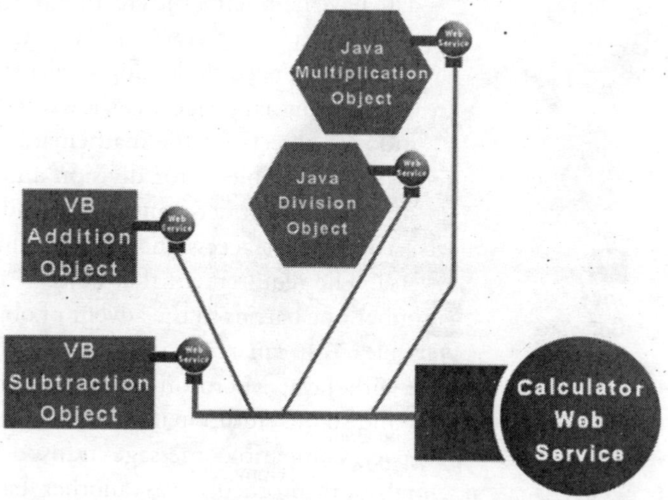

Figure 5.11 In the calculator example, exposing both the VB and Java objects for the four mathematical operations as web services renders them all compatible in a calculator web service. Unlike the example shown in figure 5.10, it is not necessary to rewrite the Java objects in VB to make them work together.

protocols, each object can now be used by any web service consumer program. In our example, we create a new calculator web service—itself an object that can be used by any web service consumer—that sends and receives SOAP message requests for mathematical functions to each of the original objects. It makes no difference to the calculator web service that addition is a Visual Basic object while division is a Java object. It only "sees" the SOAP interface.

Of course, if you are developing new software from scratch, you may expose your new objects as web services. Then, you don't have to go back and "expose" them later with standardized interfaces. It should not be a knee-jerk reflex to do so, though, because opening objects up to universal use also brings about some challenges. For instance, the functionality of an object may have to differ from what you originally intended if you decide to make it available to a much broader group of consumers than planned. Still, by encouraging reuse on a practical level for the first time, web services have great potential to make software development more efficient.

Web services also have the potential to reduce one of the greatest hassles in the IT world: the redevelopment of software to conform to migrating hardware and operating system criteria. Take the situation presented in figure 5.12, which is all too common in corporate IT. A COBOL application, developed in 1975, is rewritten in C when the company modernizes and switches to minicomputers in the early 1980s. When the minicomputer becomes undesirable for any number of reasons, the company rewrites the software in Visual Basic for Windows in 1999. Then, in 2003, a

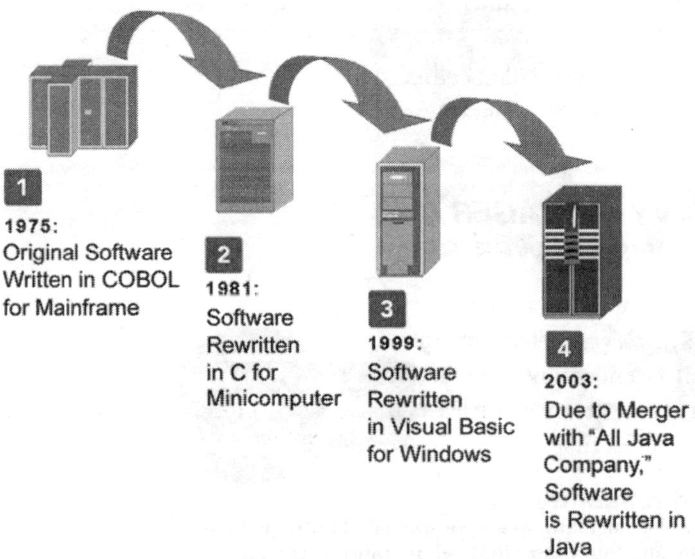

Figure 5.12 As an organization upgrades its systems or modifies them due to mergers, it becomes necessary to rewrite software programs so they can be compatible with new operating systems and programming languages.

merger with an "all Java" company necessitates the rewriting of the application again because the Windows hardware and operating systems will no longer be supported in the new company.

This continual rewriting process is costly and time consuming on many levels. Not only is it costly in real dollars—someone has to do this hard work—the process distracts from improving systems and accomplishing other pressing tasks. Each time that you migrate an application to a new language and platform, you may accidentally create bugs that elude discovery until after the new system has gone live. Rewriting the VB application in Java is an option, but rewriting is problematic. Every CTO has a nightmare story of finding out, months after launching a system, that it is calculating sales tax the wrong way, or incorrectly for a set of customers, or some such problem that might easily cost the company millions of dollars. Or the new system might cause some unforeseen conflict with other systems in the enterprise architecture, creating a breakdown in critical business processes.

By exposing the application as a web service, you can, in many cases, avoid having to rewrite programs for new platforms. In our example, when the company merges with the "all Java" company in 2003, instead of rewriting the program to create a common platform, you can instead expose key capabilities as web services. You then create web service consumer programs in your Java environment that enable the Java systems to interoperate with the Visual Basic program without "caring" if the underlying code is Visual Basic or anything else.

It is important to note that in this scenario you have to continue to support this Windows machine for as long as you support consumers of the web services it offers. Some people do not like having to manage that kind of heterogeneous operating system environment in their data center. However, when you weigh it against the issues involved in rewriting the program, web service exposure probably starts to look like a pretty good idea.

5.5 THE SAVVY MANAGER CAUTIONS: LIMITATIONS OF WEB SERVICES IN EAI

Now, if you were paying attention, you would have noticed a key phrase in the previous section: *in theory*. What an expert will tell you about web services in EAI is that they can deliver enormous benefits, but they cannot automatically replace all existing EAI infrastructure at once. At least, that is the story today. Several important issues have to be resolved first.

5.5.1 Speed and reliability

Because web services are not a software package, they have no inherent capability to manage the kind of enterprise message traffic required in EAI. EAI demands robust message management, reliability, and auditability. People need to know that their integrated applications are performing as expected. As a result, the consensus is that

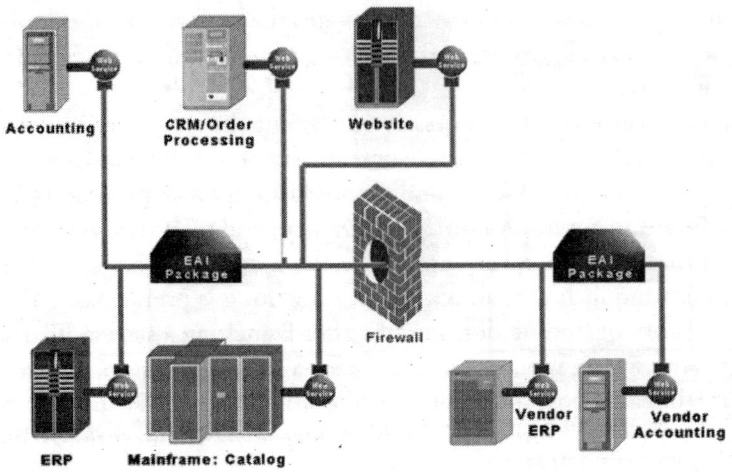

Figure 5.13 Because of their superior ability to handle enterprise-scale message traffic and related issues, some EAI packages may play a role in EAI in the SOA.

EAI packages will be around for a while. However, they will most likely be web service–based, and that makes a big difference.

You will still need an EAI package that can work with an SOA, or equivalent, to manage the interoperation of systems in an SOA. Figure 5.13 shows what this might look like. Each side of the firewall has its own EAI package assuring smooth operation of the SOA. Do you notice anything different about them, though? In the figure, the EAI packages no longer have the "lock and key" symbolism of proprietary packages. That is because in the SOA, the EAI package becomes a piece of web services–based middleware.

For the EAI vendor, this is not great news. Being web services based likely means that they will no longer be able to sell as many add-on modules to interconnect various systems. If everything is web services based, the EAI vendor cannot justify selling a proprietary package. The SOA will almost certainly diminish, though not eliminate, the business of EAI propriety integration platforms and drive a trend where EAI companies will emphasize their "process tools" rather than the underlying integration technology.

5.5.2 Security

Security is another big factor in adopting an SOA for EAI purposes. Impressive as the SOA looks in figure 5.13, it is entirely insecure. Because web services use Internet protocols for messaging, and because Internet messages are designed to go through the firewall, then web services are quite exposed to security breaches. Figure 5.14 illustrates how an unwelcome user could access web services in your SOA. There are some

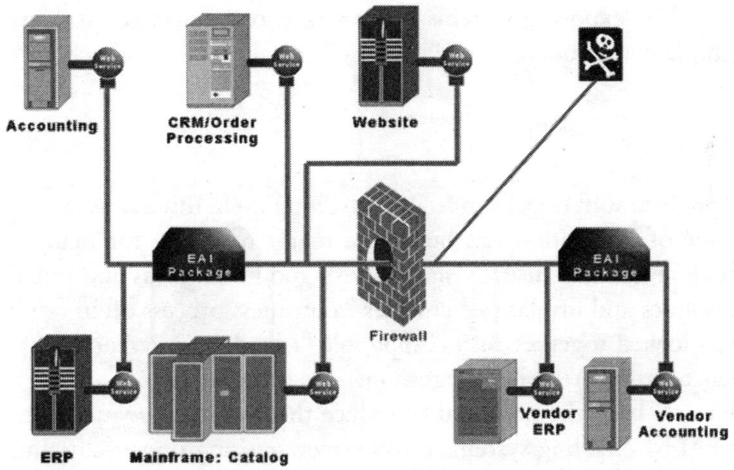

Figure 5.14 The unsecured SOA shown here is vulnerable to unauthorized use by unknown users who write their own SOAP requests.

excellent solutions to this problem, of course, and we address those later in the book. The point to remember is that web services in their natural state are completely open.

5.5.3 Political issues raised by web services EAI

Organizational politics is other reason web services are not an instant panacea in EAI. There is a reason why those "islands of integration" appear in most enterprise architectures. Often, they are the result of divergent budgetary pressures or political pull. Whether we like it or not, people in organizations tend to like their "turf" and want to expand their base of power. When these turf battles extend to IT, which they always do, the result is conflicting sets of priorities and agendas. Opening every system as a service is not going to make the issue of control, management, and budget go away. In fact, web services might compound the problems unless the organization works through the issues in advance.

For example, in our hypothetical company in figure 5.13, how is the accounting department going to react when it finds out that they have to support interoperation with the mainframe, the website, and the vendor's systems in addition to those it already supports? Who is going to figure out what kinds of information can be accessed by the new users? Who is going to pay for the increased infrastructure required to pay for the new higher message volume? Who is going to pay for and execute the changes in security policy that must accompany an increase in the pool of potential users of a web service? If the accounting department decides to charge a usage fee for access to its web services as a "chargeback," how is that issue resolved? These are but a few of the kinds of questions that automatically arise when systems are opened up in an SOA.

In sum, while exposing systems as standards-based services will bring powerful benefits, implementation requires a focused, disciplined approach to ensure effective results.

5.6 SUMMARY

With EAI projects suffering from high costs, long cycle times, and a high rate of failure, the issue of integration has become a major headache for many IT managers. Though such projects are usually started with good intentions and intelligent design, corporate politics and unplanned changes in business process often result in multiple EAI projects locked together in incompatible "islands of integration" that build further barriers to true enterprise integration.

Web services have the potential to reduce the cost, time requirements, and complexity of EAI by enabling systems to interoperate using universally understood web service standards such as SOAP, WSDL, and UDDI. Because they are based on open standards, web services also promise to deliver some degree of vendor neutrality, or lack of dependence on specific vendors. However, security and performance issues, as well as organizational political considerations, mitigate against web services as a "magic bullet" in all EAI situations.

That said, existing EAI packages are likely to endure for many years due to their ability to manage enterprise-level transaction volume and assure performance of integrated systems. It is also highly probable that these EAI packages will migrate to web services standards, a move that will permanently alter their company business models. At that point, EAI companies will primarily compete with web services "enabling" companies who offer the ability to add enterprise-class security and transactional capabilities to an SOA, as well as process tool vendors who offer industry standard-compliant visual process modeling tools.

In the portal realm, web services add flexibility by enabling portal developers to swap out content sources virtually at will. In contrast to traditional portal design, where the developer must write or acquire a separate proprietary interface to each underlying data source that feeds into the portal, with web services the developer can write web service consumer software to invoke underlying applications or data sources.

In the field of software development, web services deliver on the long-sought promise of truly reusable software code. As virtual universal objects, web services enable object-oriented software to utilize any web service–exposed object regardless of the programming language used to create the object. As a result, web services have the potential to reduce or eliminate the costly, challenging process of rewriting software programs to conform to new operating system and hardware standards as companies modernize.

CHAPTER 6

SOA for B2B commerce

We live in an era of "virtual" corporations, rapid product life cycles, and ever-changing alliances between businesses. These trends put increasing pressure on companies to find flexible, innovative ways to connect with their partners, customers, and suppliers—known in IT circles as business-to-business (B2B) commerce. However, while the Internet has proven a boon to some aspects of B2B commerce, many critical B2B operations remained mired in the rigid and costly territory of traditional enterprise architectures. In general, IT connections between businesses are difficult to maintain and complex to change.

With their inherent flexibility and vendor neutrality, web services and the SOA provide a method by which modern B2B commerce can be implemented in a flexible and economical manner. Web services and the SOA enable more dynamic and cost-effective B2B commerce, and this chapter will examine several ways in which they make this happen.

Before we get started, I want to start you thinking in terms of the interplay between business process and IT. After all, most IT exists because a business or organization requires it. In general, IT supports business processes. Too often business strategies are hostage to the rigid IT infrastructure that has developed over the years, failing to take into account that the whole reason IT exists in the first place is to make the business itself more competitive. This chapter, and indeed much of the rest of this book, deals with the ways in which IT can be made to support business processes as they evolve.

6.1 DOES TITAN DO B2B?

I ask Jay if Titan does B2B. "Yes," he answers, "Titan interacts with their agents, as well as certain government agencies, such as departments of motor vehicles." As we get into the discussion, though, Jay wants to delve so deeply into the nuances of Titan's situation that I feel he is "missing the forest for the trees." "Let's take a step back and look at some simple examples first," I suggest. "Then, we can dive into Titan's B2B situation. When two companies become partners, their respective enterprise architectures become partners, too. In customer-supplier relationships such as manufacturing supply-chain management and partner relationships such as airlines and car rental firms or auto manufacturers and dealers, traditional enterprise architectures have proven inflexible and problematic. The systems and their interfaces cannot keep pace with the changes in these relationships. Web services can enable these systems to connect with greater agility."

6.2 EXAMPLE: MANAGING THE SUPPLY CHAIN

Supply-chain management is one area of B2B commerce that provides some fertile opportunities for an SOA. To see how the SOA can improve B2B commerce in this area, let's examine a simplified example of a manufacturing company with two plants. As shown in figure 6.1, the business process for supply-chain management at this company dictates that if one plant runs out of a particular part, then its ERP system sends a message to computer at headquarters (HQ), which then automatically queries the ERP system situated at the other plant to see if it has that item in stock. If the other plant does not have the item, then the HQ computer sends an electronic order to the supplier's ERP system. The top half of figure 6.1 shows the map of this business process.

The lower half of figure 6.1 shows the enterprise architecture needed to support this business process. To support the company's inventory query and supply ordering, the enterprise architecture requires that four systems be connected using three proprietary interfaces. The mainframe at the first plant connects to the Windows-based servers at headquarters, which in turn connects with the minicomputer at the second plant and the Sun box at the supplier. As we have seen, this tightly coupled integration can prove to be inflexible as well as costly to modify and maintain. For instance, in the current architecture, the addition of new suppliers, competitive bidding on supplier contracts, and the like would be complex and expensive to implement.

Converting to an SOA opens up a number of new possibilities for conducting B2B commerce without significant reworking of the underlying systems. As shown in figure 6.2, in addition to eliminating the proprietary interfaces, the SOA makes it easily possible for the first plant to check directly with the second plant and place orders without going through the HQ computer, as it is now configured. Of course,

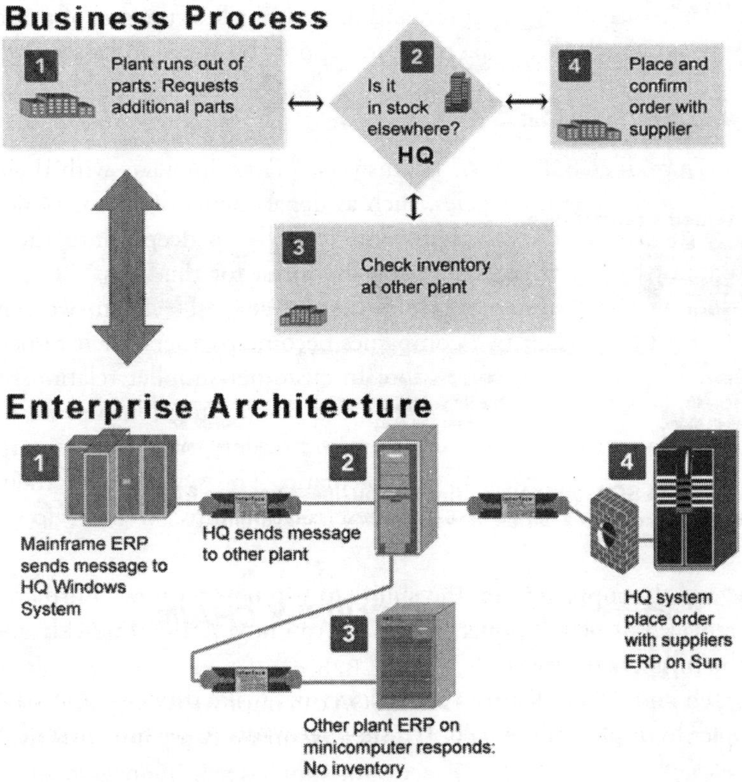

Figure 6.1 The B2B business process shown at the top is supported by the enterprise architecture depicted at the bottom. For each step in the business process, there is a matching set of system functionality or interaction between systems.

it would be possible to make that change to the architecture in the traditional method of modifying the interfaces, but that would be a far more complex and time-consuming task. The HQ system can now monitor the transaction flow passively using its own web service, which can digest the SOAP messages that travel back and forth between the second plant and the supplier.

To see how the SOA can dramatically increase the potential for B2B commerce, look at figure 6.3. The manufacturer now wants to institute an electronic competitive bidding system for its orders. The suppliers who want to bid on the opportunity to win business from the manufacturer can connect to the bidding system through a web service. Once again, this is certainly possible to do with traditional distributed computing technology, but at a much greater cost. The costs are so high, in fact, that such systems are rarely built, and when built rarely change without considerable pain. With the advent of the SOA, however, this kind of B2B commerce can easily take shape. The manufacturer gains the ability to manage its suppliers and costs more

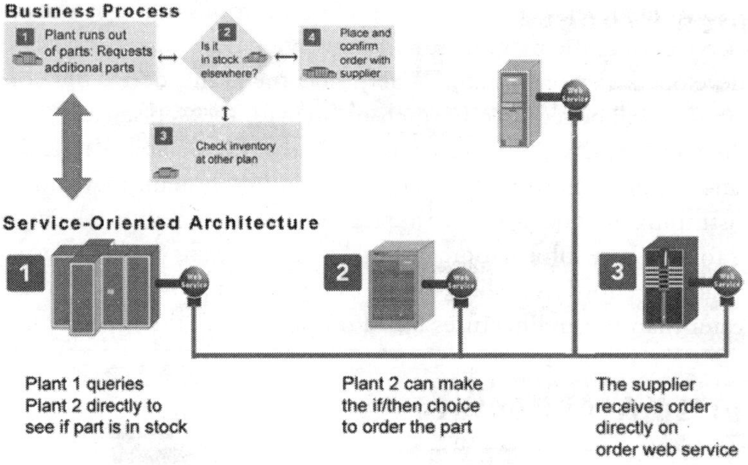

Figure 6.2 With an SOA, supporting the B2B business process from figure 6.1 takes place with a series of web service transactions.

effectively, and the suppliers gain the ability to win new business. Further, when suppliers are replaced or new suppliers added, IT can now respond quickly and inexpensively to the business decisions.

The UDDI and WSDL features of web services make the new SOA paradigm that much simpler to implement as well. If a supplier wants to become part of the bidding

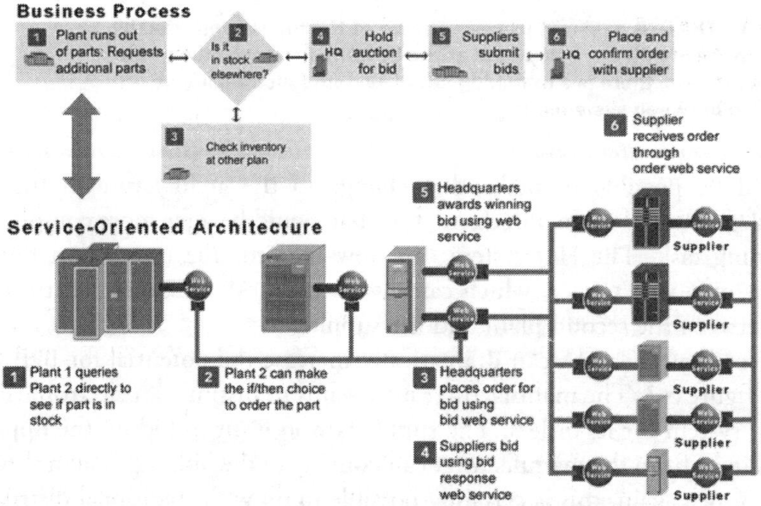

Figure 6.3 The SOA simplifies change management. When the business wants to add a multivendor bidding auction, it can require that its vendors/ suppliers adhere to web services standards when creating their bidding systems. When completed, the business can elicit multiple bids from vendors without having to use any proprietary software to make the connections.

system, its software developers can access the specifications of the manufacturer's bidding web service using the manufacturer's registry of available services. The supplier's software developers can process the WSDL document and derive the correct policy information that will be required to interoperate with the web services–based bidding system. The UDDI and WSDL gives these SOA features the ability to scale rapidly. If ten thousand suppliers need to sign on to the bidding system, they can do it largely without disturbing anyone at the manufacturer. Now, in reality, developers will call each other to exchange information and make sure they are working correctly, but in terms of relatively effortless scaling, the SOA enables improvement an order of magnitude greater than the architectures based on proprietary interoperability.

6.3 EXAMPLE: BUILDING HUBS

One trend in corporate IT that the SOA is encouraging is the development of various corporate "hubs." A hub is a web service–based center through which distributed services can be managed and secured in a central manner. Internally, hubs become the center for provisioning and management of services for the enterprise. Externally, hubs enable communication with an array of suppliers, dealers, clients, and so on. For example, in the automotive industry, thousands of dealerships must regularly receive and transmit sales information to the manufacturer. As illustrated in figure 6.4, an SOA and a hub can make this broad-based network of dealerships a reality.

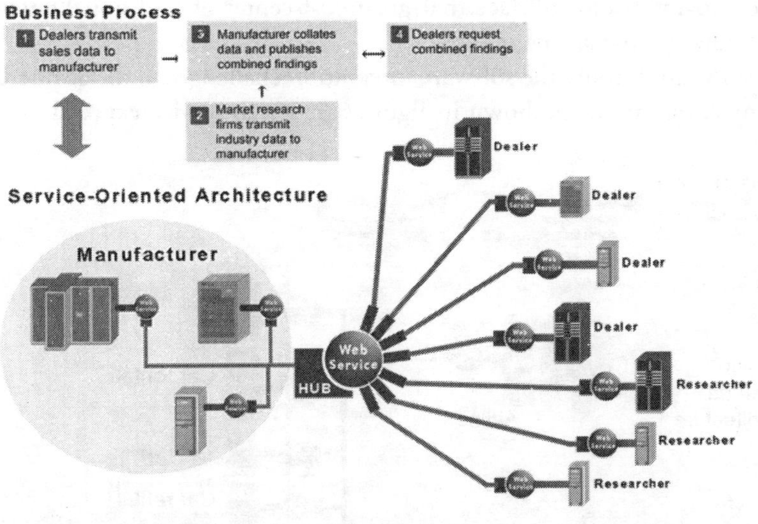

Figure 6.4 Auto manufacturers deal with thousands of vendors, dealers, and partners. To streamline the IT aspects of interoperating with so many different companies (an operation that was too expensive to even contemplate prior to the invention of the SOA), the manufacturer creates a single web services–based hub to which all vendors, dealers, and partners can connect.

The business process behind the automotive hub is a process of sales and market information sharing that has gone on for many years. On a regular basis, the dealerships report sales data to the manufacturer. At the same time, the manufacturer collects market research data from research firms. The manufacturer then combines the information and publishes it back to the dealerships. This was originally done in print, and then on the Web. However, the process was always slow and prone to errors. With the web services–based hub and SOA, it is now possible to share information in near "real time" with a large number of dealers.

6.4 PARTNER-TO-PARTNER: AIRLINE AND CAR RENTAL

The necessity for communication between companies that work in partnership with one another creates a strong potential demand for SOAs. For example, car rental companies and airlines often work together. The car rental company usually wants to know when a traveler's flight is arriving so it can best plan its operations. If someone is arriving late, or if their flight has been canceled, then the car rental company can plan accordingly.

Traditionally, if a car rental company wanted to be informed automatically of a flight time, its software developers would have to create a custom interface to tap into the airline's computer. Even if the airline provided a "kit" for doing this, as many large companies do, the work involved might still be significant. And then, the car rental company would still face that great cost center of traditional enterprise architectures: change management.

An SOA can simplify the software integration challenges in the airline-to-car rental company connection. As shown in figure 6.5, a web service exposed on the airline's

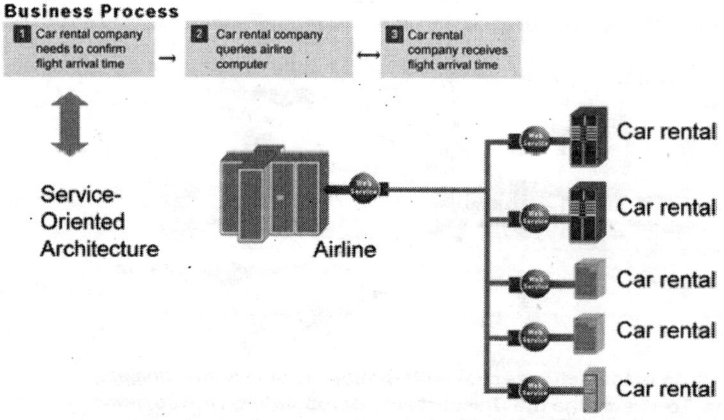

Figure 6.5 An airline can establish an SOA that links it to car rental companies and shares flight times using web service standards. As a result, the car rental company can have the latest flight times without having to resort to proprietary IT to make it happen.

mainframe can be accessed by any number of car rental companies, regardless of their hardware or software architectures. Change management on both ends becomes infinitely easier. If the airline modifies its flight arrival software, then the car rental companies can modify their web service consumer software without having to program to the airline's specific software standard.

Perhaps the most important benefit that the SOA brings to B2B commerce, however, is the flexibility that it confers on business processes. In figure 6.5, the business process is relatively simple: 1) The car rental company requests a flight arrival time from the airline, 2) the airline responds with a flight time, and 3) the car rental company receives the flight time. Now let's suppose the car rental company wants to make a special offer; for example, it tells its customers, "If your flight is going to be very late, we find out which hotels are available in the area in case you need a place to spend the night."

To realize the special offer, the car rental IT department has to implement the automated version of the following business process:

- **Steps 1–3:** The car rental company requests and receives a flight arrival time.
- **Step 4:** The car rental company checks to see if the flight is late enough to qualify for the special offer.
- **Step 5:** If the flight is late, the car rental company creates a list of nearby hotels that have vacancies.

Figure 6.6 illustrates what this process would be like as implemented through an SOA. The car rental company uses a web service consumer program to poll participating hotels, which themselves use a web service to respond.

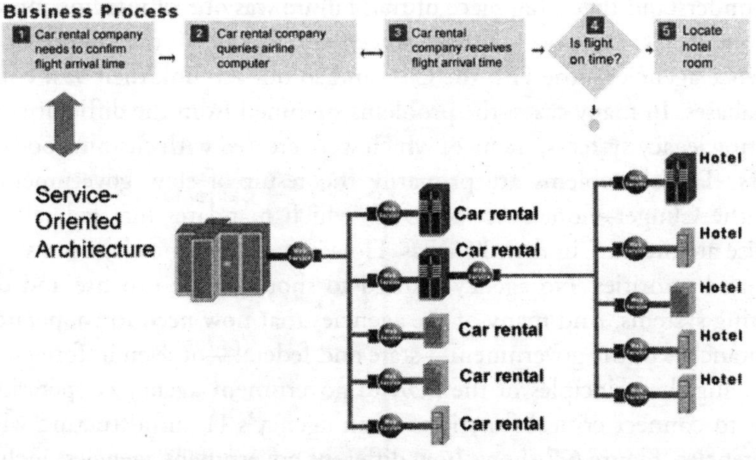

Figure 6.6 The SOA enables business process flexibility, as shown in this continuation of the airline/car rental example from figure 6.5. If a car rental company wants to add a hotel reservation capability—a new business process—it can set up a secondary SOA to handle the interoperation between its system and the systems of the hotel chains.

As with the other examples, it is of course possible to accomplish this type of integration using traditional means. However, given the effort and expense involved, it is unlikely that a car rental company and half a dozen hotel chains would make the commitment to such a concept. Why is that? The answer is that many new business ideas, especially various marketing alliances, are essentially experimental. If the idea doesn't work, then the partners drop it. The result is that most companies will not invest in trying new ideas if they bear a high IT cost burden to implement.

The SOA gives the car rental company the flexibility to experiment with new marketing ideas more cost-effectively than it could do before. While not free, it is far cheaper for the car rental company to connect with half a dozen hotels through an SOA than it would be to custom-integrate with each one.

6.5 GOVERNMENT AND SCIENTIFIC SOAS

In government, service, nonprofit, academia, and health care, there is a strong need for increased collaboration between groups, sharing of data, and ability to work together. The SOA has the potential to enable collaboration at a reasonable cost for the first time ever. At this time, the U.S. government has recognized the enormous potential of XML and web services to areas as diverse as geospatial mapping, defense, and homeland security. Indeed, several massive transformations of government system architecture are under way that will shift systems based on proprietary standards to open standards.

6.5.1 Example: coordinating government

When we hear about a "failure to coordinate intelligence" in the analysis of 9/11, we should understand that a big piece of that failure was one of information technology. Numerous articles have been written since 9/11 that detail the failures of the various intelligence agencies—the FBI, the CIA, and so on—to link their vast counterterrorism databases. In many cases, the problems stemmed from the difficulties inherent in connecting legacy systems, many of which were created with custom code over the last 40 years. These problems are primarily the result of slow government processes, despite the Clinger–Cohen Act of 1996, which mandates that federal agencies use enterprise architecture in their IT areas. However, each agency has its own technology budget and priorities. No agency wanted to shoulder the expense and difficulty of integrating systems. And many of the agencies that now need to cooperate are in different branches of the government—state and federal—or even in foreign countries.

Applying the principles of the SOA to government agency cooperation makes it possible to connect critical functions of an agency's IT infrastructure with those of other agencies. Figure 6.7 shows how different government agencies, including those in state, federal, and foreign governments, can share information using web services. In this case, the process involves searching for matches in intelligence in each separate agency database and updating the respective databases with any matches that are found. As you might notice, there is no "traditional architecture" example in figure 6.7. That

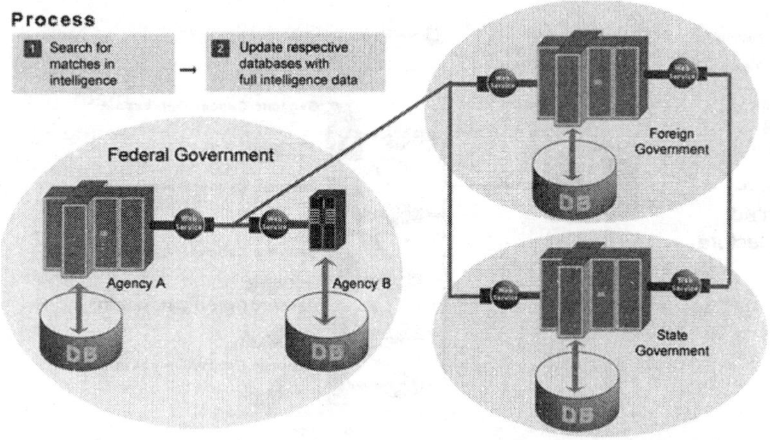

Figure 6.7 An SOA can enable more effective, as well as cost-effective, interagency collaboration. By exposing critical databases and process functionality as web services (assuming proper security will be in effect), multiple government agencies can share information efficiently.

is because the kind of interoperation described in this scenario simply didn't exist before it became possible through the use of the SOA.

Of course, IT is not the only factor in interagency collaboration. A wide range of political and budgetary issues must be resolved before the agencies can cooperate effectively with one another. However, the SOA provides a set of tools for collaboration that never before existed. As a result, they have the potential to produce dramatic results in government. The example shown here is but one of the hundreds of ways that SOAs can improve the government's management of taxes, health care, and law enforcement, among many other areas of concern.

6.5.2 Example: integrating scientific data

Of the myriad opportunities to transform scientific and academic research through the use of SOAs, perhaps the most intriguing is the area of biomedical informatics. Biomedical informatics involves the application of IT to improving medical knowledge and the practice of medicine.

Cancer genome research is an example of an area of biomedical informatics that stands to be greatly enhanced by the SOA. Cancer researchers around the world have begun to notice that different patients with the same kind of cancer respond differently to the same treatment. In other words, two men might have prostate cancer, but only one of them has success with radiation treatment. The researchers have discovered a correlation between a specific genomic characteristic of the patient and the success of a particular treatment regimen. The resulting implications for cancer treatment are profound. If the doctor knows what kind of treatment is best suited to treat a person with a given genomic characteristic, then he or she can provide that

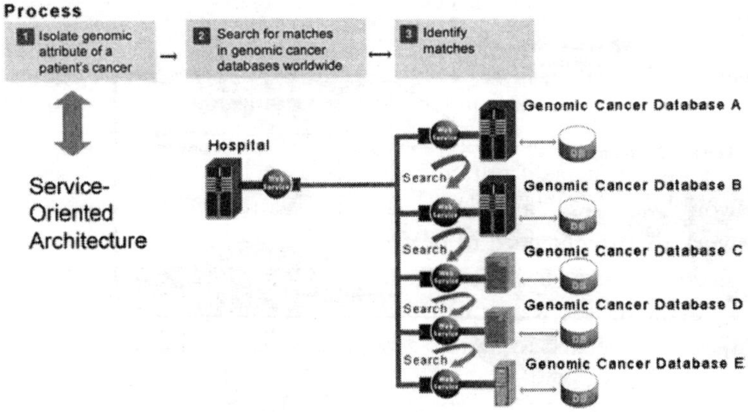

Figure 6.8 Genomic cancer research illustrates an innovative use of the SOA in the medical/scientific arena. When a genomic-cancer treatment link is discovered at a hospital (i.e., when success in treating a particular kind of cancer is linked to an instance of a specific genotype in the patient), that discovery can be compared to other cancer/genome treatment links stored throughout a series of linked databases worldwide. The data sharing enabled by the SOA can help other cancer patients get the treatment they need by identifying potentially powerful treatments for their cancers.

treatment and avoid wasting time with an ineffective one. The trouble is that this area of research is quite new, and the data available on the correlation of genomic traits and cancer treatment is highly distributed. There might be a cancer patient in New York who could benefit from a cancer treatment finding that was recorded on a computer in Brazil. How do you get the patient's physician in New York to learn about the genomic treatment correlation in Brazil? The answer: an SOA.

By linking distributed cancer treatment and genomic correlations databases worldwide, a biomedical informatics SOA can help save lives and advance cancer treatment research. As shown in figure 6.8, a hospital computer could send out a worldwide query requesting possible matches between a type of cancer treatment and a specific genomic trait. With each system exposed as a web service—in this case a web service that takes the genome and cancer data and matches it against its own database of treatment/genome correlations—it becomes possible to find genomic/treatment matches from any participating medical database.

6.6 THE SAVVY MANAGER CAUTIONS: YOU MAY STILL NEED PROPRIETARY STANDARDS

Here's a question: Are there times when you are better off using proprietary standards than open standards? The answer is a resounding yes, in certain kinds of situations. Though I am one of the greatest fans of open standards, I do not advocate them as a cure for all IT problems. For example, what would the difference in operating experience be if the airline and car rental company in the previous section needed to share a large database of information to reconcile the monthly transactions?

It would certainly be possible to create a web service that, upon request, transferred that large set of data from the airline's computer to the car rental company's computer. The car rental company's computer would receive the table in the form of a SOAP document, parse it out, and then transfer it to its database application. This process would work well, and the users would get to save money on any custom integration work that might need to be done.

But... the performance of such a web service would be atrocious. Because of the nature of XML and the way it is processed by computers today, the amount of processing firepower needed to handle a large database table in SOAP form would make the operation highly inefficient. Instead, the task would be far better served by the implementation of whatever native database procedural languages and integration standards are required to share the table from "machine to machine." In general, it is important to consider the performance ramifications of any SOA decision. In some cases, the challenges stemming from proprietary standards may be worth contending with if the performance concerns for an SOA are serious enough. Figure 6.9 contrasts the two approaches.

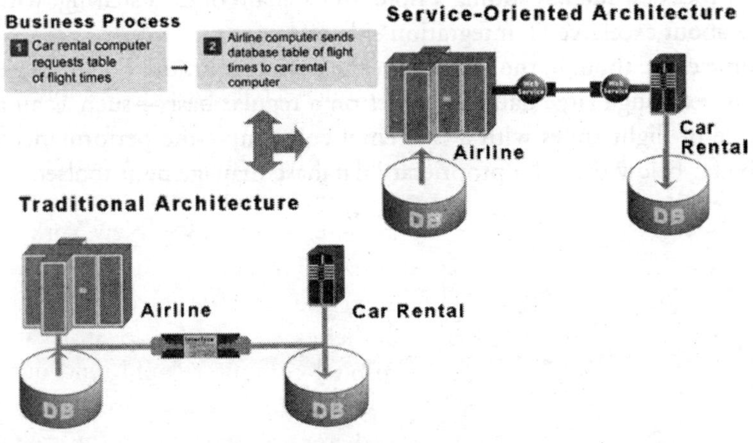

Figure 6.9 In some situations, it is preferable from a performance perspective to use proprietary standards. For example, periodic large-scale exchanges between databases are far more efficiently accomplished using the RDBMS's proprietary tools for exchanging tables than they would be with a web service.

6.7 SUMMARY

Web services and the SOA are enablers of greater B2B (business-to-business) commerce. By simplifying the process of connecting one company with another, and making it cheaper as well, the SOA facilitates partnership of many different kinds.

Examples of B2B commerce enabled by the SOA include, among others, supply-chain management, corporate hubs, partner-to-partner information exchange, and government/scientific applications. In supply-chain management, the SOA simplifies coordination between manufacturers and their suppliers. A corporate hub is a web services–based system through which multiple partners can connect. In partner-to-partner information exchange, partner businesses can improve their mutual functioning by updating each other with relevant data, for example, an airline sharing flight arrival times with a car rental company.

With each B2B scenario, there is a corresponding business process model. In addition to simplifying the IT side of the B2B transaction, the SOA provides for greater flexibility in business processes by reducing the complexity of adapting IT to changing business processes. For example, if a car rental company and airline share flight times, the business process is relatively simple. If the car rental company wants to then share those flight times with a hotel, the business process just became incrementally more complex. However, with the SOA, the car rental company can experiment with new business processes, such as adding a hotel to its chain of data sharing, without having to worry about excessive IT integration side effects.

In some cases, though, the SOA is not the perfect solution. For example, when systems must exchange large database tables on a regular basis—such as an airline sharing a table of flight times with a car rental company—the performance of the SOA would be far below that of a proprietary database management toolset.

CHAPTER 7

SOA: improved business processes

Jay looks glum. "It's all extremely cool," he says, "but I don't know how I'm going to sell this to my management."

"You lack a clear-cut business driver for SOA," I respond, and Jay nods as if he understands. "You're in good company," I add. "A study conducted by *InfoWorld* in early 2005 showed that 48 percent of its readers found 'lack of business justification' to be their primary inhibitor of SOA adoption at their company."

"Well, show me the business justification," he says, "and maybe we can actually look into to doing some of this stuff."

"There are many routes to payoff in SOA," I explain, "but several of the most respected consultants in the field—the global players—tend to see return on investment for SOA through its ability to help you improve business processes." Jay is giving me the "I don't want you to know I don't know what you're talking about nod" again. I go on.

"Much of what we call business is actually a collection of processes, such as purchasing, manufacturing, selling, billing, and so on. As companies grow larger, more complex, and more global, the efficient management of business processes can have an impact on profitability. Beyond the day-to-day management, business process management [BPM] can also help provide top management with an overview of business health and a read on strategic momentum. Effective BPM, and the ability to modify business processes dynamically, is a sought-after goal in that it provides business agility. In this context, agility means the ability to change and adapt to market conditions faster than the competition."

Wal-Mart is a good example of a company that works hard at business process optimization, especially in its merchandising area. Wal-Mart studies the rate of sales for different products at different stores and determines an optimum mix of merchandise to be stocked at each store based on an analysis of sales patterns. For instance, Wal-Mart may sell less lawn furniture in a region that has a lot of rainfall. An analysis of lawn furniture sales at that region's stores will tell management exactly how much lawn furniture to stock so as to avoid excessive inventory and wasted shelf space. The result is greater profitability and more satisfied customers.

In recognition of the efficiencies that attention to process can bring, many business leaders have begun to pay close attention to how their organizations manage those processes. In turn, the IT industry has developed a number of tools to help businesses manage their processes. They are called, not surprisingly, business process management (BPM) software packages.

Web services and the SOA are poised to make an impact on the way businesses conduct BPM. BPM software packages work from the premise that most business processes involve both human workflow activities or are tied to underlying IT systems. And, in the majority of modern businesses, this is mostly true. Figure 7.1 shows a simple business process—the marketing of credit cards at a financial services provider—and the subsequent enrollment of new cardholders, with each process supported by an IT system. Little happens in a major corporation without an IT system being utilized at some stage of the process. Because web services have the potential to improve the way IT systems communicate and interoperate with one another, the SOA stands to enhance the effectiveness of BPM efforts.

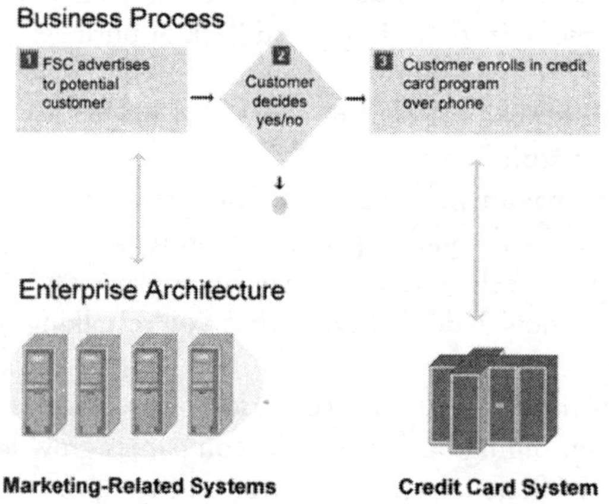

Figure 7.1
Business processes and supporting IT systems in a financial services company

7.1 THE "INTEGRATION-CENTRIC" ENTERPRISE

I call companies that use system integration as a vehicle for businesses analytics "integration-centric" enterprises. What do I mean by this? Assuming that knowledge of a particular business process is captured by the underlying IT system that supports that process, then a business manager can investigate the nature of that part of a business process by examining its supporting IT system. In the Wal-Mart example, the point-of-sale (POS) system captures information about the "sales" business process that it supports. By examining the data captured by the POS system, Wal-Mart's management can gain insight into its operations. If more than one IT system supports a business process, as is often the case, then it becomes necessary to integrate those systems. By default, virtually all businesses today are integration-centric because, heretofore, there has been no alternative to system integration as the path to BPM or business analytics.

To illustrate the concept of the integration-centric enterprise further, let's continue with our example of the financial services company using system integration to analyze the profitability of its credit card business. Today's financial services companies spend vast sums acquiring customers for such services as credit cards, bank accounts, retirement accounts, and insurance. Typically, a customer must be exposed to a number of solicitations—coming in the form of direct mail, phone calls, television and magazine ads, and other media—before making the decision to choose the service. The result can be a high cost of customer acquisition.

In addition to suffering from high costs of customer acquisition, the company may expend unnecessary resources servicing customers who have complaints, problems, disputed charges, or stolen cards. The provider may struggle with trying to understand who among their customers is the most profitable and who is the least desirable to retain. For instance:

Customer A

- Customer A is acquired for a credit card account after being exposed to $200 worth of media.
- Customer A enrolls for his credit card online, a process that costs the financial services provider $10, and proceeds to charge $5,000 to the card without a single customer service phone call, charge-back, or late payment.
- The provider earns $1,000 in interest on Customer A's card balance, making a profit in the first year of $790 on Customer A.

Customer B

- Customer B is acquired for a credit card after being exposed to $300 worth of media.
- Customer B enrolls on the phone, taking half an hour to ask questions and discuss the service. The phone enrollment costs $35.

- Customer B charges $500 to his card, but calls customer service three times to complain about errors on his bill at a cost of $15 per call.
- Customer B cancels his card after six months, during which time the financial services provider has earned $50 in interest.
- The provider has lost $330 on Customer B.

In addition to the challenge of understanding whether a customer is desirable (like Customer A) or undesirable (like Customer B), the financial services company must analyze whether it makes sense to market additional services to existing customers. When and if they do market additional services to the existing customer, they must decide how much to spend. When the customer enrolls in additional services, the company must evaluate whether or not the decision to market in the first place was a good idea. Should they continue to market further services, or stop? The answer to these questions can be found in silos of data that exist in systems that support steps in the credit card business process.

Figure 7.2 shows the business process involved in marketing credit cards, enrolling customers, and providing them with customer service. Each step in the process is linked to an underlying IT system. Each system, therefore, contains valuable information about the quantitative results of that particular process. For example, the call center's system might tell you how much time the call center has had to spend servicing Mr. Smith. The credit card system mainframe can tell you how much Mr. Smith has charged on his card, how on-time his payments are, and so on. The marketing-related systems can tell you how much has been spent to recruit Mr. Smith as a credit card customer.

The primary question, of course, is whether Mr. Smith is Customer "A" or "B." Was it worth the money spent to recruit him as a customer? If the financial services company wants to market additional services to Mr. Smith, will it be a wise investment of marketing dollars? (And the sums can be quite large—hundreds of dollars per customer signed up, in many cases.) The issue of individual customer profitability

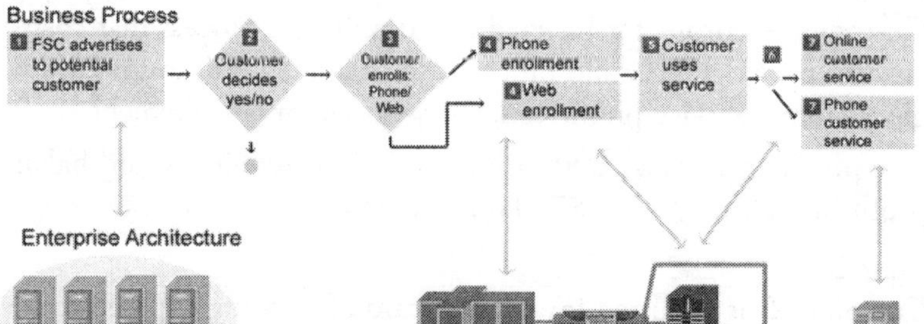

Figure 7.2 Customer acquisition and follow-on business processes, as well as supporting IT systems, at a financial services company

manifests in other areas as well, such as how the company handles incoming customer service requests. Should Mr. Smith be sent to the front of the phone queue, or made to wait? Theoretically, the best customers should wait the shortest time, but how do you identify them? The answer is you have to integrate the systems in order to correlate the data contained in them and figure out just how much money you have made or lost on Mr. Smith. In the integration-centric enterprise, there is one likely path to accomplish this task: data warehousing.

7.1.1 Data warehousing

One way to analyze sets of data that come from separate systems, as a financial services company would need to do in order to determine profitability of its credit card customers, is to dump the data from those separate systems into one common database. This common database is known as a "data warehouse." Figure 7.3 shows how such a data warehouse might be created at the financial services company. The company would create custom interfaces between the system that housed the data warehouse and the various systems that support the credit card business.

The result of a collection of the data into the data warehouse is a set of database tables that resemble those in table 7.1. The power of the data warehouse is its ability to link information from separate systems in one database. In the example of Mr. Smith, we can see the following:

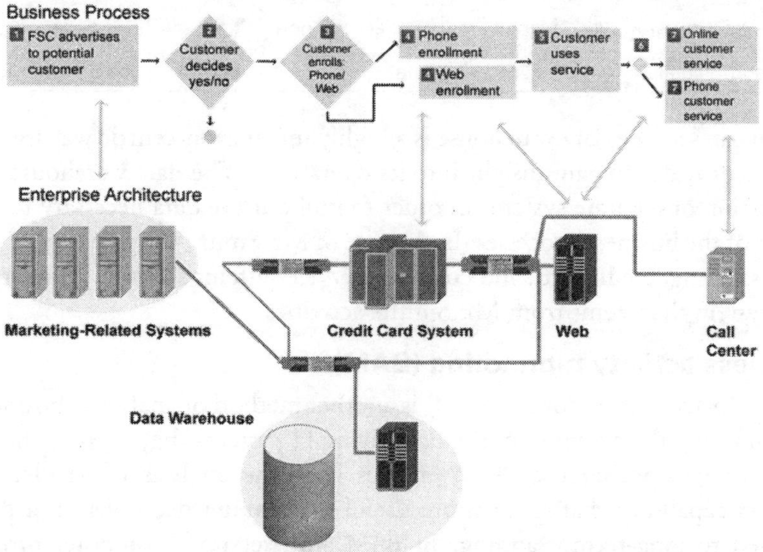

Figure 7.3 A data warehouse collects data created by various systems. In this example, the financial services provider's data warehouse collects information about credit card customer acquisition and subsequent card use. Once stored, the data can be analyzed.

- It cost the financial services provider $250 to acquire him as a customer—we see this in the data from the marketing systems.
- He has generated interest earnings of $80 for the provider—we see this in the data from the credit card system.
- He has used customer service three times, costing the provider $37.

The data warehouse makes it possible for the provider to calculate the value of Mr. Smith as a customer. In his case, he has made the provider $43, but considering the $250 cost of acquisition, he will have to continue charging on his card for quite a few months before the company makes back its initial investment. (This is why, incidentally, when you want to cancel a credit card the bank tries very hard to keep you as a customer. They know it could take a year or more for them to recoup the cost of acquiring you as a cardholder.)

Table 7.1 Data Warehouse Tables That Correlate Information about a Single Customer Across Three Source Systems

Data from Marketing Systems			Data from Credit Card System			Data from Customer Service		
Name	**Mode**	**Amount**	**Date**	**Balance**	**Interest**	**Name**	**Mode**	**Cost**
Joe Smith	Telemarketing	$100	June	$1,000	$20	Joe Smith	Call	$10
Joe Smith	Direct Mail	$100	July	$2,000	$40	Joe Smith	Web	$2
Joe Smith	Other media	$50	August	$1,000	$20	Joe Smith	Call	$25
Joe Smith	Total	$250	Total		$80	Joe Smith	Total	$37

As you can see, the data warehouse is a highly integration-centric way for the financial services provider to gain insight into its operations. The data warehouse relies on the integration of separate systems in order to pull out the data necessary to examine the results of the business processes. In the case of Mr. Smith, the provider has to integrate the marketing, credit card, and customer service systems so it can correlate the data in each system that stems from Mr. Smith's activities.

7.1.2 Business activity monitoring (BAM)

Business activity monitoring (BAM) is another method of analyzing business processes by examining the activities of the underlying IT systems that support those processes. Unlike a data warehouse, BAM enables real-time analysis of smaller amounts of data—a capability that is far more useful for making decisions on a daily basis as opposed to long-term planning. In BAM, you set up a computer program whose whole purpose is to "study" a specific IT function, or set of functions, that supports a particular business process. From the information gleaned in the process, business managers can gain insight into their operations and make decisions accordingly. As figure 7.4 shows, BAM is like holding a "microscope" up to an IT function. Management can also use BAM to conduct status checks on processes.

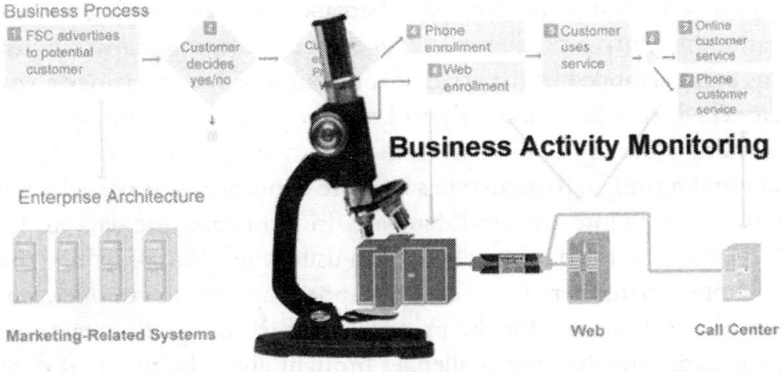

Figure 7.4 Business activity monitoring (BAM) is the IT equivalent of holding a "microscope" up to a specific operation. A BAM software program monitors the activity of a system or function that supports a particular business activity.

In the financial services provider example, a BAM program might be configured to monitor one aspect of credit card processing. So, for instance, the company's managers might learn from this BAM program that suddenly people are responding to a particular marketing program, perhaps due to other events in the news. From this insight, the managers might decide to strike while the iron is hot and increase the spending on this campaign while decreasing other less effective measures. The result is a reduction in wasted telemarketing.

There can be overlaps between data warehousing and BAM, too. A BAM program might feed data into a data warehouse. Continuing with our example, the BAM program that observes when people sign up for credit cards could be configured to submit its findings to the data warehouse. The data warehouse then could be programmed to correlate the date of signup with other data, and provide an historical analysis of trends. The financial services provider might then learn, for example, that women over 40 are twice as likely to sign up for a credit card on a Sunday morning versus a Sunday night. Again, this is a business insight that management can use to market its credit cards more effectively.

However, like the data warehouse, BAM is also an integration-centric approach to business process management. If the provider wants to analyze business activities that occur in multiple systems, it must integrate those systems in order to conduct its BAM program.

7.1.3 Issues in integration-centric enterprises

Though the integration-centric approach to business process management and business analytics can be effective, its reliance on system integration makes it costly and complex to implement and maintain. Once a business has elected to use data warehousing or BAM, it is likely to be locked into a custom or proprietary software platform that manages the data warehouse or BAM program. License and maintenance fees abound, and change management becomes time-consuming and expensive. In many cases, the expense of change management results in data warehousing or BAM programs being scrapped in the wake of some kind of system change a year or so after being launched. It is just too costly to keep the data warehouse up to date with the changes taking place in the IT environment from which it draws its data.

Data warehousing in particular has its share of problems. It typically relies on batch importation of data into a central database. In most cases the data in the warehouse is not "real time," so the data warehouse can usually tell you something that happened the day before. Then, there is the cost of supporting the growth of a data warehouse.

The acid test, however, for the practicality of the integration-centric approach to business analytics involves the challenges brought about by the need to analyze business processes across multiple lines of business or divisions. In many companies, it is necessary to be able to analyze business processes that occur in separate lines of business to be able to manage effectively. The same could be said for business processes that occur in separate divisions that were once separate companies prior to a merger. These situations severely test the abilities of the integration-centric approach to deliver a cost-effective and adaptable business analytics solution.

Our hypothetical financial services provider has the need to analyze business processes that occur in different divisions. As shown in figure 7.5, the provider has a credit card operation, a brokerage, and a bank. To calculate the "lifetime value" of a customer, the company must be able to draw data from each of the three lines of business. As we discussed previously, with the integration-centric approach, the financial services provider can either create a data warehouse or implement a BAM program to capture this information. Theoretically, that is no problem. In reality, though, it is quite a challenging proposition.

If the financial services provider were to create a data warehouse to capture the customer value information from each of the three lines of business, it would have to create custom interfaces to nine systems, as opposed to just three as it did in the case of credit card processing alone. It would have to connect to the marketing, operations, and customer service systems of each of the three divisions. That means the company would have three times the licensing and maintenance expense. And, assuming that the nine systems are heterogeneous (which they may well be, especially if each set of systems comes from a formerly separate company that was acquired), then the level of complexity involved in managing the integration becomes substantially higher. Change management is exponentially more difficult with nine systems requiring testing and debugging versus three systems.

The result of the enormous challenges and costs associated with cross–line of business (LOB) integration is that it is seldom done. And, it is even more seldom done for the purposes of business analytics. Business management may decide that the cost of integration is not justified by the advantages conferred by greater insight into business operations. This is a disastrous outcome, as business visibility and insight is an increasingly important factor in a company's ability to survive.

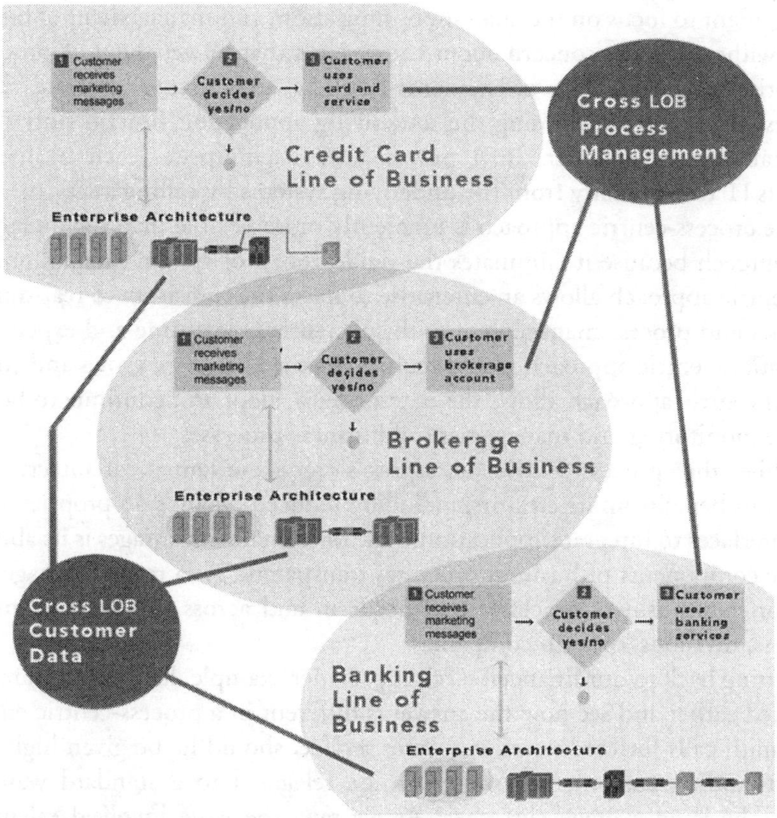

Figure 7.5 Multiple lines of business (LOB) create customer data that is challenging to analyze because the data often resides in separate sets of systems. In many cases, it is so costly and complex to integrate the separate LOB systems that it is simply never done and the business loses the opportunity to analyze customer behavior across multiple LOBs, often with a negative impact on the bottom line.

The ultimate issue with integration-centric business analytics, however, is who is in charge? Are the IT considerations governing the choice of what business processes management will look into? Or does the business management decide what processes they want to analyze without regard for IT considerations? Ideally, a business ought to be able to look into any process that it deems relevant without concern for the IT issues involved.

7.2 THE "PROCESS-CENTRIC" ENTERPRISE

The service-oriented architecture gives business managers the ability to improve their analysis of business processes by simplifying the manner in which they can monitor the IT systems that support business processes. In contrast to the integration-centric enterprise, a "process-centric" enterprise, which is based on an SOA, enables management to focus on the analysis, optimization, and management of business processes without undue concern about the systems that power them. A process-centric enterprise takes advantage of standards-based IT architecture to create visibility for business processes by exposing the underlying application functionality in an open and standardized manner. In a process-centric enterprise, each business process requests IT functionality from the underlying systems by calling a service.

The process-centric approach is inherently more flexible than the integration-centric approach because it eliminates the rigid process of system integration. The process-centric approach allows an enterprise to make the transition to real-time business analytics and process management with substantially less time and expense than the integration-centric approach would require. As the enterprise grows and changes, the process-centric approach allows the enterprise to adapt and continue to benefit from flexible monitoring and management of business processes.

While the process-centric enterprise's service-oriented architecture bestows numerous benefits on its creators, including reduced reliance on proprietary and custom interfaces to integrate applications, one of its main advantages is its ability to render the components of business processes transparent. As a result, managers can link and correlate business processes that occur in and across separate systems, lines of business, divisions, or even companies.

Getting back to our financial services provider example, let's ask the same question we asked earlier and see how the answer is different in a process-centric enterprise. If Mr. Smith calls for credit card customer service, should he be given high priority as an outstanding customer or should he be relegated to a standard waiting queue because he is an average customer? As we saw, the issue involved calculating Mr. Smith's value to the financial services provider across multiple lines of business. Mr. Smith might be a good credit card customer, but he might also be a terrible banking and brokerage customer. If he scores average points as a banking and brokerage customer, should he not be made to wait while other, more profitable customers are given priority? Yes, he should, but as we saw, the mechanics of setting up a system that could make those observations across multiple lines of business using system integration was prohibitively expensive. Not any longer.

Now, with the process-centric enterprise, management can use the inherent flexibility and openness of the SOA to measure business process results across multiple lines of business. As shown in figure 7.6, the provider can pick which services it wants to monitor. Because all the services that power the functioning of the company are based on the same open standards, little custom programming is required to link and correlate the analysis of the business processes that the web services support, even if they take place across different lines of business.

Linking the customer retention costs and customer values across business lines and using the data gathered from those links to determine the optimum customer service routing response leads to true profit maximization and retention of the most profitable customers. The financial services provider can figure out right away if it

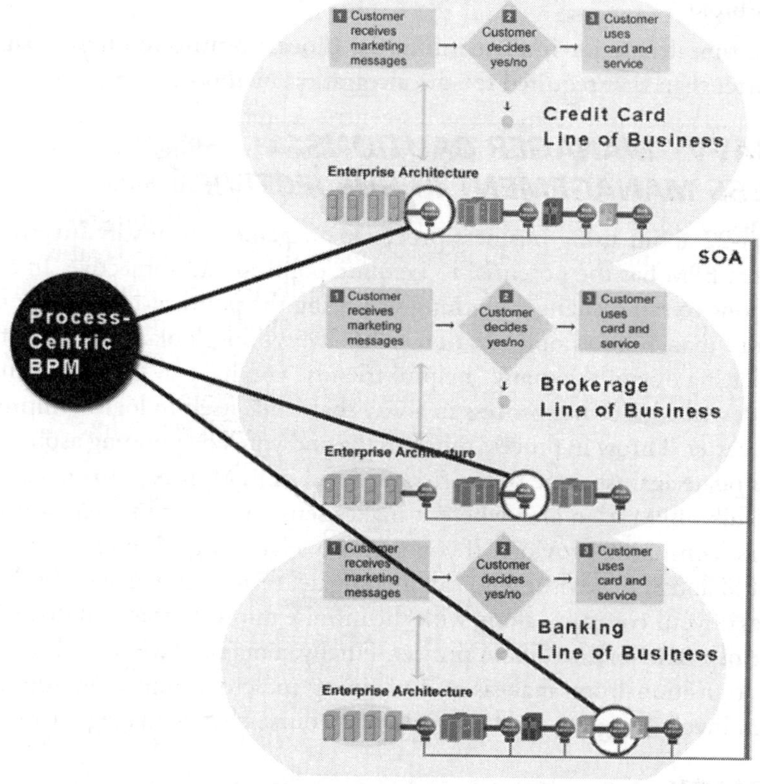

Figure 7.6 In the process-centric enterprise, management can easily link and correlate business process in order to gain insight into business operations, even if they occur across multiple lines of business.

wants to make Mr. Smith wait, or not, with the resultant improvement in its business performance that comes with favoring one's best customers. The advent of the process-centric enterprise enables organizations to radically shift their focus and resources away from technology and integration and toward developing and optimizing business strategies and processes.

The process-centric approach to business analytics offers several clear advantages over its predecessor, the integration-centric approach:

- It is more flexible and economical than the integration-centric approach.
- It enables business process optimization through logical process modeling.
- The enterprise is not reliant on proprietary interfaces that are costly to maintain.

- It obviates the need for an expensive, heavy footprint, proprietary message bus/broker.
- The time frame for implementing the process-centric solution is significantly shorter than that required for the integration method.

7.3 THE SAVVY MANAGER CAUTIONS: PROCESS MANAGEMENT IS SUBJECTIVE

The catch-22 about using business process management to justify investment in an SOA is that BPM has the potential to be quite political and subjective. In addition, it can be prone to rapid change. Nothing will bring the political-technology nexus into focus more than process optimization talks. Everything looks simple on the whiteboard. Getting one of the many "helpful friends" you have in the accounting department to describe his or her process in a way that lends itself to logical improvement is another matter. Throw in process outsourcing and you'll be popping aspirin like crazy.

To mitigate against some of the risks entailed in BPM, it pays to choose your partners carefully. BPM is an area where it makes sense to invest in a relationship with a world-class consulting provider. If you are with a large organization, you will need to have a BPM and SOA advisor who can investigate, review, and analyze both the global objectives of your company along with the infinite minutiae that will drive the success or failure of a BPM-oriented SOA project. Finally, a major player can also facilitate the complex transition from analysis and planning to actual implementation, a process that often involves a great need for agile mid-course change management.

7.4 SUMMARY

As companies struggle to compete in the global economy, many of the best management teams are stressing the importance of analysis and management of business processes. Continuous analysis and optimization of business processes confers the advantages of business agility to its practitioners. Agility gives management the power to implement strategic cost cutting and revenue-generating opportunities within a time frame that will bring the desired results.

Until now, most companies could only analyze business processes through methods that required expensive system integration. Given that analysis of business processes necessitated the examination of the underlying IT systems that powered these processes, custom integration was needed to effect such examination. I call these companies "integration-centric" enterprises.

Use of the service-oriented architecture delivers the ability to focus on the management of business processes without regard for the specifics of the underlying IT systems. When business processes are supported by web services based on open standards, then it is radically simpler to monitor those web services than it would be to monitor their proprietary analogues. I refer to companies that use an SOA to implement business analytics as "process-centric" enterprises.

The process-centric enterprise enables business managers to enjoy a high degree of flexibility in the management and analysis of business processes. They can concentrate on business processes without undue concern for the IT considerations of conducting an analysis of business processes. Business management goals, not IT agendas, drive BPM. The process-centric enterprise makes possible a high level of business insight and resulting agility in the management of business operations—a desirable goal in today's business climate.

CHAPTER 8

Real-time operations

Jay needs a coffee break. I allow him a cup, but then continue to move forward with our discussion. There is so much to go over. "Have you ever had the experience of making a bank deposit and then, a few minutes later, checking your account balance on the bank's website?" I begin. "You don't see your deposit, do you?"

"I have had that experience," he replies. "It always frustrates me."

"Where is that data?" I ask. "Let's say you call the bank's IVR system, and you are able to confirm the deposit, but it's invisible on the website. It's in the bank's computer, for sure. It just has not made its way to the database that supports the website. It will probably show up there later in the day, or even the next business day. It would be great if your deposit could appear instantly on the website. That would mean that the bank's information systems were operating in real time, as opposed to the delayed mode in which they work today."

I continue: "In some computing circles, the term 'real time' refers to a system's reaction time to a specific input. For our purposes, however, we use the phrase to describe how promptly distributed systems interoperate. For me, real time has to do with the synchronicity of data in distributed systems. If data in two systems is supposed to match but doesn't because of a delay in data exchange, then those systems are not interoperating in real time."

8.1 WHAT IS YOUR COMPANY'S TIME FRAME?

I ask Jay, "Do you get involved with the IT aspects of Titan's time frame?"

He replies, "We have thousands of transactions occurring every hour. Information technology events occur every fraction of a second, and many of these events are related. I wish we had a better handle on what was happening at the moment."

"Well," I say, "let's see if we can learn from the bank example. When you make a deposit at a bank, the teller enters the transaction into a computer terminal at the branch. In most cases, that transaction data is transmitted almost instantly to some central computer at the bank's headquarters. Later in the day, you transfer funds from your brokerage account at the same institution to your checking account. In the majority of cases, you will not see the results of these transactions online on the bank's website (if you can see them at all) until later in the day or even the next day."

Figure 8.1 shows the delayed data transfer process that occurs in most enterprises. The deposit clears to the bank's central computer at 2:30 P.M., right after the customer makes the deposit. The brokerage transfer occurs at 4:40 P.M. However, neither transaction gets sent to the web server/combined account database until 10:00 P.M. If you checked the website at 9:30 P.M. it would not show either of your transactions, even

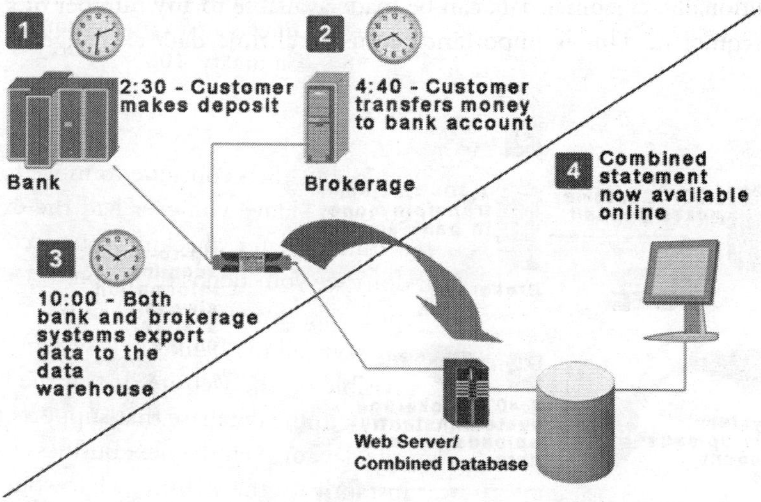

Figure 8.1 Banks provide an example of non-real-time transactions. In most cases, when you make a deposit at a bank, the data about that deposit is transferred to the online database that supports the bank's website in a batch process that occurs at regular intervals during the day. Your deposit will not show up in that database for some period of time. You do not have "real-time" awareness of your deposit data.

though they occurred hours earlier. Thus, even though the activities of the website and the banking branch systems are correlated, they do not operate together in real time.

8.2 THE GOAL OF THE REAL-TIME ENTERPRISE

A small disclaimer is needed here. In reality, there is no such thing as true "real-time" computing. There are always delays of some sort in computer interoperation, even under optimum circumstances. For this reason, some use the term "near real time," but I hope you will indulge me in the use of the more idealistic vision of "real time." In addition, just because something *can* happen in real time does not mean that it *has* to happen in real time, and therefore the term "right time" is also used to describe a process that can unfold in accordance with the mandates of the business and no slower. For our purposes, I will use "real time" for simplicity, and to get at the heart of the issue of how new SOA opportunities enable a different model of business operation than in the past.

In a real-time enterprise, data moves from its place of origin to wherever it is needed as soon as it is created. In our example, the bank deposit data is transmitted from the bank's central computer to the web server at 2:30 P.M. to be available online at 2:30 P.M. The brokerage transfer is transmitted at 4:40 P.M. to be available online at 4:40 P.M. Figure 8.2 shows how this looks. Instead of a batch upload of data at fixed times of day, the updating of the web server occurs constantly. The result is the virtually instantaneous availability of customer data online.

Additionally, customer data can be made available to any number of systems that might require it. This is important because real-time data exchange is more than

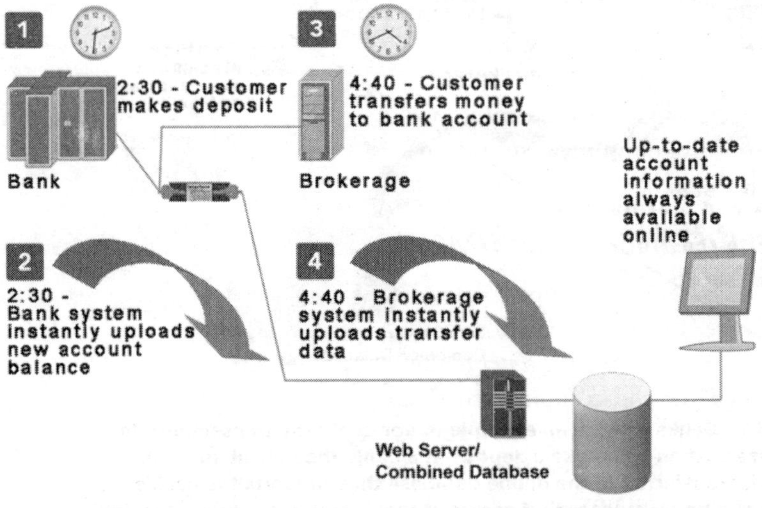

Figure 8.2 In order for a bank to deliver real-time deposit data, it must set up an interface that allows the deposit data to flow immediately into the online database.

a convenience for the customer. While it is inconvenient for the customer to be denied instant, accurate combined account information online, it may be bad for the bank's business as well. Banks are regulated by the government, and the law forces them to keep certain "reserves" on deposit. If a customer withdraws a substantial amount of money, but the bank is not aware of it until the following day, there is the risk that the bank might accidentally violate the reserve regulation. There is the potential for costly errors, or even fraud, when accurate information is not available due to time delays.

Right now, you're probably wondering why all enterprises don't just change to real-time operations right away. It seems so obvious that real time is preferable to delayed action. Well, if only it were that easy! Like so many tasks in IT, getting data to flow in real time is a lot easier said than done, especially in legacy and proprietary messaging environments.

Many of the older computers and software programs that run large enterprises are not well designed for real-time data exchange. When many of these legacy systems were established, they were programmed for batch uploading of data. Once they've been configured that way, modifying that process is complex and costly. As we have seen earlier in this book, the decision to implement a custom or proprietary solution—in this case to enable real-time data exchange—brings with it an overhead of maintenance and a permanent change management headache. In addition, using custom or proprietary solutions to effect real-time data exchange put the enterprise at risk for uncertainty of results as the new software is tested. For example, a simple error in programming could convert decimals points so that the number 10,000,000 becomes 10,000. If undetected, even for a few hours, such a bug could be disastrous.

Delayed data uploads and other forms of non-real-time interoperation also prevail for infrastructure reasons. Large "data dumps," such as uploading a whole day's worth of transactions to a web server, often occur at night because they would strain system resources and hamper performance if they were conducted during the business day. Mostly, though, delayed interoperation stems from the cost and complexity of the custom programming required to make it work. Delayed interoperation is simpler and less expensive to manage in a traditional, custom-coded environment.

8.3 DELIVERING REAL TIME WITH THE SOA

The SOA enables simpler, more cost-effective real-time interoperation and data exchange. In contrast to most batch upload models, which typically rely on the creation and transfer of a *flat file* that contains a mass of data in a format specifically designed for the computer that receives it, web services function by sending and receiving discrete, universally understood SOAP XML messages. The SOAP message is easily intercepted in real time and diverted to whatever system may also need the same data that it contains.

SOAP interception, a process of electronic pipes and filters about which you will be hearing a great deal in subsequent chapters, involves placing a special piece of software called a "SOAP interceptor" in the path of the SOAP messages that travel back and forth between a web services consumer and a web service. Because of their ability to digest, monitor, copy, and forward the data-rich SOAP messages, these interceptors figure very prominently into real-time enterprises, SOA management, and SOA security.

In an example of SOAP interception enabling real-time operations, the bank could expose the "update account balance" function on its central computer as a web service. If the customer made his deposit at 2:30 P.M., then the branch computer would instantaneously update the customer's balance on the central computer by invoking the "update account balance" web service at 2:30 P.M. As the SOAP message traveled on the bank's network from the branch to the central computer, a piece of SOAP interceptor software that monitored that network would pick up the deposit transaction data and copy it. The SOAP interceptor would then send the copy of the SOAP message that contained the deposit data to the bank's web server (or whatever system needed the information). This would also occur at 2:30 P.M. The web server or other destination system would receive the deposit data at 2:30 P.M. instead of waiting until 10:00 P.M. for the batch upload of all deposit data. Figure 8.3 illustrates this process. For the moment, for purposes of simplicity in illustrating our basic point, let's pretend that security is not an issue. We discuss securing these SOAP message streams in great detail in later chapters.

Let's look at a more involved example to show how the flexibility and universality of web services enables a real-time SOA enterprise on a larger scale than our simple bank deposit scenario. At a global manufacturing company such as the one depicted in figure 8.4, management may have to coordinate parts purchasing on a

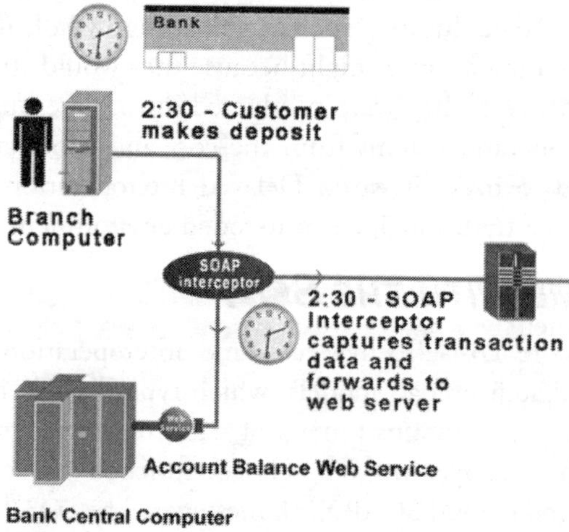

Figure 8.3 When the deposit IT function is exposed as a web service, it becomes possible to intercept the SOAP message and forward the deposit transaction data to the online database in real time.

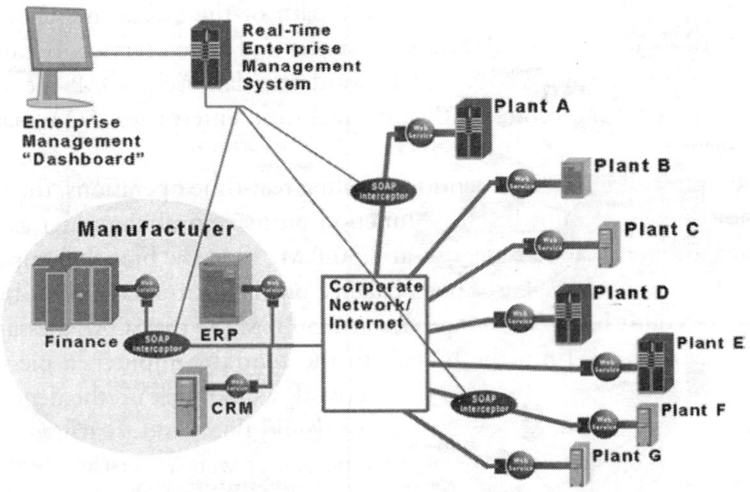

Figure 8.4 A global manufacturing company can operate in real time using an SOA. By placing SOAP interceptors at locations where business-critical SOAP messages are traveling, the company can monitor important transactions right as they occur.

"just-in-time" basis among a number of plants located around the world. To improve its management of the parts-ordering process, the manufacturer places SOAP interceptors at places on the network where they can report on manufacturing activities at specific plants. For example, let's say that the manufacturer has had difficulty ordering parts to arrive on time at plants A and F. By monitoring their SOAP message traffic and reporting their results in real time to an enterprise management "dashboard," the manufacturer's managers can improve performance in parts ordering and delivery for those two plants. For our purposes, a *dashboard* refers to a visual presentation of high-level operational data for use by managers.

8.4 GETTING AGILE WITH A REAL-TIME SOA

Ultimately, the SOA-based real-time enterprise confers the benefit of *business agility*. Agility is the ability to adapt business operations quickly and accurately in response to changes in the business environment. Agility is a principle that has relevance for both day-to-day tactical issues such as parts inventories as well as for strategic, big-picture matters such as expansion and capital investment.

The SOA creates the conditions necessary for managers to act in an agile fashion because it gives them a powerful and flexible tool to monitor and analyze their operations and processes in real time. The SOAP interceptor, the prime ingredient of the SOA-based real-time enterprise, can be placed virtually anywhere on the network of an SOA. As figure 8.5 shows, there are many potential configurations for SOAP interception and the resultant real-time business operations analysis. The manufacturer

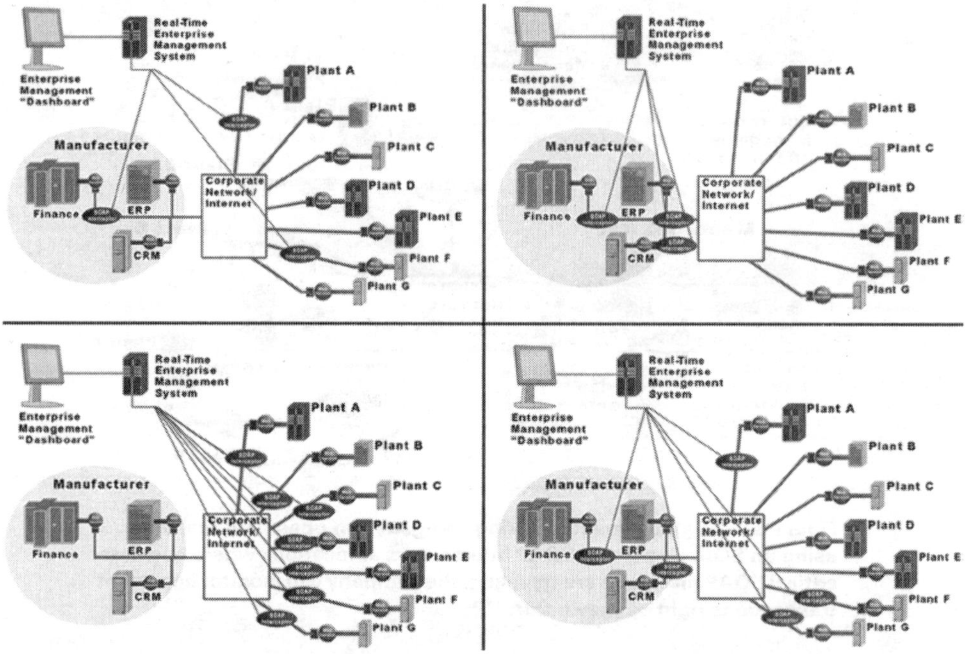

Figure 8.5 This quad graphic shows multiple SOAP interceptor placement scenarios for a manufacturing company. These images reveal the utter flexibility in SOAP message monitoring made possible by the standards-based SOA.

may choose to monitor two plants, as it does in the top-left square. Alternatively, it has the flexibility to monitor and analyze its internal computing operations at headquarters, as shown in the top-right square. Or it can place SOAP interceptors at every plant and obtain accurate operational data on those plants in real time, as the bottom-left square depicts.

Real-time business operations analysis based on SOAP message interception is potentially an incomparably flexible process when contrasted with the traditional custom/proprietary approach shown earlier. With an SOA, you can analyze where you want, when you want. Changing analysis patterns is relatively easy because you don't have to mess around with any custom code. You do not run the risk of disrupting the functioning of applications because you are not interfering with their core processes. You are merely "eavesdropping" on the message traffic.

Returning to the credit card customer example we used in chapter 7, figure 8.6 shows how an SOA-based real-time enterprise can help realize the goal of determining the value of a credit card customer across multiple lines of business. By linking disparate systems and correlating the data belonging to a specific customer, the SOA-based enterprise can tell you, in real time, what the value of the client is, as of that specific time.

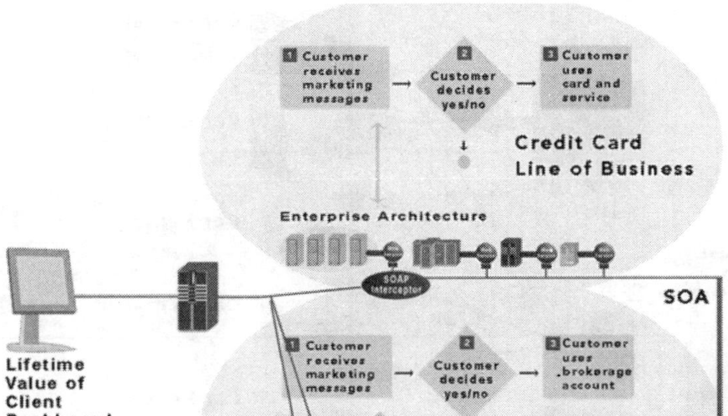

Figure 8.6 This SOA-based enterprise enables the financial service provider to determine the true value of a customer in real time by tracking the customer's behavior across multiple lines of business simultaneously.

8.5 THE REAL-TIME VIRTUAL DATA WAREHOUSE

By intercepting and correlating the data-laden SOAP message traffic, you can use an SOA-based real-time enterprise to construct a "virtual" data warehouse. A virtual data warehouse provides all the analytical power of a traditional data warehouse without the burden associated with actually building and maintaining one. The enterprise can "grab" critical data from the SOAP message stream and store it for analysis. In the case of the financial services provider shown in figure 8.6, the virtual data warehouse can compile a customer value database using the transaction data it collects as it intercepts the SOAP messages. In the airline and car rental example in figure 8.7, the airline can collect performance data on its car rental partners. In both cases, you can create a robust data warehouse without having to design a huge set of custom data-importation software programs.

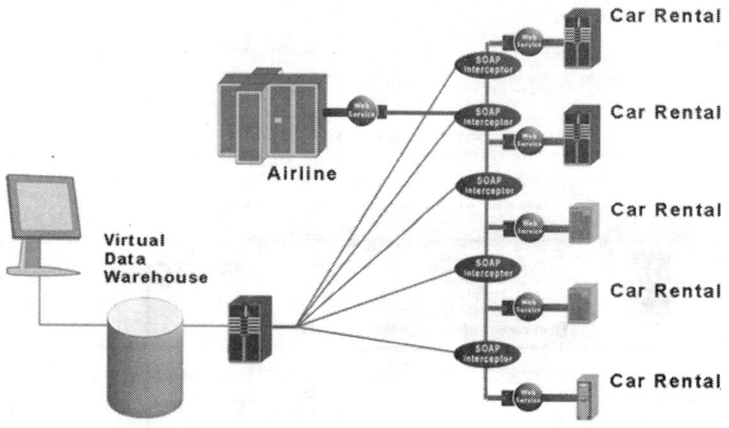

Figure 8.7 A "virtual" data warehouse created by capturing data in SOAP messages in an SOA

Virtual data warehouses deliver further business agility as well. The same flexibility that enables you to selectively monitor business operations and processes gives you the ability to collect operational data selectively. In contrast to traditional data warehouses, which typically cause challenges when they need to be changed, the virtual data warehouse can be adapted to changing circumstances with relative ease. When you need to analyze your virtual data warehouse, though, you will still probably need to rely on a proven data warehouse analytics package such as Cognos or Business Objects. The virtual data warehouse will concern itself with real-time analytics and populate a traditional data warehouse for archival purposes and historical analysis.

8.6 SETTING BUSINESS-LEVEL AGREEMENTS

Another interesting potential of the SOA-based real-time enterprise is the opportunity to create and manage business-level agreements (BLAs) among the various components of your business. In the same way that a service-level agreement (SLA) establishes a rule for performance of a system or network (e.g., a network must be up 99.9 percent of the time or the SLA has been breached and thus repercussions occur), the BLA is an enforceable agreement that sets out the standards for business processes. The CEO of a company does not want to be called at 3:00 A.M. to be told that "Server 643 is running slow"—that's an SLA violation; however, if the effect of some problem in the network is causing inventory to pile up at the cost of $100,000/ minute, he'll gladly take the call. The latter example is a BLA violation; a business metric has been crossed that affects the health of the operation. The BLA is enforced through the monitoring of the SOAP message traffic that supports the process that is the subject of the BLA.

In our bank example, the real-time monitoring of SOAP messages that support the deposit transaction can be used to set up and enforce a BLA. As shown in figure 8.8,

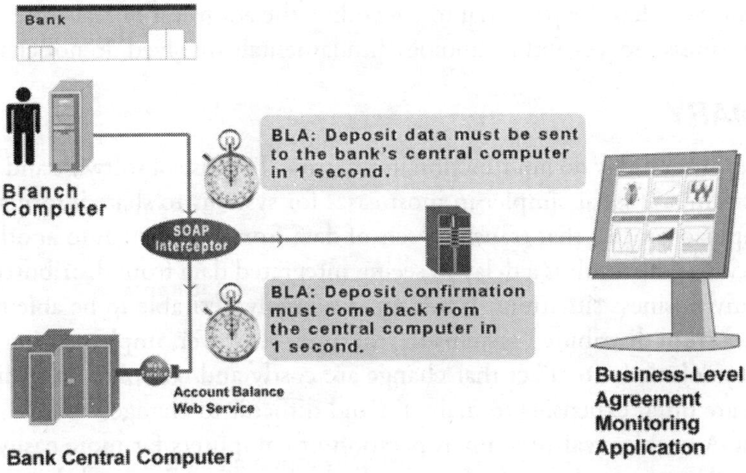

Figure 8.8 By monitoring the time elapsed between the SOAP messages related to deposit transactions, the SOAP interceptor can manage a BLA set up to ensure that deposit transactions are cleared within a predefined period of time.

the SOAP interceptor can track the timing of the deposit transaction. The SOAP interceptor, and its related systems, can track whether or not the BLA has been honored. In this case, one BLA states that deposit data must be sent from the branch computer to the central computer in one second. The second BLA states that the central computer must send back a deposit confirmation message in one second as well. If either message is delayed by more than one second, the SOAP interceptor will catch it. Depending on how the SOAP interceptor and related systems are programmed, a violation of a BLA might trigger an alert of some kind or stimulate the activation of a secondary backup system that will help manage the SOAP message load.

8.7 THE SAVVY MANAGER CAUTIONS: REAL TIME IS AN OVERUSED TERM

"Real time" is one of the worst offenders in the IT buzzword lexicon. The timing of IT transactions is the result of many interdependent factors. As such, timing issues, as well as coordinating business processes with IT resources for timing purposes, can be the source of many political and technological challenges. Once again, outsourcing can create multiple layers of headaches, especially if you are trying to synchronize operations and IT transactions among a changing roster of outsourced vendors. My advice to you is similar to what I suggested in the previous chapter: be selective about the partners you choose, and think carefully about where you want or need to invest in real-time operations. Finally, be sure you have nailed the business process objectives firmly before you get into a discussion of technology. Many IT vendors use the phrase "real time" as if it were a plug-and-play piece of functionality in their products. Trust me, it's not. SOA has the potential to streamline the adoption of real-time operations, but the business process and technology fundamentals involved do not change.

8.8 SUMMARY

Most enterprises today do not function in real time. Because of software and infrastructure constraints, it is far simpler in most cases for systems to share information using a batch upload process that transmits sets of data from one system to another at periodic intervals. The result is a delay in seeing integrated data from distributed systems.

In many business situations, however, it is highly desirable to be able to see integrated data from distributed systems in real time. However, implementing custom or proprietary solutions to effect that change are costly and complex. In addition, such solutions are often expensive to maintain and difficult to change.

The SOA enables real-time interoperation of computers far more easily and cost-effectively than the traditional approach. Because web services and the SOA depend on discrete SOAP messages traveling between computers to accomplish their given tasks, it is relatively simple to intercept those SOAP messages and monitor the transactions they support in real time. A SOAP interceptor software program, and its related systems, can send copies of intercepted SOAP messages to a business analysis software application, management "dashboard," or "virtual" data warehouse that management can view in real time.

The SOA-based real-time enterprise can also facilitate the creation of business-level agreements that establish operating parameters for systems that support specific business processes. SOAP message interceptors and their related systems can measure the time frame and other characteristics of transactions that support business processes and alert management when a system is not complying with the agreed-upon performance parameters.

CHAPTER 9

Security in a loosely coupled environment

I ask Jay if he recalls an aftershave commercial from a few years back where a man gets a crisp slap on the face but responds by saying, "Thanks, I needed that!" I tell him that's how I feel whenever the subject of SOA security comes up. It's a slap of cold, hard reality that wakes us up to the kinds of serious challenges we have to overcome to fulfill the vision of the SOA. Indeed, from this point on the book deals with the pragmatic but crucial considerations brought on by developing and implementing an SOA in real life. Yet, we should welcome the slap on the face. We need to know what stands in our way. So now that we have spent eight chapters building up the SOA, we have to look at a very real and troubling issue that has the potential to be a "showstopper" for the entire trend: security.

Although the IT community is embracing service-oriented architecture because of its promise of efficiency and improved IT management, security problems are causing many to proceed slowly, or not at all, with SOA implementations. Security has always been a concern for IT managers at large companies. Major systems have typically been designed to protect against unauthorized use, intrusion, and viruses. Today, however, the issue has taken on even more seriousness in the wake of terrorist attacks and global viruses.

While SOA security concerns abound, virtually all IT managers are realizing that they must soon identify and implement security solutions for SOAs because their developers are exposing applications as web services using the new generation of development tools. A pressing need exists, therefore, to solve the security risks in the SOA.

9.1 Risks of loose coupling

The SOA's inherent security problems stem from the ways in which the SOA replaces traditional security parameters with new, open standards. The security problem is twofold in that not only are the new standards completely open—no one owns them—but they were also developed without security in mind. Web services were developed over a period of years by industry consensus as a way to, among other things, enable the creation of reusable code, simplify development, and streamline system integration. While these goals were met, the open standards that emerged have not yet fully addressed security. Specifically, XML, SOAP, WSDL, and UDDI are open standards that enable the transmission and description of data and procedure calls between systems. However, none of these open standards contain any inherent security aspects of their own. If left alone, they are completely nonsecure. In fact, web services were designed to be able move efficiently through firewalls. This very loose coupling actually decreases their usability in this regard. In the past, a company's own employees could hardly access needed data, let alone the "bad guys." Now, with open standards, any 12-year-old with an Internet connection can access openly exposed transactions as readily as your authorized personnel.

To illustrate the security problems inherent in SOAs, let's look at the example of a supply-chain management process that involves a manufacturer and three vendors. Figure 9.1 represents the traditional B2B security environment. Each trading partner communicates with the manufacturer using a private network. Encryption may be used, but the manufacturer and vendor can both be fairly confident that their communication is private. Authentication (the user is who he says he is) is coded into the application, so the manufacturer can be relatively confident that Vendor A is actually Vendor A. Authorization (the user is allowed to use the system) is coded into the applications themselves as well as being handled by the security infrastructure of the entity originating the transmission.

Though secure, this traditional setup is costly and complex to maintain. Modifications to the manufacturer's application will automatically require custom revisions to the vendor's application or else they will not be able to communicate. Flexibility in extending the functionality of these connected applications is limited to the amount of custom interface development that each trading partner wants to finance.

If the manufacturer and its vendors decide to expose their applications as web services in an SOA, depicted in figure 9.2, they benefit from greatly increased flexibility

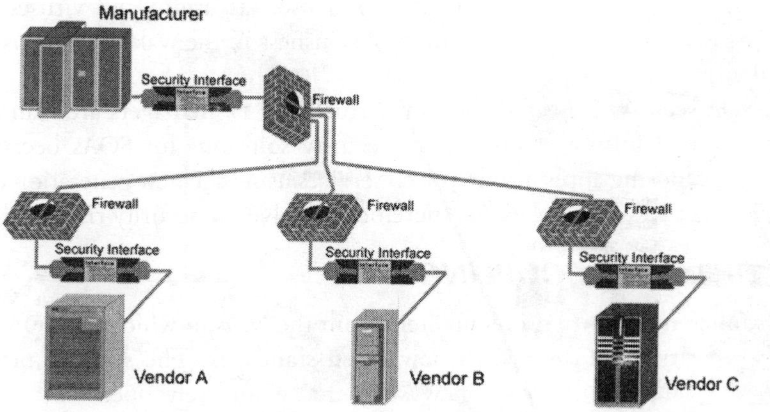

Figure 9.1 Traditional security arrangements in an architecture that connects a manufacturer and its suppliers might involve a separate firewall and proprietary security interface for each system.

but face security risks. Applications developed in this environment have numerous potential functional advantages over the traditional model, including "pulling" order data out of the system based on anticipated demand. Unfortunately, however, the SOA shown in figure 9.2 also contains a variety of security risks. Let's look at each of these risks in turn.

9.1.1 Machine to machine

To get a good grasp of SOA security issues, it important to understand that most security infrastructure is geared to human-to-machine interactions while web services involve scalable machine-to-machine interaction. Until recently, the majority of attention and product development has been given to the fairly well-understood human-to-machine web access space. This includes products that provide identity

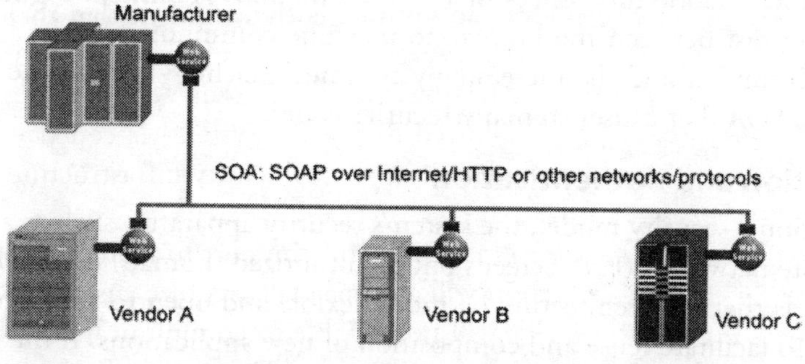

Figure 9.2 This is an unsecured SOA version of the EA shown in figure 9.1. It is completely open, and as a result is vulnerable to security problems related to authorization, authentication, privacy, integrity, and auditing.

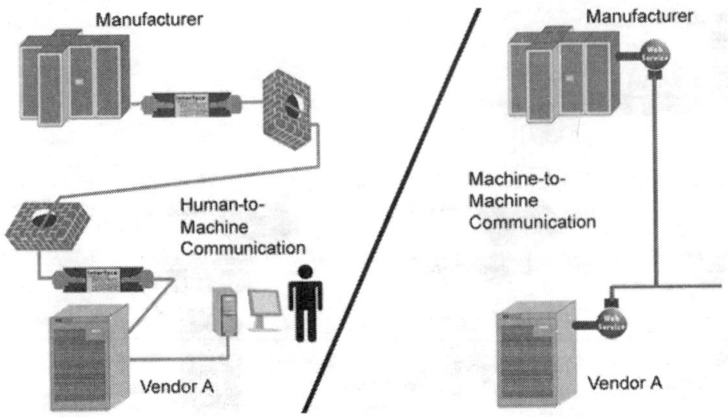

Figure 9.3 Contrast between human-to-machine and machine-to-machine communication. In most machine-to-machine scenarios, security is more coarse-grained than in human-to-machine interactions. The result is a less secure infrastructure.

management and single sign-on (SSO) solutions for users accessing systems via a web browser. The machine-to-machine interactions have received less attention, relying on their essential obscurity, a network security apparatus, or a binary security mechanism such as super-user access or key exchange, both of which are typically embedded in the applications themselves.

The reason for this is simple—the majority of applications were monolithic, thereby minimizing the number and complexity of machine-to-machine interactions. If organizations begin deploying an SOA without giving due consideration to alternative security mechanisms, unauthorized users may find it simple to penetrate and evade detection because the systems are now directly exposed in a standards-based manner and the security mechanisms used are either nonexistent or very simple and "large-grained." When we refer to a system as being *large grained*, we mean that its ability to discern subtle differences in security situations is limited. Figure 9.3 illustrates the contrast between the human–to-machine communication in a traditional security environment and the increasingly common machine-to-machine communication in the SOA that causes so many security issues.

).1.2 Authorization and authentication

In the traditional security model, the system's security apparatus, such as a firewall or virtual private network (VPN), screens out unauthorized (human) users. However, an SOA demands that the architecture be more flexible and open to access from multiple systems to facilitate reuse and composition of new applications. If the systems are exposed as services but a new security mechanism is not enforced, a hacker could configure a machine to impersonate a vendor's system and make erroneous or fraudulent service calls. Because of the large-grained nature of the security mechanism, the manufacturer has no way of knowing that the machine requesting the user of the

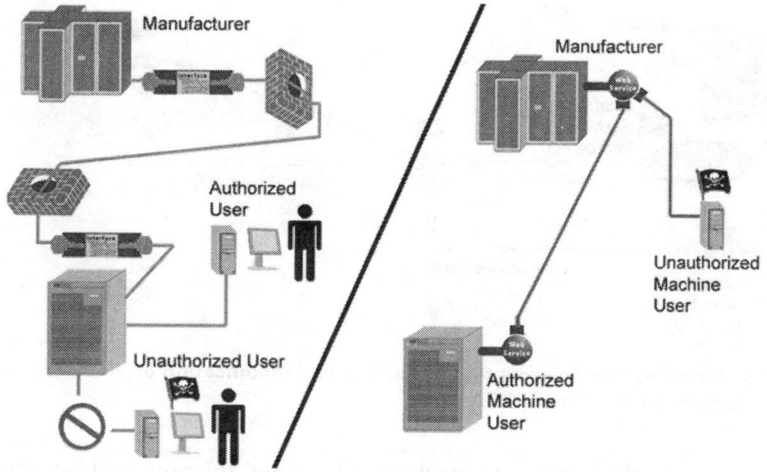

Figure 9.4 In the unsecured SOA, the often coarse-grained security mechanisms of machine-to-machine interaction raise the risk of unauthorized use of web services.

web service is neither authorized nor authenticated. Figure 9.4 illustrates the structure of this risk. Obviously, unauthorized use of a mainframe computer is a serious security breach.

Authentication, the process that verifies identity, is a distinct issue but one that is related to authorization. In authorization, you establish whether a particular user has the permission to proceed with the task it is requesting. In authentication, you prove that the user is actually the user it claims to be. In the unsecured SOA, achieving reliable authentication is difficult. In the example shown in figure 9.4, the unauthorized machine user might also be faking its identity.

9.1.3 Privacy and integrity

Privacy, the ability to conduct business without unwanted eavesdropping, and integrity, the ability to have confidence that messages are not modified in transit, are major factors in IT security. As we have seen in numerous incidents, hackers and others often listen in on message traffic and modify those messages for purposes of mischief or crime. An infrastructure that cannot guarantee a high level of privacy and integrity is not adequately secure.

In an unsecured SOA, as shown in figure 9.5, an unauthorized machine can intercept and "listen in." This unauthorized SOAP-intercepting machine can pass the messages along to other unauthorized users for the purpose of fraud or malicious mischief. For example, if the manufacturer were making something related to national security, then it would be concerned that information about inventories, delivery dates, materials and so on would fall into the wrong hands. The unauthorized SOAP-intercepting machine can also modify the SOAP message in transit and deliver

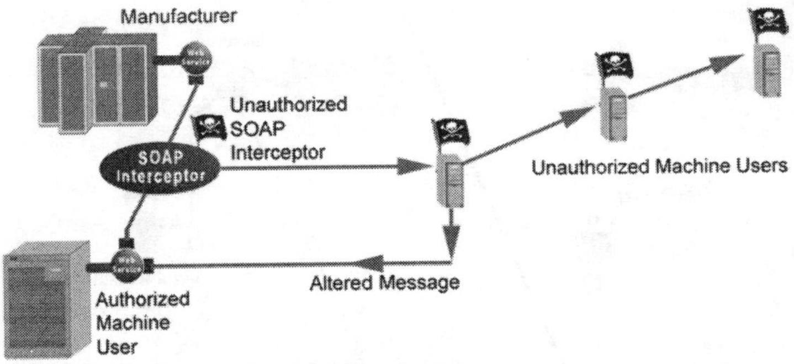

Figure 9.5 Unauthorized interception, rerouting, and modification of SOAP messages in a nonsecure SOA

a false message to the requesting machine. Therefore, the potential for fraud and misuse in this scenario is great.

This scenario highlights the need for encrypting the SOAP messages between systems. In the past, this has typically been handled by a network security apparatus like a VPN. However, due to the open and distributed nature of an SOA, it quickly becomes impossible to secure each machine-to-machine interaction in this manner. In the absence of SOAP encryption, an intercepted SOAP message can be understood, literally, by everyone. SOAP was designed to be universally understood, so a SOAP message can be received by a legitimate user or hacker without any distinction.

9.1.4 Flooding

With an unsecured SOA open to all comers, malicious, unauthorized users can "flood" it with service requests and render it inoperable. In the same way that hackers brought down such websites as Amazon.com with bogus requests, a malicious, unauthorized user can bring about a denial of service (DoS) attack on an unsecured SOA. Figure 9.6 illustrates this risk. One factor that makes the risk of DoS very serious is the inability of the SOA to monitor or assure the service levels of its web services. (A web service's service level is a defined measurement of the web service's performance. For example, a web service might have to adhere to a service level of responding to a SOAP request in 10 milliseconds.) If hackers attack, the unsecured SOA has no inherent way of telling if it is being overloaded. The unsecured SOA cripples the ability of system administrators to identify and respond to security problems in a timely manner.

9.1.5 Auditing

An *audit log* is a fundamental tool of IT security. To examine security performance and diagnose security problems, security personnel must have access to accurate logs of system behavior. The unsecured SOA has no message and transaction logging mechanism. After a service has been invoked, there is no way to determine who has used the service and from where the request originated. As a result, no audit trail exists

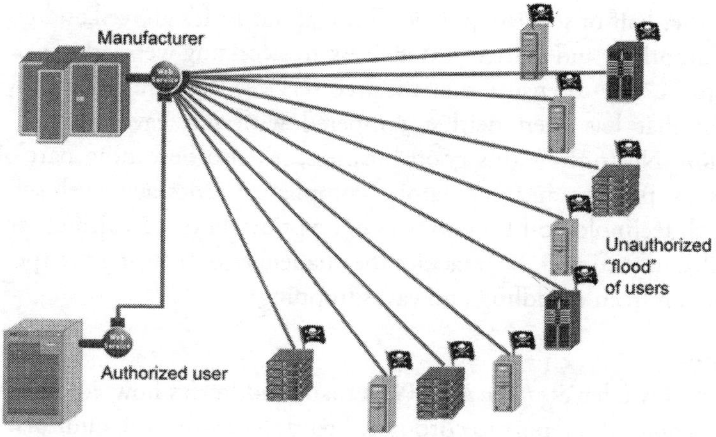

Figure 9.6 Unauthorized "flooding" of web service requests in an unsecured SOA

that can be used later to investigate possible breaches in security; there is no way to determine who has done what and at what time.

9.2 LAYERS OF SOA SECURITY

From another perspective, each aspect of SOA security outlined above should be addressed as a separate layer of security. In my discussions with clients, I have found the following three conceptual categories to be quite helpful in sorting out the major challenges in securing an SOA. If you engage in a discussion of security with a vendor, partner, or colleague, you may hear security issues referred to in this framework. Before we look at actual SOA security solutions, let's go over security policy, message-level security, and governance.

9.2.1 Security policy and provisioning

Security policy refers to the issues that arise around authentication and authorization. In general terms, any SOA security discussion is going to have a component of security policy. Who is allowed to use the web service, and who is not? How can you establish the identity of a user (or a machine that functions as a user)? How can you systematically manage the policies that you have created for security? For example, you might set a policy that all users with the role of VP can use a specific web service. How do you enforce that policy? Another way you may hear this question is in terms of "provisioning"—that is, who will be provided with a specific web service. Many vendors and analysts talk about provisioning issues and systemic provisioning capabilities.

9.2.2 Message-level security

Message-level security is a group of technology issues that relate to the integrity of the actual web service that is traveling across the network. Message-level security is the necessary other half of security policy. Think about it: It's all well and good to ensure that only authorized and authenticated users are accessing web services. However, you also want to be able to ensure that the web services they are using provide accurate information that has been neither tampered with nor eavesdropped on without authorization. Not only is this good business, it's also becoming part of the law in such areas as privacy and regulatory compliance. Message-level security, which involves such technological functions as encryption, keys, certificates, and signatures (more on this in section 9.3.5), tackles the challenges of securing the specific web service interaction from meddling and eavesdropping.

9.2.3 Governance

At a high level, we have *governance*. Governance addresses how enterprise IT systems are run by people who report to corporate boards and answer to auditors. Governance refers to the broad combination of security policy, provisioning, message-level security, corporate IT policies, human resources (HR) policies, compliance, and other administrative aspects of managing enterprise IT. Governance affects many areas of IT, and with SOA, governance has particular relevance for security. In the age of Sarbanes–Oxley, corporate boards and auditors are quite interested in knowing that the information they use to run the company is drawn from IT systems of high integrity. The goal of SOA security in the context of governance is to provide assurance that the SOA can deliver verifiable data that will stand the test of an audit.

9.3 SOLUTIONS TO SOA SECURITY

Now that we've been "slapped in the face" by security concerns in the SOA, and said "Thanks, I needed that!" it's time to look at some possible solutions to these challenges. The short answer for SOA security problems is that you need to buy or develop a security solution for your SOA. The long answer, which follows, is quite subjective and complex. The goods news, however, is that most major security issues in the SOA can be resolved by a correctly designed SOA security solution. The solution itself may consist of a number of sub-solutions, each dealing with a certain aspect of SOA security. Depending on your needs, and the existing security infrastructure, you will probably require a specific set of solutions that might differ from those of another entity.

Let me repeat my earlier disclaimer: It is my goal here to give you a way to evaluate how security may affect your SOA planning. I am a vendor of SOA security products. And yes, you may detect some bias on my part for one solution approach over another. At the same time, you should be aware that I compete with many other companies that also approach SOA security in the same manner as I do. In effect, the market has validated some approaches to SOA security more than others.

9.3.1 SOAP message monitoring

SOAP message monitoring based on SOAP interception is one way to build the foundation of an effective SOA security solution. SOAP interception involves placing a special

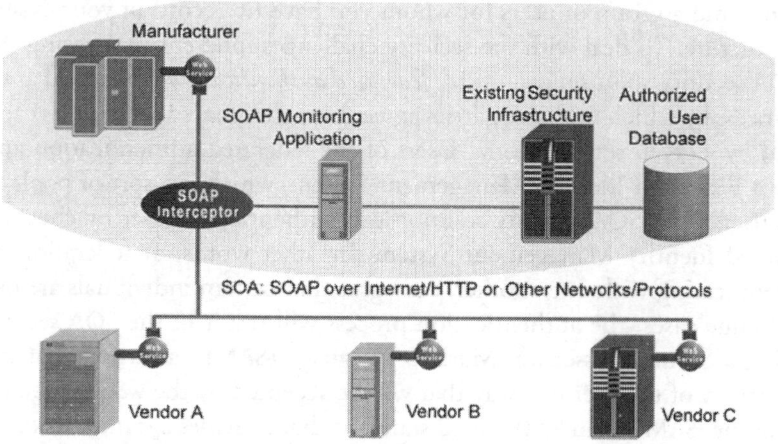

Figure 9.7 A SOAP interceptor monitoring SOAP messages serves as a foundation for security in this SOA. The SOAP interceptor analyzes the user identities contained in the headers of the SOAP messages it monitors and compares them with those names stored in the existing security infrastructure. The result is authentication and authorization of SOAP message senders and receivers.

piece of software called a "SOAP interceptor" in the path of the SOAP messages that travel back and forth between a web services consumer and a web service. Because of their ability to digest, monitor, copy, and forward the data-rich SOAP messages, SOAP interceptors figure very prominently into SOA security. As shown in figure 9.7, an SOA security solution "watches" the SOAP invocation messages approaching the web service as well as the responses to those service calls. When it "sees" a message, the SOA security solution checks to make sure that the requesting entity is authenticated and authorized to use the web service. The SOA security solution accomplishes this by checking the user data contained in the SOAP message header.

In most cases your SOA security solution will be augmenting an existing security solution that you deployed to secure your entire enterprise before beginning transitioning to an SOA. In all likelihood, as a result, your SOA security solution will have to connect to and communicate with the existing security infrastructure. As shown in figure 9.7, the authentication and authorization of users on the SOA occurs when their credentials are checked with the enterprise's database of authorized users. Authentication and authorization are achieved by intercepting the SOAP messages and comparing the users listed in the message header with those users stored in the existing security infrastructure.

9.3.2 SAML and federated authentication

What happens when you need to authenticate and authorize SOA users who come from outside your enterprise? The openness of the SOA makes this scenario more likely than it has been in the past. You may be faced with the challenge of figuring out who is who, amid a group of users for whom you have no record in your existing security infrastructure. To deal with the security challenges inherent in securing third parties, an SOA security solution can utilize *federated authentication*. Federated authentication is a process by which multiple parties agree that a designated set of users can be authenticated by a given set of criteria. Users of the federated authentication approach can create a Federated Identity Management System, which is a sort of pool, of authenticated users. The SOA security solution can authenticate a user by checking with the Federated Identity Management System. In other words, a "federation" of systems, communicating with one another, can agree that certain individuals are okay.

In some cases, the authentication process will result in the SOA security solution creating a Security Assertion Markup Language (SAML) assertion that expresses the authenticity of the user in a way that will be accepted by the web service that the user is invoking. SAML is an XML-based standard that provides a framework for describing security information about a user in a standardized way. WS-Security is the name given to the set of security standards that have been ratified to date. Many SOA security solutions take advantage of these emerging security standards. As shown in figure 9.8, the SOA security solution can intercept the SOAP message, and then route it through an authentication process wherein the user is authenticated. Then, the SOA security solution passes the SOAP message along to the destination web services, but with a SAML assertion tacked on. Note: SAML assertions do not rely on federated authentication processes.

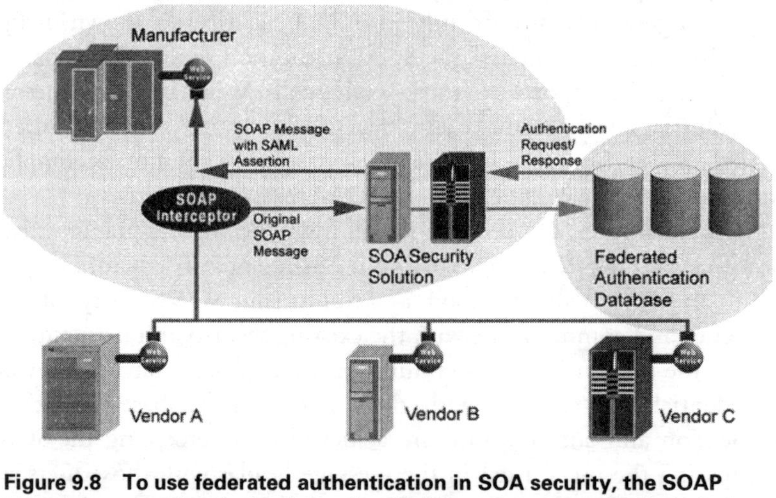

Figure 9.8 To use federated authentication in SOA security, the SOAP interceptor must forward an incoming SOAP message to a security solution that checks the identity of the user contained in the SOAP message header with the users listed in the federated authentication database. Once approved, the SOA security solution creates a security "assertion" that the user has been authenticated in a Security Assertion Markup Language document that is appended to the SOAP message as it travels to the web service it was intended to invoke.

9.3.3 Application proxy

One highly effective way to protect the security of core systems is to avoid letting anyone reach the service hosting platform. This can be done by deploying a proxy for the web services within your SOA. As shown in figure 9.9, a secured proxy can receive and respond to all web service requests on behalf of the actual web services, and is therefore protected from malicious intent. An added advantage of the proxy approach is its ability to reduce the load on the enterprise's security infrastructure. Instead of generating a lot of message traffic across the network to authenticate and authorize each user every time it wants to invoke a web service, the proxy reduces the traffic by centrally managing and caching the authentication and authorization of web service requests. The proxy also inserts the authentication and authorization SAML assertions into the message, thereby eliminating the need for the actual web service instance to query the security system directly.

9.3.4 Contract management

We'll spend a lot more time on this subject in the next chapter, but contract management, which is primarily an SOA management issue, also plays a significant role in SOA security. A *contract* is a set of rules that governs the use of a web service. For instance, a contract might stipulate that a particular user has the right to invoke a specific web service ten times per day. And, upon invocation, the service level must meet certain parameters, such as a one-second response time.

In security, contracts are helpful in determining whether the SOA is functioning properly or whether it is being misused due to a security breach. As shown in figure 9.10, the SOAP interceptor sends the web service request and response data to the SOA security solution, which then calculates whether the contract has been met or broken. If a security problem, such as a DoS attack, has slowed a web service to the point where it is not meeting its contractually agreed-upon service levels, the SOA security solution can alert management that there is a possible problem. Of course, a severe enough attack could bring the whole network to a halt, but the

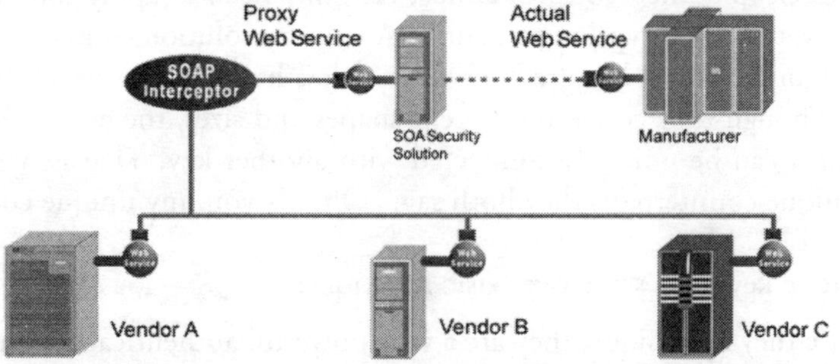

Figure 9.9 The web service proxy helps secure an SOA by handling the SOAP message traffic, reducing the load on the enterprise's security infrastructure and protecting the web service from malicious use.

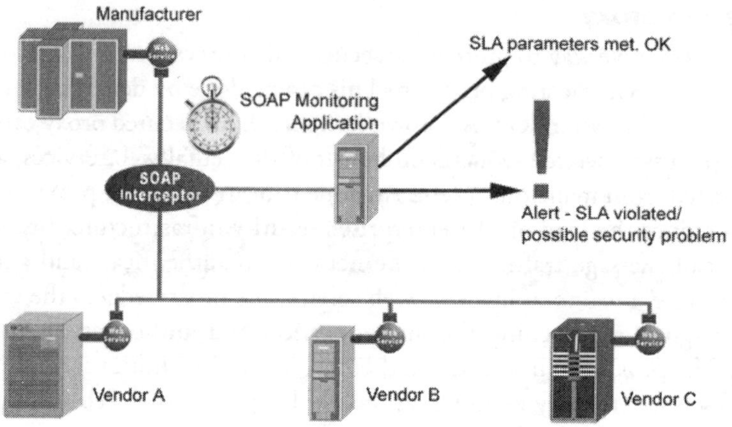

Figure 9.10 The SOA security solution monitors service levels and sends an alert when a security problem has caused a web service to miss its contractually set service level.

security solution would at least have the capability of issuing a notification that something is wrong.

9.3.5 Certificates, keys, and encryption

Over the years, the IT world has embraced a number of message-level security techniques involving cryptography. Now, you can apply these same techniques to your SOA. These processes, involving digital signatures, certificates, keys, and encryption, can play a role in securing your SOA. A quick disclaimer here: One could easily write a book or even several books about each of these four security techniques. Please look at this section as a brief overview of encryption-based security as it relates to the SOA.

If you want your SOA to have robust security, where you are confident that the users of your web service are properly authenticated and that the information flowing back and forth between web service and their invoking applications is not read by unauthorized people, then you will almost certainly need to apply the powerful tool of public/private key encryption to your SOA security solution. A key is a large number (humongous, really—hundreds of digits) that has certain special mathematical properties. Though they come in different shapes and sizes, the essential property of a key is that it can be uniquely connected with another key. That is, when one key meets its unique counterpart, they both say, "Oh, it's you, my unique counterpart… and no one else."

The unique key pairs serve two basic functions:

- Because they are unique, they are a very powerful authentication tool.
- Because of their mathematical properties, they can be used to create unique, impenetrably encrypted messages that can only be "read" by a user who has both of the unique, matching keys in the pair.

Here's how it works when two users want to exchange encrypted information: User A creates a unique pair of keys. He then keeps one hidden within his own system (the "private key") but posts the other key (the "public key") at a location on the network where User B can access it. User B then takes the public key and uses it to encrypt the information he wants to send to User A. How this is actually done involves so much math that I get a headache just thinking about it, but basically the public key and message data are run through an encryption algorithm that produces an encrypted file that is impossible to open without the private key. User B then sends his encrypted message to User A, who uses the private key he hid at the beginning of the process to "unlock" the encrypted data. The bottom line is that User A is the only person in the world who can unlock the encrypted data because he has the unique matching key to User B's public key.

Now, if you're paranoid like I am, you might be thinking, great, but how does User A know that User B is actually User B? What if someone hacked into the system and found the public key that User B was meant to use? To answer this valid question, a number of entities have come into existence that assure the authenticity of specific users and grant them digital certificates that attest to their authenticity. These entities are known as *certificate authorities* (CAs). A well-known example of a CA is VeriSign, which issues certificates for use in e-commerce transactions.

Thus, an SOA security solution that uses keys, encryption, and certificates to enforce privacy and authentication might resemble the one in figure 9.11. In our manufacturer example, the vendor system wants to send a SOAP message to the manufacturer's web service. To make this possible, the manufacturer has to first send a public key to a CA. The vendor system then requests a certificate from a CA. The certificate that the vendor receives contains the public key that matches the private key residing on the manufacturer's system. The vendor then uses the certificate's public key to encrypt its message and transmits it to the manufacturer. However, as in the previous examples, the SOA security solution intercepts the message and checks the validity of the certificate with the CA. This serves to authenticate the vendor's identity. Only after this authentication has been completed does the encrypted SOAP message travel to the manufacturer. Once there, the manufacturer uses its private key to decrypt the message and process it.

If you think this sounds like a lot of work just to send a message, you're right. Security in the SOA, as in other areas of IT, creates a lot of "overhead." Each message has to travel to several places before it reaches its destination. Certificate files can be large and taxing to network infrastructure, and the whole process tends to slow down performance. Still, it is an unfortunate necessity.

9.3.6 XML encryption

To preserve the openness of your SOA while instituting tight message-level security standards, you will probably want to use XML for your encryption. When the SOA security solution uses a key to encrypt a message, it transforms the message into a

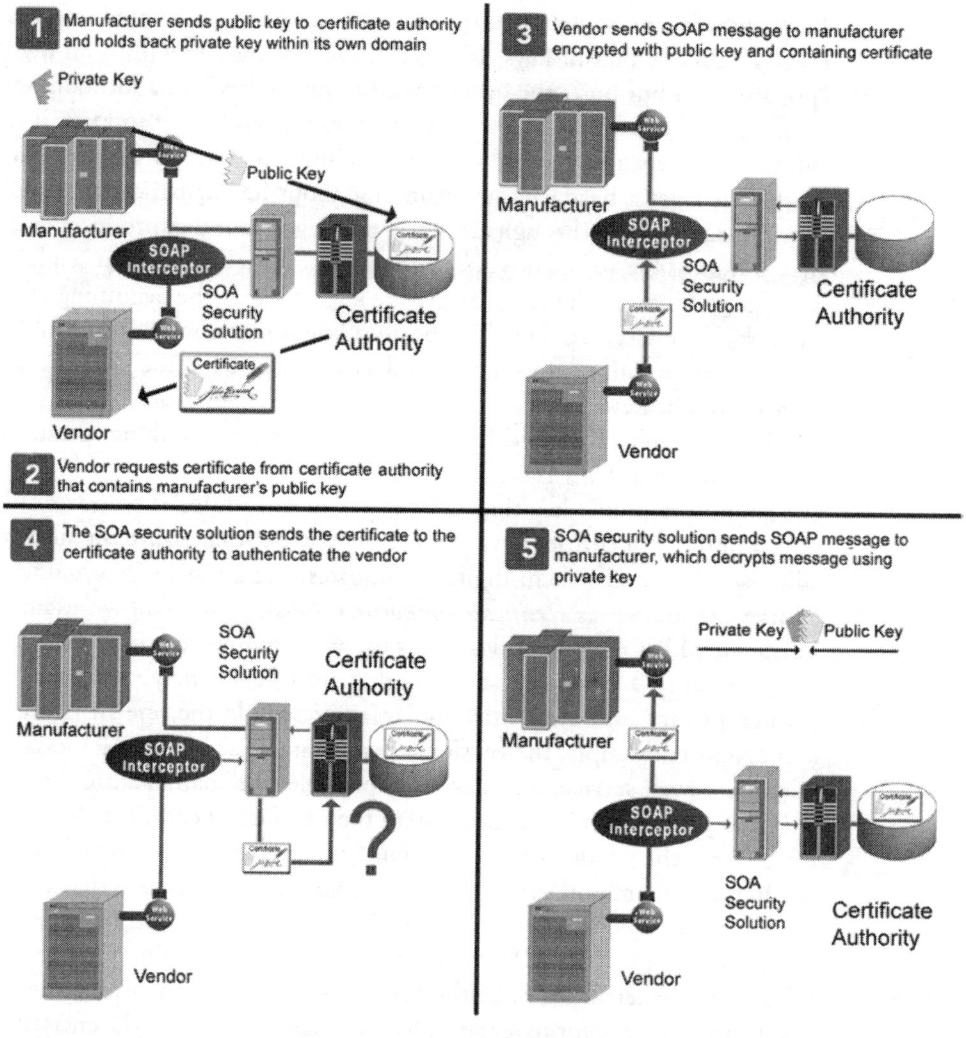

Figure 9.11 The step-by-step process of using public/private key encryption and certificates in a secure SOA

piece of XML that is encrypted. The message is in XML format, but the content is not apparent because it is hidden through the use of an encryption algorithm. The benefit is that the system that receives the message can accept it, decrypt it, and process it as XML without relying on custom or proprietary messaging standards. You get security, but your system remains based on open standards.

9.3.7 Digital signatures

Digital signatures, another form of message-level security, are a variation on the certificate, key, and encryption approach to security. A *digital signature* is a mathematical statement of authenticity that you attach to a SOAP message. Based on keys, the digital signature is a number (again, a very large number) that uniquely captures your identity and the content of your message, by running the two sets of data (the key and the message) through a special algorithm. So, to take a simplified example, if your message is "hello" and your key is 12345, the algorithm will process those two inputs—the digital value of the world "hello" and the key number 12345—and produce a third number, which is your unique digital signature. When the receiving system gets the message and attached digital signature, it can use the key to verify that

- You are the true author of the message (authentication).
- The SOAP message has not been altered in transit.

If it had been altered, then the unique signature number would no longer match the key and the original message used to create the key.

The difference between digital signatures and the complete encryption process described earlier is that in the digital signature case, you do not have to encrypt the entire message. As a result, the performance of the system improves. As long as you don't mind if someone can see your message in plain text, then the performance considerations of digital signatures provide a high degree of security and integrity of data in your SOA.

Signatures can be a component of *nonrepudiation*, an important aspect of security that needs to be addressed in an SOA context. Nonrepudiation refers to an organization's ability to authenticate that a particular transaction occurred, and thus deny the sender the opportunity to repudiate (a fancy word for "deny") that the transaction went through. For example, if you placed an electronic order for merchandise, and that order was not authenticated in some way, such as with a digital signature, then it might be possible to repudiate the order. If the merchant's system provides for nonrepudiation, then the merchant can affirm that the order was indeed placed.

9.3.8 Replay attack protection and auditing

Finally, your SOA security solution should provide a facility for tracking SOAP requests in order to limit the potential for damage in DoS attacks. Usually, a tracking feature will monitor the sender of the SOAP message and the time that it originated. In some cases, the SOA security solution will "stamp" the SOAP message with a unique identifying number. If the solution is set to block duplicate messages, it then becomes impossible for the same message to be sent twice. Eliminating this potentiality helps reduce the change that hackers could flood the SOA with duplicate requests—a favored technique used in DoS attacks.

Auditing is a further use of SOAP message tracking capabilities. If the SOA security solution is configured to track messages, then it should be able to generate usage logs and audit reports for SOA message traffic during specific periods of time. The audit has many uses, but in security it serves as an important record of what has happened that can be used to investigate security problems and diagnose potential security weaknesses. This type of log has become essential to achieve regulatory goals such as Sarbanes–Oxley compliance.

9.4 THE SAVVY MANAGER CAUTIONS: DON'T LET SECURITY PARALYZE YOU

SOA security is a massive subject. I could write a whole book on it. In fact, that's not a bad idea... My intent in this chapter is to give you an overview that provides a basic toolset for evaluating information presented to you on the subject. If you are a business executive, my suggestion is to avoid becoming overwhelmed by security issues. It is easy to become paralyzed by security—security people can also do it to you—and balk at doing virtually anything for fear of security concerns. Indeed, I could probably take a proposed IT solution you are contemplating and walk you through enough security nightmares around it to scare you away from it.

Instead, I recommend that you seek high-quality counsel on security and explore what your enterprise already has in effect. Chances are, your company probably already has a pretty robust security system (or systems). The challenge with SOA is to figure out how to extend those existing security measures to the web services that comprise your SOA. Many SOA security solutions are designed to interconnect effectively with existing security functionality. At that point, the security risks might begin to look a bit more manageable and you can proceed with your plans.

9.5 SUMMARY

Security is a pressing issue in SOAs because the SOA stresses machine-to-machine interaction, while most IT security is based on human-to-machine interaction. Authentication and authorization become more challenging in this environment. It is virtually impossible to block unauthorized use of web services in an unsecured SOA; it is quite simple for an unauthorized user to access web services. Web services have no innate ability to track who is using them or who is permitted to use them. And you cannot stop unwanted listening in and message interception. The unsecured SOA presents hackers with the ability to eavesdrop on SOAP message traffic and see information that may be private. In addition, it is relatively easy to intercept a SOAP message in an unsecured SOA and reroute it or transform its content for purposes of mischief or fraud.

You cannot secure unknown third parties in an SOA because of the architecture's open nature. It is possible for secondary or tertiary users—the partners of your partners, for example—to access an unsecured SOA. As a result, the unsecured SOA is vulnerable to overload. With no access controls, an unsecured SOA is open to being "flooded" with excessive SOAP message traffic from hackers. The result can be a DoS attack that harms the ability of your systems to function. Finally, you have no transaction logging. The unsecured SOA cannot keep track of its users or its messages. Thus, there is no auditable record of usage that can be used to investigate security problems or diagnose security weaknesses.

There are both prepackaged and custom solutions to SOA security that can potentially address all of these issues. As you examine your SOA security needs, consider implementing an SOA security solution that enables SOAP message monitoring; federated authentication; application proxy; contract management; certificates, keys, and encryption; and audit logging. It seems like a long list, but the truth is without any one of these in place, all the benefits from your SOA will evaporate.

SOAP message monitoring utilizes a SOAP interceptor model to intercept and monitor SOAP messages as they travel from invoking systems to web services. SOAP message monitoring is the foundation of SOA security because it gives your security solution the ability to stop and examine each message for user authentication and authorization. To secure third parties, your security solution can take advantage of federated authentication. You should offer the ability to authenticate users on the system through a federated authentication process. The end result is an SAML assertion that provides credible authentication of the user to the web service.

A web service application proxy aids security by receiving and processing SOAP requests in place of the actual web service. It can keep all users away from the actual service. Along with moderating the load on the network, the proxy provides an additional layer of security to the SOA.

Contract management is an SOA management feature that also contributes to security. Contracts establish who has the right to use a web service and when they can use it. By eliminating usage by noncontracted parties, the contract adds security to the SOA.

Certificates, keys, and encryption are also essential for a truly secure SOA. The most robust SOA security results from the implementation of encrypted messaging authenticated by private key/public key pairs from a certificate authority. XML encryption allows a web service user to send an encrypted SOAP message that retains its XML formatting. As a result, the system is secure but remains standards based. Digital signatures, a variant of the encryption model, offer the web service user the ability to create a unique, authenticated digital "signature" that serves the dual purpose of verifying the identity of the user as well as assuring the integrity of the message data.

Finally, in order to track the use of an SOA, it is necessary to employ an SOA security solution that maintains an ongoing audit log of all SOAP message requests and responses. The audit log is necessary for investigating security problems, diagnosing security weaknesses in the SOA, and achieving government regulatory compliance.

C H A P T E R 1 0

Running an SOA

"Service-oriented architectures are chaotic places," I warn Jay. "Left alone, web services have no intrinsic manageability. The kind of management tools you have for your overall IT infrastructure generally can't handle the sort of distributed, heterogeneous services you get in an SOA. And if your web services are operating as processes across your enterprise and that of your trading partners, it'll be even more complex to get a grip on. Managing an SOA—that is, the ability to operate an SOA so it performs reliably and delivers consistent service on a variety of levels—is a significant challenge to IT professionals today. You'll definitely face it at Titan. The issues are comparable to those we just discussed regarding web services security. Indeed, the unmanaged SOA is a sort of evil twin to the unsecured SOA. The two situations share certain similar problems, and similar solutions as well."

10.1 PROBLEMS IN THE UNMANAGED SOA

When an organization exposes its application functionality as web services but provides no mechanism for the management of those services, it has created an unmanaged SOA. At first, it may not appear to present too many problems. However, as it exposes more and more systems, including mission-critical business applications, the organization stands to face a range of problems that will dramatically affect operational performance.

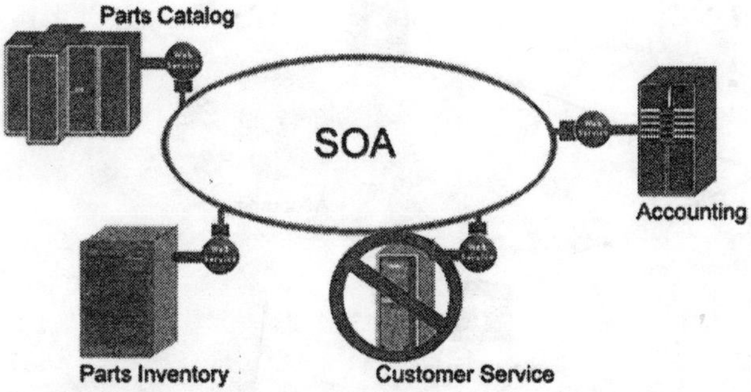

Figure 10.1 If a web service goes down in an unmanaged SOA, there is no reliable way to alert users that the service is unavailable.

10.1.1 Quality of service

Quality of service (QoS) is perhaps the most basic issue in web services management. QoS refers to the availability of a web service to respond to invocations and its performance in carrying out those responses. In figure 10.1, which shows an SOA for a parts distribution business, the customer service (CSR) web service is down. Let's assume that the other web services in the SOA need the functionality of the CSR service to help the business complete its transactions. If the web service is down, they cannot do their business. However, how do they know that the service is down?

In an unmanaged SOA, they have no way of knowing. The CSR web service is simply unavailable, a situation that will have a negative impact on all the other web services that need it. Compounding the problem, there is also no way of knowing how well a web service is supposed to perform in this unmanaged SOA. If the CSR service is usually very slow, then the systems that invoke it may not even realize that it is out of commission.

Bottom line: there are no service-level agreements (SLAs) in an unmanaged SOA. Each web service operates independently with no controls or methods to establish how, when, and if the web service will respond to an invocation. If it does respond, no parameter exists to determine whether the response time is acceptable. If it does not respond, no tracking system alerts the invoking system that it never got a response. This is a situation that is inevitably perilous for the organization that set up the SOA.

10.1.2 Transaction monitoring and web service orchestration

Until now, we have mostly discussed extremely simple scenarios where the entire transaction involves a single computer invoking a single web service. In a real business, however, transactions tend to be more complex. In many situations, web services must perform their tasks in an orchestrated sequence to complete a specific transaction. The process of arranging for multiple web services to act in a predefined sequence is therefore known as "orchestration."

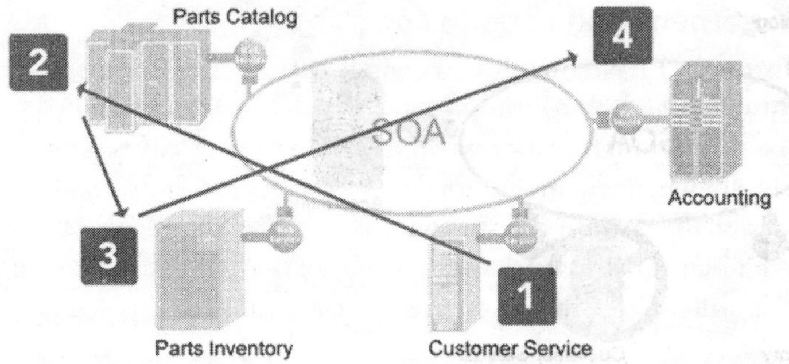

Figure 10.2 Web service orchestration for taking and fulfilling an order

As shown in figure 10.2, the part order fulfillment transaction requires that all four web services in the SOA be orchestrated in a specific order. First, customer service receives the order and invokes the parts catalog service to determine if the part that has been ordered is still officially being offered for sale. The parts catalog service responds to the invocation. If the part is still in the catalog, the parts inventory service is invoked to find out if the part is in stock. If the part is in stock (or not), the order then goes to the accounting web service, which creates either an invoice or a back-order form, depending on the status of the part.

In the unmanaged SOA, it is impossible to deliver reliable orchestration. Though you can establish a web service orchestration sequence in an unmanaged SOA using various web service–authoring tools, you cannot manage the orchestration or ensure its reliability. Once you have set it up, you will have no way of knowing if it is performing correctly. In our example, if the inventory check web service takes 20 minutes to respond to an invocation instead of two seconds, the SOA has no automatic way to detect the problem. Or if transactions are not being completed—for example, if orders are placed but never fulfilled or invoiced—there is no reliable way to diagnose the problem.

10.1.3 Context sensitivity

Processes invoke web services in a specific business context, so their management should take this context into consideration. For example, in a hospital, one process might be responsible for turning on the lights in the parking lot when it gets dark. Another process might be responsible for ensuring a smooth flow of oxygen to patients who need it. Which one is more important? The oxygen process is critical to life and death. The parking lot lights could go off and no one would die. Therefore, in terms of SOA management, you would probably want to be able to differentiate between a highly urgent web service problem and a low-priority one. If the oxygen-managing web service went down, you would want someone paged instantly. If the parking lot lights went out, it could be handled in the normal course of activities. Without management, every service looks the same and errors that may be detected cannot be prioritized for your attention.

10.1.4 Change management and version control

Throughout this book, I have mentioned change management as a problematic area for traditional distributed architectures. Guess what? If it is not handled correctly in an SOA, it can be just as much of a problem as it is in older architectures. Change is a constant factor in IT management, and the SOA is no exception. As requirements and business processes change, so do the systems that support them. While the SOA alleviates many of the painful stresses that come with change management in the traditional model, it is still an area that demands close attention and proper management to work effectively.

Change management in the SOA brings about similar challenges to those in the traditional model. When a web service changes, both the invocation and response aspects of the new web service must perform as promised or there will be a problem. As shown in figure 10.3, if the company replaces the accounting web service with a new web service, the administrator of the SOA must be able to assure users that each system that invokes the new web service will get the results it needs.

In practical terms, this means that each invoking system (in this case there are three) needs the URL for the new web service so that it knows where to send its invocation SOAP messages. The new web service, in turn, must be able to process these invocations and respond correctly. This might require that each invoking system receive instructions on how to formulate a SOAP request from the WSDL document for the new web service.

If the SOA is not managed, there is no automated way of updating the information the invoking systems need to use the new web service. It is quite possible that one or more systems in the company will continue to "hit" the old web service. However, in the unmanaged SOA, these unfulfilled SOAP requests will not cause any alerts to be issued.

You might be thinking, "What's the big deal?" You have three invoking systems and one new web service. How hard could it be to check whether they are all working? In this simple example, you would be correct. However, keep in mind that as

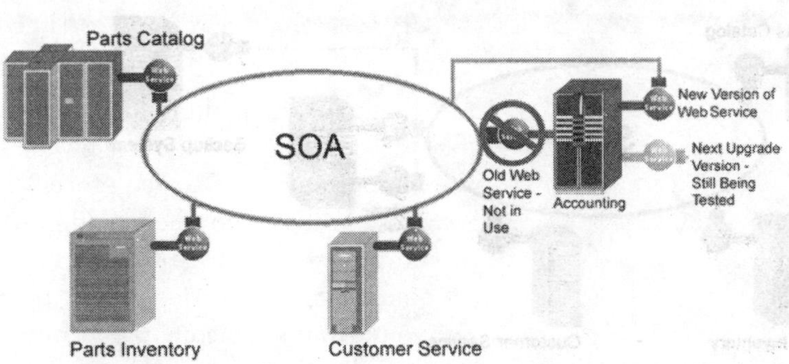

Figure 10.3 When a web service is replaced by a new version in an unmanaged SOA, users have no reliable way of knowing how to access the new version.

web services grow in popularity, your organization and those of your partners might contain thousands of web services. Management at that point is absolutely vital. Even if you had only a few dozen web services distributed throughout your SOA and those of your partners, change management and version control could be a major problem without proper SOA management.

10.1.5 Load balancing and failover

As your SOA grows, it will likely face the kind of load balancing and failover challenges that you find in traditional IT infrastructure. A web service, after all, is software, and it has to be treated as such. To achieve a high service level, you must be able to control the load of SOAP requests hitting each web service and also provide a failover backup in the event of a failure.

In our example, let's assume that the load of SOAP requests hitting the accounting web service is highly variable. One day, there are ten requests per minute; the next day, there are five hundred. If the web service can stay within defined service-level parameters only if it processes fewer than three hundred requests per minute, then you will have to create a second instance of the web service—ideally on a second machine—to handle the increased load on the busy days. If you do that, your SOA will start to look like the one in figure 10.4. If the load on the primary web service exceeds three hundred invocations, the SOA needs to know how to route the excess SOAP requests to the second web service. If the computer containing the primary and secondary web service fails, the SOA has to be able to reroute the SOAP requests to an entirely different computer that has been established as a backup. This condition is known as a *failover*.

The unmanaged SOA does not have any way to facilitate these load balancing and failover circumstances. Web service standards contain no provisions for load balancing and failover. If left alone, a failed or overloaded web service has no way of routing SOAP requests to alternative web services. Imagine the challenge of coordinating change management and version control when you have multiple instances of the web service for load-balancing purposes!

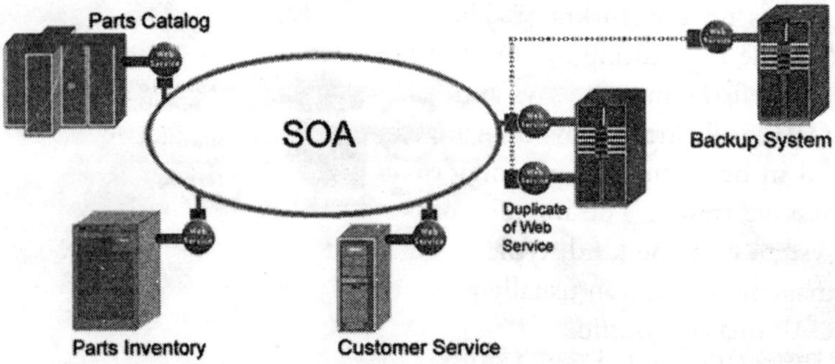

Figure 10.4 It may be necessary to create duplicates and backups of heavily used web services in a busy SOA. Then, you will need to manage load balancing and failover to ensure consistent quality of service.

10.2 WEB SERVICE MANAGEMENT SOLUTIONS

You can choose among a number of products and solutions for managing your SOA. Some of the major application server companies are beginning to offer SOA management features on their products. This has naturally started a debate in the technology community as to the suitability of application servers as a basis for hosting distributed intermediaries for web services security. A number of companies, including mine, are releasing web services and SOA management solutions that address some or all of the SOA management issues we have discussed in this chapter so far. You may look at today's offerings and conclude that some combination of solutions may work best for your SOA management needs. To clarify my point on this, let me reiterate my earlier disclaimer: I am a vendor of SOA management solutions. However, I think you will find that I have approached the issues related to running an SOA in broad enough terms to enable you to make a relatively unbiased decision for what is right for your particular enterprise.

10.2.1 SOAP monitoring

Most of the credible SOA management solutions on the market today function based on the same kind of SOAP message interceptor model used by the SOA security solutions discussed earlier in this book. This is not surprising, because many of these solutions handle both security and management of the SOA. Security and manageability seem to go hand in hand in the SOA. Though they are different issues, they are related to the extent that you cannot really have security without manageability, and vice versa. After all, a secure SOA that is subject to chaotic, unmanaged problems would not be much use to anyone. A well-managed but nonsecure SOA would leave its owner vulnerable to improper use and lack of privacy.

Monitoring of SOAP messages is the basis of SOA management. To understand the necessity for SOAP monitoring in SOA management, think of an IT riff on the old riddle about the tree falling in the forest: If a SOAP message crosses a network, and no interceptor is able to monitor it, does it actually get through? The answer is, of course, there's no way to know! The core functionality of most SOA management solutions is the monitoring of SOAP messages, a process that generally includes "listening" to what the message says and recording its coming and going.

Figure 10.5 illustrates how SOA management solutions work. SOAP interceptors positioned in between each potential invoking system and web service monitor the SOAP message traffic. The interceptors feed the monitoring information back to a central system of some kind, typically a combination of software and database. The SOA management solution usually requires a database because it needs to maintain a log of SOAP message traffic.

Ultimately, if recorded in a database, SOAP monitoring provides an audit trail for the SOA. An SOA management solution's audit log generally provides rich information to administrators regarding the performance of the web services within the SOA.

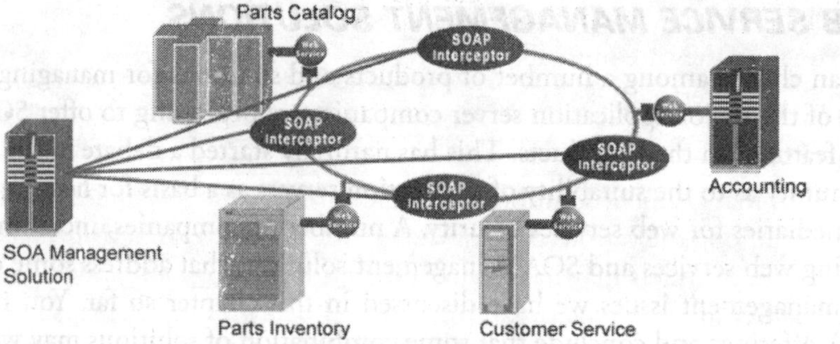

Figure 10.5 SOA management solution using SOAP interceptors

In addition to security issues, which we discussed previously, the audit is essential to complete SOA management. The audit log is a record of all the goings-on in the SOA. As such, it provides the data needed to assess load and infrastructure demands, investigate problems that have occurred, and check web service performance against guaranteed service levels and contracts.

10.2.2 Quality of service and SLAs

Once SOAP monitoring is in place, the SOA management solution can track QoS for web services in the SOA. To make this work, the SOAP interceptor sends time-stamped data to the SOA management solution that measures how quickly a web service responds to an invocation. Then, the SOA management solution compares the response time to response time that has been established for that specific web service, or all the web services in the SOA. (Most SOA management solutions have an interface where an administrator can enter QoS parameters for each web service in the SOA.) For example, the accounting web service might list a standard response time of one second. If it takes two seconds to respond to an invocation, the SOA management application will notice that the QoS is suffering and send an alert to the administrator.

In addition to monitoring QoS and alerting administrators to problems, most SOA management solutions offer administrators the ability to establish SLAs. Under an SLA, the provider of the web service guarantees that the web service will perform according to certain parameters. In our example, let's assume that the accounting web service is run by the IT staff of the accounting department on a computer in the accounting department's data center. The divisions of the company that invoke the accounting web service require a specific service level, such as a one-second response time and guaranteed availability. The SOA management solution enables the account IT staff to enter an SLA with the users of their web service. If they violate the SLA, there may be repercussions for the IT staff. It is their job to assure the users of the web service that it will always perform under the terms of the SLA. The SOA management solution measures whether the IT staff is doing their job honoring the SLA. Remember, a key goal of an SOA in the first place is to encourage "reuse" in the enterprise.

If developers of new applications are not convinced that a service is going to function up to quality, they are more likely to "recode" the capability from scratch than to risk relying on the service.

10.2.3 Contracts

Most SOA management solutions enable administrators to establish web service usage contracts among the various parties who use the SOA and the providers of the web services. These contracts may have a number of different components. The SLAs we discussed earlier are one type of contract. Additionally, the SOA management solution may allow providers of web services to dictate who may use the service, for how long, and how often. For example, the accounting department might permit the customer service system to use its web service one thousand times a day. If the thousand-use limit is attained, the accounting web service will not respond to subsequent invocations.

Contracts are an important ingredient of SOA management because they erect barriers to misuse and overuse. In addition, contracts allow consumers of services to "get what they pay for," as services can also be offered to third parties on particular business terms. In a process that overlaps with security, the contract aspect of SOA management sets limits on web service usage. As a result, the contracts protect against system overload, flooding, and malicious attacks. Furthermore, they enable administrators to plan for web service use. If the administrators know, for example, that a specific web service has ten users with contracts for one million uses per day, then they know they have to have computer and network capacity capable of handling that load.

Contracts can also quantify web service usage for the purpose of payment or charge-backs. In many companies, one division charges other divisions for services it renders. Even though they are part of the same company, each division has its own separate budget and income statements. As a result, a division may want to recoup the expense it incurred setting up a web service by charging for its use. For example, the accounting department might decide it wants to charge a penny to customer service every time customer service invokes the accounting web service. Or accounting may decide to charge the penny after a certain limit of "free" invocations has been reached.

10.2.4 Caching

When a web service provides an identical response to a frequently repeated request, it may make sense to cache the response. For example, if the accounting system has to verify the product codes for the ten most popular items that the company sells, it is a waste of computing and network resources to have the parts catalog web service respond to that same question over and over again. Those product codes can be cached in the SOAP interceptor as an autom atic response to the SOAP message that asks for them. The cached responses spread the load away from the parts catalog web service, enhancing the manageability of the SOA. Figure 10.6 shows what this might look like.

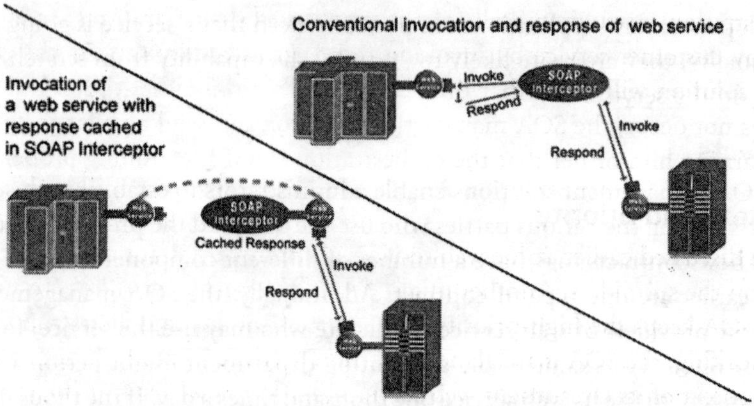

Figure 10.6 Cached response to frequent, identical SOAP requests using a SOAP interceptor

10.2.5 Orchestration

In the unmanaged SOA, we saw that there was no way to be sure if an orchestrated sequence of web services was acting according to the instruction set laid out for them by the software developers who put the orchestration together. With an SOA management solution, you can establish the correct sequence of actions that need to occur for the orchestration to produce the desired result. The SOA management solution can monitor the activity of the web services and verify that the orchestration is proceeding correctly.

As depicted in figure 10.7, the SOA management solution checks each web service invocation and response against its set of orchestration instructions. If the

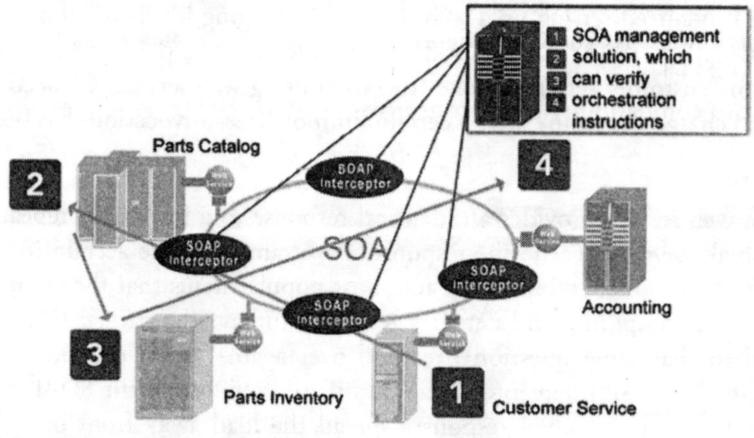

Figure 10.7 An SOA management solution can verify orchestration instructions by intercepting the SOAP messages that travel between each orchestrated web service and comparing them to an established set of instructions.

orchestration instructions call for the parts catalog service to respond to an invocation by customer service by invoking the parts inventory service, the SOA management solution will verify that this sequence of actions either did or did not occur. If it does not occur, the SOA management solution can send an alert to the administrator warning him or her that the orchestration is not functioning properly.

10.2.6 Context and priority

As we discussed earlier, some web services are more important than others. One might turn on the sprinklers. Another might detonate a nuclear warhead. To make sure that your SOA keeps the high-priority web services running and alerts you when they are not working, the SOA management solution needs to be able to assess relative priority and context of its constituent web services. To do this, the SOA management solution provides an interface where the administrator can input data relating to the relative priority of each web service. The SOA management solution then monitors the performance of each web service and responds to problems based on priorities. For instance, if a low-priority web service goes down, the system may send an email alert to the administrator. If a high-priority web service goes down, the SOA management solution could be programmed to page ten different people at the same time. Further, the same web service, invoked by different processes, could have completely different contexts. For instance, a weather service can be used by one process to plan a wedding and the other to monitor cloud cover for a bombing run. An effective web service management system can help monitor not only the services themselves for prioritization, but the processes that invoke them as well.

10.2.7 Change management

Because your SOA inevitably changes over time, you will want your SOA management solution to abstract your developers and your services from the challenges that changes brings. As shown in figure 10.8, a good SOA management solution keeps track of which version of a web service is the correct one to use, and offers real-time backward compatibility so no consumers are denied when a service upgrades. In the

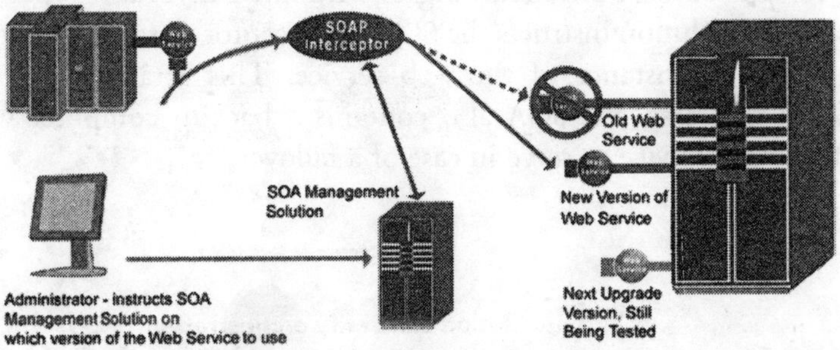

Figure 10.8 The SOA management solution directs a SOAP request to the correct version of a web service.

example shown in the figure, an administrator has the ability to instruct the SOA management solution about which version to invoke. When the SOAP interceptor receives the invocation for the web service, it automatically checks with the SOA management solution for information about versioning. In this case, the SOA management solution tells the SOAP interceptor to route the SOAP request to the new version of the web service. This may not seem that profound in such a simple example, but to understand the benefit of this kind of solution, you have to imagine the change management headache that would occur if this SOA had ten thousand web services, all changing over time. Similarly, this challenge would be enormous if a single service was being used by thousands of consumers. When a change is made, you do not want the thousand developers who run the consumer applications banging on your door demanding your head.

10.2.8 High availability

Depending on the priority level of a web service in your SOA, you may arrange different options to handle increases in load or failover. For a critical web service, such as the nuclear bomb activation, you'd probably want a backup system available as a failover option. Or, at the very least, you'd arrange a second instance of the web service to handle overflow load. To direct the SOAP requests to the right place, you need to make your SOA management solution "know" how to handle a high-load or failover situation. The result you want is a circumstance known as "high availability." *High availability* is a term that describes some distinct level of availability performance for a piece of software or hardware. You might insist, for example, that a web service be available 99.999999 percent of the time. In that case, you would absolutely require a backup computer for failover. Ideally, that computer would be on a separate power grid and maybe in another state. (I live in earthquake country, so this is frequently on my mind.)

To create a high-availability situation, the SOA management solution has to know how to measure the load on a web service. To realize this goal, the administrator inputs a load parameter into the SOA management solution that can be measured against actual activity. So, for example, if the administrator establishes that a web service needs to split its load after reaching one hundred invocations per minute, the SOA management solution instructs the SOAP interceptor to route the overflow invocations to a second instance of the web service. This arrangement is shown in figure 10.9. In this case, the SOA also contains a backup computer with another instance of the web service to serve in case of a failover.

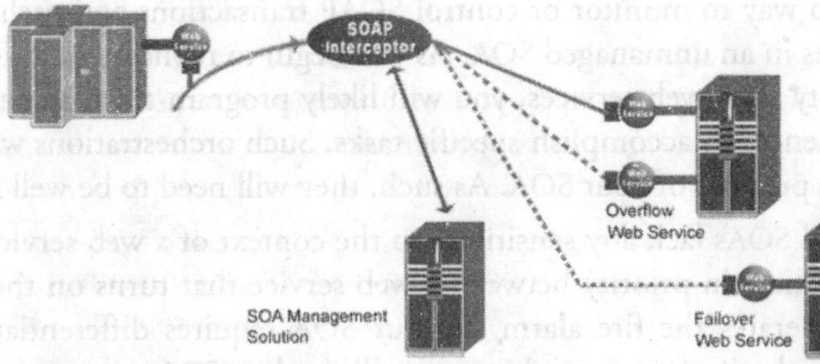

Figure 10.9 An SOA management solution can enable high availability by routing SOAP messages to less busy "overflow" versions of the same web service.

10.3 THE SAVVY MANAGER CAUTIONS: CHOOSING AN SOA MANAGEMENT SOLUTION

If you're thinking that all of these management challenges are a lot to handle, you're right. Like security, SOA management can be a bear for IT administrators and system architects. For this reason, the solution you select or create for SOA management may be one of the most critical decisions you make as you create your SOA. Luckily, you have a number of good choices. However, you'll really have to do your homework and due diligence on proposed solutions. As in other areas of IT, but especially in the case of an emerging and poorly understood set of standards such as SOAP XML, vaporware abounds. Watch outfor hype. (Mea culpa, though I will not confess to anything specific…) When choosing a solution, it is vital to consider not only the capabilities of the software package you select but how well it integrates with your existing infrastructure. Remember: an SOA is not a replacement for your infrastructure; it is simply a more efficient way to organize and interoperate with your existing investments. To that end, partnerships and alliances with your existing vendors will be critical.

10.4 SUMMARY

SOA management is a serious challenge. However, for each problem there is a solution. A range of SOA management solutions are beginning to mature as the market has advanced. These specialized software programs solve many of the following problems:

- Quality of service (QoS) is impossible to effectively measure performance in an unmanaged SOA. If a web service takes one second, or five minutes, to respond to an invocation, you have no way of centrally controlling it. If you have a small SOA with a handful of web services, this problem may not seem that serious. However, as your use of web services become even slightly more sophisticated, QoS can become one of your biggest concerns.

- There is no way to monitor or control SOAP transactions and orchestration of web services in an unmanaged SOA. As you begin to replicate traditional system functionality with web services, you will likely program them to act in orchestrated sequences to accomplish specific tasks. Such orchestrations will probably be the core purpose of your SOA. As such, they will need to be well managed.
- Unmanaged SOAs lack any sensitivity to the context of a web service. You cannot differentiate in priority between a web service that turns on the lights and one that operates the fire alarm. If your SOA requires differentiating service issues on the basis of context, then you will need an SOA management solution that handles this problem.
- Change management and version control can cause problems in an unmanaged SOA environment. In small SOAs this is not a big issue, but in a large-scale SOA, IT administrators may have to manage thousands of changing web services at one time. Without management, this is a virtually impossible task.
- Load balancing and failover are also problematic in an unmanaged SOA. Depending on priority, you may need to develop multiple instances of web services to serve increased load or provide backup in the case of a failover. If there is no management in the SOA, there is no way to manage the load.

SOA management solutions, comprised of software packages, combinations of software programs from different vendors, and custom solutions, offer some or all of the answers to these challenges. Most SOA management solutions utilize the same SOAP interceptor model as the SOA security solutions discussed in the previous chapter.

The SOAP interceptor/centralized SOA management solution setup makes it possible for administrators to input instructions on how to manage the SOA. As SOAP messages travel to web services, they are intercepted. With interception, the SOA management solution can measure response times, alert administrators to problems in QoS, check orchestration instructions, reroute invocations to correct versions of web services, and manage the load and failover.

The distributed set of interceptors (or "policy enforcement points" as they are sometimes called) combine to offer an "abstraction layer" that separates the services themselves from the consumer applications. This abstraction layer is what is commonly referred to as a "services fabric"—it is the place in the network where the complexities of management and security are pushed so that the services can be invoked easily, with agility and flexibility. A well-managed and secure "fabric" is the key to exploiting the advantages of a service-oriented architecture.

CHAPTER 11

Assembling SOA networks

"Shouldn't we deploy web services, get the hang of them on a small scale, and then worry about all the complexity?" Jay asks. "We need to crawl before we walk."

"True," I reply. "You'll probably do a pilot, and we'll get into that. However, you need to be able to think through the eventualities of an SOA. Today, most organizations have started to deploy small numbers of web services so they can accomplish discrete tasks. However, it's likely that the numbers of web services in most companies will grow as the technology matures. I like to call this concept an SOA network—a whole lot of web services in simultaneous use across multiple network domains. I realize, of course, that when I talk about SOA networks, I'm making a prediction for the future. But I hardly think this a risky or even controversial bet. There's so much momentum behind these standards as key enterprise building blocks that pronouncing the advent of SOA networks would be like guessing that the telephone was going to catch on in 1900. The more people who use it, the more others need to follow, and so on, in an accelerating, virtuous cycle of adoption."

11.1 TITAN'S POTENTIAL SOA NETWORK

An SOA network is a networked set of SOA environments, including their respective web services, functioning interdependently. SOA networks might come into existence

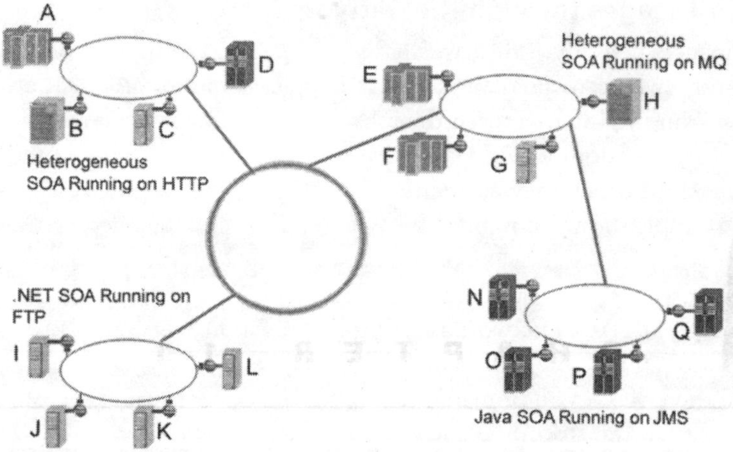

Figure 11.1 A simple SOA network consists of multiple SOAs connected by a common network infrastructure such as the Internet or private networks.

between organizations, within them, or both. I encourage Jay to envision what would happen if Titan's SOA had to connect with those of other companies and government agencies—a standard issue in the insurance industry. Figure 11.1 shows a simple example of what Titan's SOA network might look like. It connects four separate SOAs. Each SOA runs off a different set of communication standards and operating platforms. Going clockwise, you have a heterogeneous platform SOA running on HTTP for messaging, a heterogeneous SOA running on MQ for messaging, and a Microsoft .NET SOA using FTP to transmit SOAP messages.

What I want Jay to see in the example is how web services may have to interact with web service consumers that span different communication protocols, security systems, and network routing configurations. Just because groups are using "standards" in some areas is hardly a recipe for compatibility—in the same way that if you get a man and woman to both speak Spanish, it will certainly help them connect but is a far cry from predicting their ability to relate. Coming from different platforms, protocols, and so forth, the expectations of consumers and providers of web services need to be massaged and handled independently of the end points themselves.

11.2 MANAGING THE SOA NETWORK

If an SOA is challenging to manage, then imagine how complex it can get when you have multiple SOAs to keep track of, some of which may be in other companies, or even other countries. Message management, transport, routing, and security are several of the many management issues that arise when trying to manage a reliable SOA network. Even if each individual SOA in the network is well managed, the network as a whole can remain unmanaged.

11.2.1 Passing messages through the network

What happens when SOAP messages have to travel across the network? How does a message know where to go? While many people assume that SOAP always travels across HTTP on the Internet, even the most minor forays into SOAs in the real world show that this is seldom true. In real life, SOAP messages travel on a multiplicity of networks, each of which may have different transport and routing conventions.

In the example shown in figure 11.2 (where I have swapped out Titan with a Java- and JMS-based SOA for the sake of simplicity and teaching), in order for Computer D to invoke a web service on Computer E, its SOAP request must travel from a network running HTTP to a network running MQ. Two management issues arise out of this transaction. First, the SOAP message must be able to adapt to transport over HTTP and then MQ. In an unmanaged SOA network, SOAP, as is, does not have any innate capacity to transform itself to be carried correctly over multiple transport protocols. Second, there is the matter of routing. How can you be sure that the message knows how to get from point D to point E?

Figure 11.3 shows a typical routing scenario in an SOA network. When the SOAP requests emanates from the invoking computer, shown on the left, it can follow one of two paths to the responding web service. It can travel a path that is fast, or it can take a path that is known to be more reliable, if a little slower. Remember the web service that controls the nuclear warhead? Obviously, you'd probably want that message traveling on a reliable path. Trouble is, SOAP in its native form has no mechanism to handle routing decisions. In the unmanaged SOA network, routing is problematic.

And let's not forget SOAP message management basics. How does Computer D know that Computer E has received the message? How fast is the response? Are there

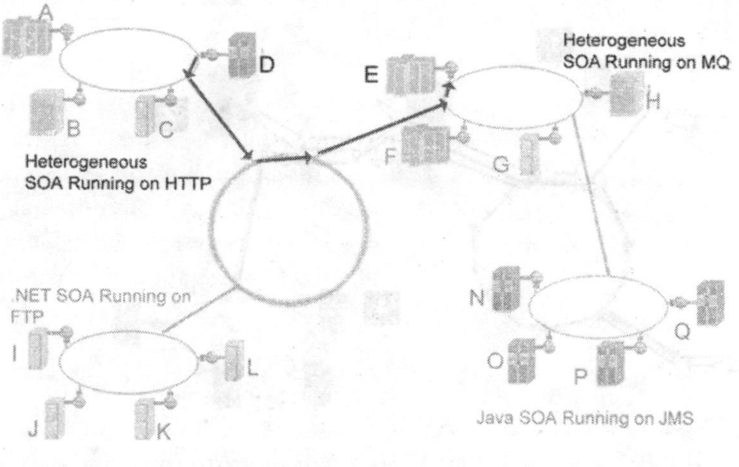

Figure 11.2 When a SOAP message has to pass through an SOA network, it may have to make its way successfully through multiple network hops.

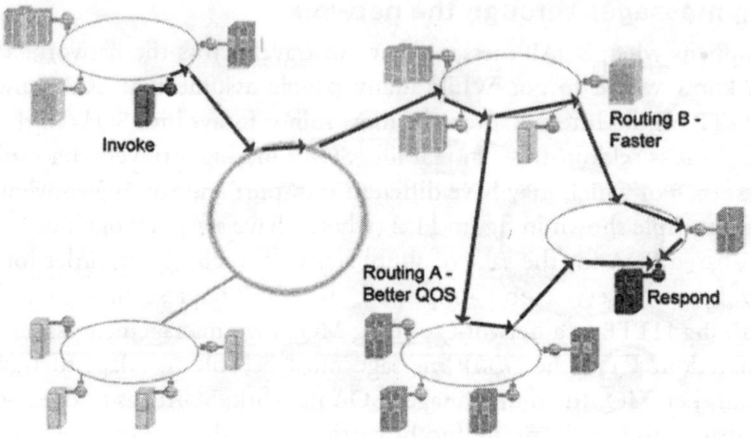

Figure 11.3 There may be more than one way for a SOAP message to reach its destination web service. In all likelihood, one route may be faster, and the other might be more reliable. Depending on your priorities, you may want to be able to designate the better route.

SLAs and QoS guarantees, contracts, or charge-backs? All of these questions still need to be asked—though in an SOA network, the answers are typically much more complex than in a standard SOA.

In an orchestrated process, like the one shown in figure 11.4, the management issues multiply. In this four-step orchestrated process, SOAP messages must travel

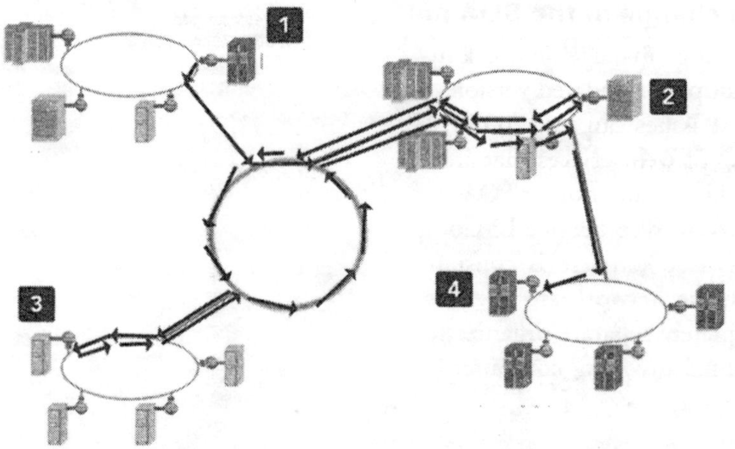

Figure 11.4 A four-step orchestrated web service process in an SOA network

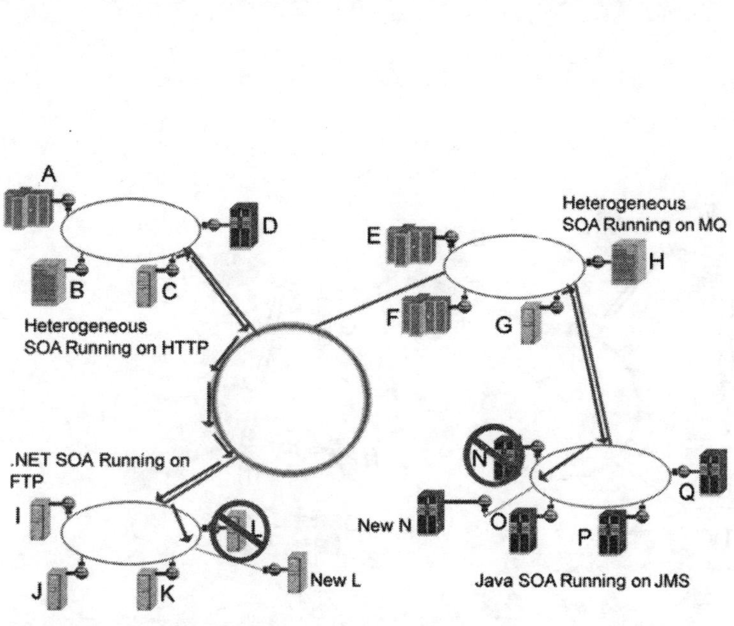

Figure 11.5 Keeping track of change management in the SOA network is a major challenge. As web services change, move, or get upgraded, you will need a way to update any potential consumer of that web service. If you fail to do this, then those consumers will continue to invoke web services that no longer exist and experience inferior quality of service.

back and forth several times across four different networks, each of which runs on a different transport protocol. The SOAP messages must be transformed, and transformed again as they move from point to point. With routing, change management, and security challenges factored in, it is probable that this orchestrated process would not work at all in an unmanaged SOA network.

11.2.2 Managing change in the SOA network

As always, change management is a major bugaboo in an SOA network. In the same way that multiple or updated versions of web services can cause confusion, in an SOA network these issues can lead to outright failure of performance. Figure 11.5 shows two instances of web services that are changed. If Computer C wants to invoke Web Service L, which is in another SOA, how does it know that Web Service L has been replaced by New Web Service L? Computer G and Web Service N present the same problem. Because software is constantly changing, the web services that comprise each SOA in the network are likely to change over time. Because the services exist within completely separate organizations, if the changes cannot be reported reliably to any potential invoking computer in the network, then the network will cease to function properly.

11.3 SECURING THE SOA NETWORK

Security is also a big hurdle that you face when you put together an SOA network. As is the case with management, security in the SOA network confronts all of the same

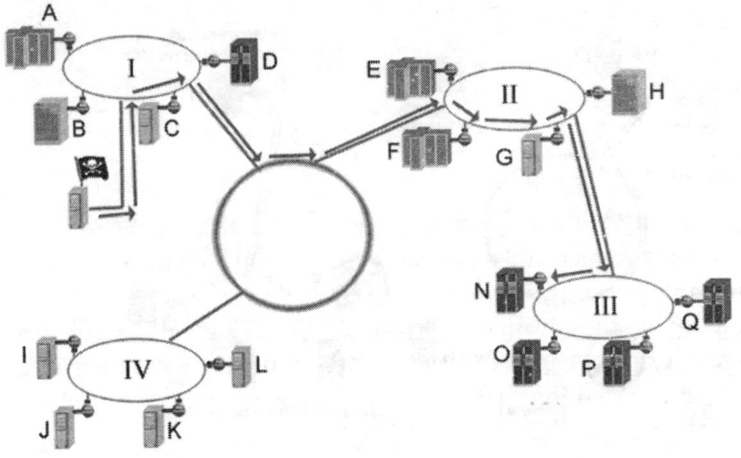

Figure 11.6 SOA networks present multiple challenges in securing third parties. In this example, Web Service N in SOA Network III will have to be able to authenticate a user from Network I if it is meant to operate securely. If an unauthorized user is able to simulate being a user of Network I, then Web Service N will be vulnerable to unauthorized use.

issues that you find in a standard SOA, only more so. The SOA network compounds all of the authentication, authorization, privacy, and message integrity challenges inherent in the SOA.

Figure 11.6 depicts an SOA network security scenario that shows how each SOA in an unsecured network is vulnerable. If SOA Network III is set up to permit any request emanating from Network II, and Network II is set up to allow requests from Network I, then any user on Network I can access Network III, even if they lack proper security credentials. At best, there is the potential for unintentional misuse of web services by users in Network I. At worst, outright intrusion can take place without detection or consequence.

Even if each SOA has its own security mechanism, the network as a whole is vulnerable because there is nothing to secure the interactions between the component SOAs. Assuming that the respective security mechanisms are not correlated, if an unauthorized user on Network I wants to access Web Service N on Network III, Web Service N has no way to authenticate the user and no way to establish whether that user is authorized to use the service. Privacy and message integrity are also at risk in an unsecured SOA network. As the SOAP messages travel between the "hops" on the network, they can be intercepted, copied, rerouted, or changed before they reach their intended destination.

11.4 FINDING THE RIGHT SOLUTION

Now, at this point, a reasonable person might be wondering if an SOA network is worth the trouble. It's enough just to establish management and security in a single

SOA. When you combine SOAs into a network, as you have seen, the challenges become much more complex. And remember, the SOA management solution must handle all the issues we have raised all at once. It has to handle routing, transport, message management, change management, and security simultaneously—and do so not only within one SOA environment but also between multiple environments.

Believe me, it is worth the effort to overcome the struggle to secure and manage your SOA network(s). If you restrict the reach of your SOA to those services available only within your domain, then you are limiting your SOA's ability to interoperate with systems in other organizations or branches of your organization. This limitation will begin to nullify the advantages of your SOA in the first place and ultimately leave you in no better shape than if you had never adopted the standards in the first place.

Luckily, several solutions are available for managing and securing an SOA network. In fact, many of the SOA management and security solutions also have SOA network management and security features as well. When you evaluate these products and solutions, you may want to bear their network features in mind.

11.5 USING SOAP INTERCEPTION FOR SOA NETWORK MANAGEMENT

Though there are a number of approaches to managing SOA networks, the most effective seem to be those that are based on SOAP interceptors reporting to a centralized solution. After all, the SOAP message—its header, to be specific—is the unit that drives the functioning network. The message is the little piece of XML that must traverse the network with all of its hops, routing decisions, and transport protocols. It is the SOAP message that must successfully pass through security policy checkpoints. A distributed manner of enforcing the policies of the SOA therefore would appear to be both logical and necessary.

Figure 11.7 depicts an SOA management solution based on SOAP message interception. At each juncture in the network, a SOAP message interceptor processes incoming and outbound SOAP messages. The SOAP interceptor communicates with each web service in its respective SOA network. The SOAP interceptor, therefore, can transmit totally accurate information about each web service in its network to the central SOA network management solution. The SOA network management solution, as a result, "knows" everything it needs to know about every web service in the entire SOA network.

Where does the SOA network management solution store all this knowledge about the web services in the network? Options abound, but one of the most effective solutions involves a robust metadata store that can make information about the services readily available. Further, taking advantage of a standard that already exists, you can begin with a basic UDDI (web services registry) and expand it to serve a comprehensive SOA network management role. A UDDI, which contains basic information about a web service with the goal of making that service easier to locate and use, can

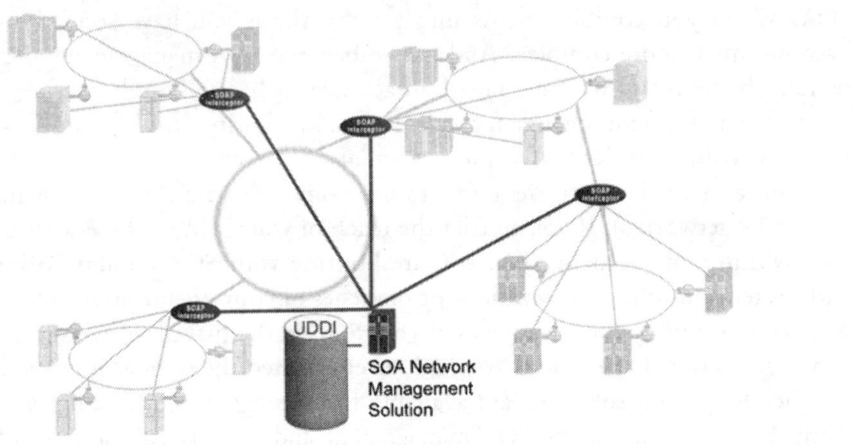

Figure 11.7 SOAP interceptors can serve as the basis for an SOA network management solution.

be enhanced and plugged into a powerful database management system (DBMS) such as Oracle or IBM DB2. The net result is a complete repository of information about the web services in the SOA network. The SOA network management solution draws on this information to manage the network.

The SOA management solution's enhanced registry stores metadata about each web service, including

- Transport protocols rules
- Network routing rules
- Security policy information
- QoS and SLA rules
- Change management status

When a web service invocation emanates from a computer on the network, the SOAP interceptor grabs it and adds the information it will need to get to its destination web service and receive an answer.

For example, figure 11.8 shows a SOAP request coming from the computer on the left. Before it can reach the web service that it is trying to invoke, it is stopped by the SOAP interceptor. The SOAP interceptor then "asks" the SOA network management solution to verify the information in the SOAP request's header. It makes sure that the request is not heading toward a defunct web service that has been replaced with an upgraded version. It ensures that security policies are in force and then verifies the routing plan for the message, checking whether the message should be routed according to QoS dictates or speed. It then transforms the SOAP message into whatever

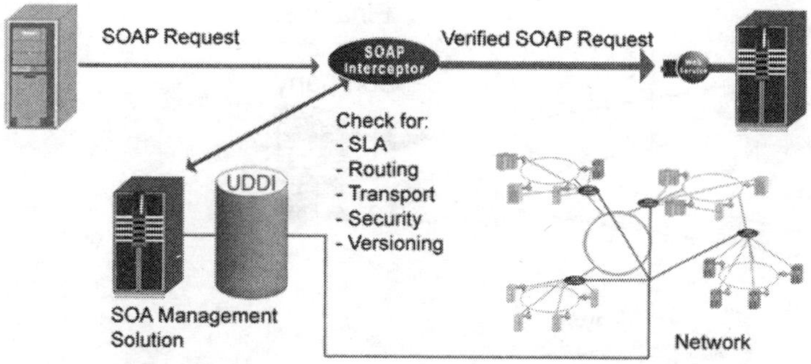

Figure 11.8 When a SOAP message crosses an SOA network, the SOAP interceptor stops it, checks it, and possibly modifies it to comply with service-level performance, routing instructions, transport protocol transformation, security, and versioning.

transport protocol is required at the other end. After that process has been completed, the verified SOAP request is forwarded to its intended destination. The information necessary to make the verification is stored in the SOA network management solution's metadata repository.

11.6 XML VPNs

One of the great benefits of an SOA network is its ability to let you extend programmatic, integration capabilities to business partners. Going beyond simple sharing of data with partners, the SOA network enables true B2B application integration. At the same time, this capability creates a truly vexing security policy enforcement dilemma. How can you be sure that a user from a partner organization is authorized to integrate with your applications? How can you authenticate that user? Do you even want that headache in the first place?

There is a solution approach that removes many of the administration ownership issues from the equation. The XML virtual private network, or XML VPN, enables multiple enterprises to interoperate without the necessity of having to know much about each other. Like a traditional SSL VPN, which creates a "tunnel" of encryption across public networks so two machines can interoperate securely, the XML VPN allows secure connections between web services and their consumers across the Net. An XML VPN mitigates certain security policy enforcement issues in B2B SOA implementations.

For example, let's say that you have a financial services company that enables various partners to participate in a credit card "Reward Points" program that allows cardholders to redeem reward points for merchandise at participating partners. A retailer can enable its customers to apply their credit card reward points toward purchases. To make this work, your company sets up web services that provide rewards point account balances to participating partners. Each of your partners develops web service

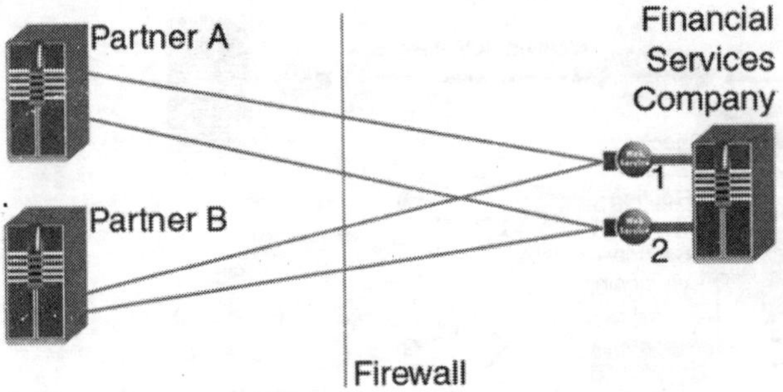

Figure 11.9 A financial services company sets up a credit card user rewards program that allows cardholders to redeem reward points at participating partners. Web services provide reward point balances to partners, who must develop web service consumer applications to find out how many reward points each cardholder has. This presents a security challenge. The financial services company must authorize and authenticate developer users at each partner without knowing any of the users.

consumer applications that invoke your reward points web services. Figure 11.9 illustrates the consumer and web service relationships that must be maintained in order for your partners to be able to gain access to reward point account data exposed as web services at your financial services company.

The reward points program creates a security challenge for your company. First, in order for the program to work, you have to offer programmatic access to your web services to software developers at your partner firms. This is because each partner needs to develop a web service consumer application to be able to participate in the reward points program. Here's the problem: How does your company know who each developer user is? To assure the security of your systems, you have to be able to authorize and authenticate any developer user who wants access to the web service for development purposes. Even in this extremely simple example, your company has to maintain up-to-date authorization and authentication information for two partners and two web services. What happens if a partner developer quits? How does your company keep track of that? More important, do you want that responsibility? You can imagine how complex and time consuming this arrangement could become.

By deploying an XML VPN, your financial services company can reduce many of the security headaches associated with maintaining its partner interactions in the reward points program. As figure 11.10 shows, each partner routes its web service requests through a secure proxy. All access rules and user identities are maintained in an XML VPN controller, which accepts or rejects the web service requests. The web services, too, are represented in a proxy, which interacts with the controller. In this way, the XML VPN reduces security to the level of the proxy. No specialized administration or software development is needed to track individual users at each partner firm.

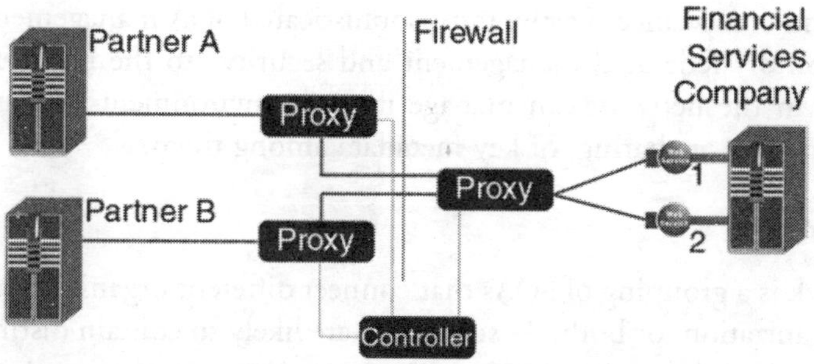

Figure 11.10 An XML VPN creates secure proxies for both the web service consumers and the web services themselves. Security is maintained at the level of the proxy, with any web service request or programmatic user login from a trusted partner that matches the preset rules stored in the controller being automatically approved.

11.7 THE SAVVY MANAGER CAUTIONS: WHO'S IN CHARGE?

One major issue that is sure to come out of the development of large SOA networks is that of ownership. Who is in charge? Who owns the data related to the management of the network? It can become a thorny issue. In order for SOA networks to exist, there will have to be some level of cooperation between the entities that comprise the network. This is not a simple matter. In some ways, the technological aspects of building an SOA network are the easy part—getting multiple organizations to agree to participate in the SOA network might be challenging.

However you do it, you have to build intelligence into your SOA network, or it will quickly cease to function. There are simply too many moving, changing parts for it to run itself. This notion of "abstracting" the complexity from the end points of an SOA and into the network is the basis of the "services fabric" management solutions that have recently come to market. As these networks grow—and I believe that they will become immense—there will be no way for each computer in the SOA network to know the status of every web service in the network and how best to reach it. The management solution has to be able to absorb a comprehensive set of information about the SOA network in its entirety. The management solution must have the intelligence to help the component SOAs and web services function as intended.

A number of possible solutions are emerging as this issue becomes better defined. One option is to have external third parties handle these cooperation tasks. Some of the large telecom carriers are already exploring this as a line of business with which to augment their corporate services. These entities will operate web services "hubs" and manage the security and auditing issues that would normally hamper commerce between parties. Another likely scenario for larger companies is that they will become the driving forces in rallying their suppliers and partners, mandating widespread participation and compliance. Lastly, most sophisticated SOA management solutions bring the notion of "federated management and security" to the table. This means that each SOA in the network can manage its own environments but interoperate through a federation, or sharing, of key metadata among them.

11.8 SUMMARY

An SOA network is a grouping of SOAs that connect different organizations, divisions of the same organization, or both. As such, they are likely to contain distinct message transport protocols and security policies. SOA networks present a number of significant management challenges that surpass those involved in standard SOA management in complexity. These challenges include SLA and QoS monitoring across multiple domains, assuring effective routing of SOAP messages, transforming SOAP messages to successfully travel across multiple transport protocols such as JMS and HTTP, and managing version control. Security is also a big factor in SOA networks, as each network is likely to have its own unique security policies.

Solutions are available, and can be evaluated on their ability to offer a comprehensive and scalable approach. Several SOA management solutions also provide features that help manage a network of SOAs. The most prevalent models rely on "message interception." Some SOA network management solutions rely on enhanced UDDI to serve as a repository of information about every web service in the SOA network. With a metadata repository or "smart" UDDI, the SOA network management solution can ensure reliability of the SOAP messages traveling across the network, and effectively abstract the consumers and services from the complexities of interacting with one another. In addition, the emerging technology of XML VPNs promises to add another security solution for managing networks of independent, and interdependent, web services and consumers.

C H A P T E R 1 2

Utility computing

Utility computing, also known as "on-demand" computing, is a new paradigm for computing infrastructure that organizes IT resources so that they may be accessed—and paid for—as needed, just like traditional utilities such as gas, water, or electricity. Right now, utility computing models are being advanced by every major player in the IT field. While the efforts are quite early in their maturity, utility computing is more than just empty hype. It has potential implications for the way organizations purchase and use computer resources. It will also likely have a major impact on software as well, with web services and the SOA playing a pivotal role in its adoption.

12.1 WHAT TITAN WOULD GAIN FROM UTILITY COMPUTING

As I explain to Jay, the basic idea behind utility computing is to enable systems to perform only when needed, and for cost models to rise and fall according to usage as well. I ask him, "Do you ever have one set of servers sitting largely idle while another rack is being worked so hard there's steam coming out of the blades?" Jay nods in agreement. "Yes," he says, "it's a common problem at Titan. The IT budget always contains requests for more hardware to alleviate overtaxed systems while others remain underutilized."

I put it to Jay this way: To understand that value of utility computing, we have to look at the way most IT infrastructure is deployed today. As shown in figure 12.1, demand for applications tends to be variable. At any point in time, much of the infrastructure that has been deployed to meet peak demand remains unused. In technical terms, the server capacity has a low rate of utilization. In financial terms, the low rate of asset use results in lower ROI for IT infrastructure, an area that is a favorite target of corporate cost cutters.

Thus, the appeal of utility computing is two-sided. For consumers of IT infrastructure (the application users), utility computing offers the possibility of paying for application use only when a particular application is actually being used. Like utility consumption in the home, where we expect to pay for electricity, for example, when we have the lights on, and expect not to pay when we have the lights off, the utility computing user pays for actual usage and does not pay for downtime. From the point of view of IT infrastructure providers, whether they are outsourced services or in-house IT departments that function on a charge-back basis, the foundation of utility computing is the ability to maximize the utilization of IT infrastructure assets.

For utility computing to make sense financially, it has to benefit both the user and provider of the IT infrastructure. The onus of making utility computing viable, however, falls on the IT infrastructure provider because infrastructure users assume that they will pay less for a utility computing solution than they currently pay for fixed IT infrastructure that supports demand inefficiently. Indeed, if the costs of utility computing to infrastructure users were the same or higher than those of existing setups,

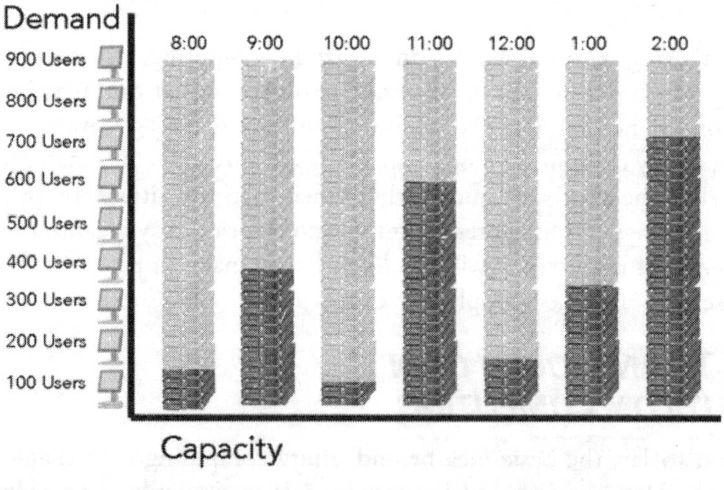

Figure 12.1 Demand for applications tends to be variable, rising and falling throughout the day. However, most IT infrastructures are designed to meet maximum demand. The result is a low utilization of IT assets, which translates into high expenditures for infrastructure that is seldom used, except in high-demand periods.

then few would bother with it. Therefore, the infrastructure provider has to be able to justify utility computing in financial terms. What this means, in a practical sense, is that the infrastructure provider has to use utility computing to increase utilization of infrastructure assets.

The goal of utility computing is to maximize infrastructure load by juggling available capacity in response to demand. As figure 12.2 illustrates, a utility computing infrastructure places multiple applications on the same infrastructure. As demand for one application rises (or falls), the utility computing infrastructure increases (or decreases) usage of that application on sets of available, interchangeable servers. In the simplified example shown in figure 12.2, the infrastructure that was inefficiently used to service just one application in figure 12.1 is now configured for utility computing and has the ability to provide two applications, A and B, with the same amount of infrastructure assets. Overall utilization of IT assets is higher, which means financial return on assets is higher, and the application becomes less expensive to provide to users.

Ideally, utility computing takes place in an infrastructure where computers can switch tasks between themselves and automatically transfer demand for functionality from one machine to the next as demand rises or falls. The word "utility" is meant to connote the universal, (mostly) unquestioned availability of utility services in our lives such as electricity, water, and phones. The idea is that computing infrastructure can mimic the automated capacity response of the electric grid. When you turn on the

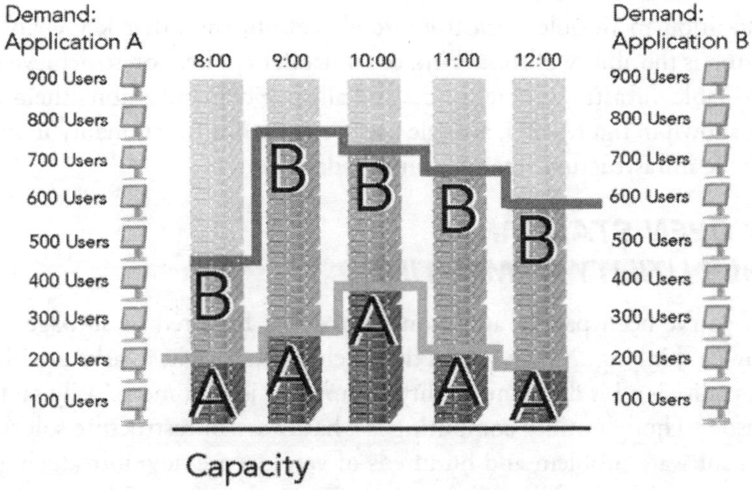

Figure 12.2 Utility computing requires the ability to juggle demand for applications between interchangeable servers. In this example, applications A and B share the same set of servers. As demand rises and falls for each application, the utility computing system allocates server capacity within the infrastructure on a dynamic basis. The result is higher utilization of infrastructure assets, higher ROI, and lower costs to users.

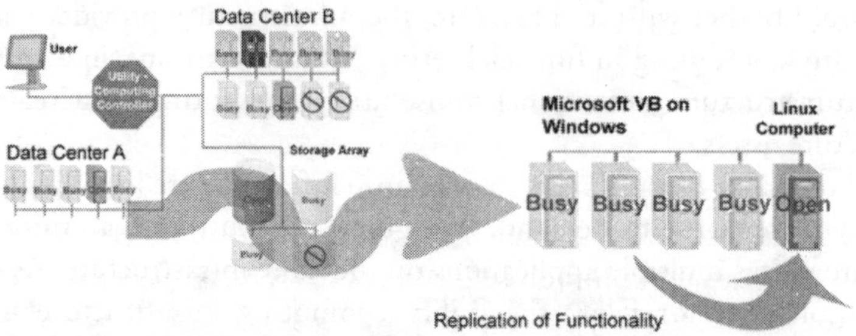

Figure 12.3 Replicating functionality between computers is a challenging proposition in a heterogeneous environment. In this example, it would be necessary to replicate a Microsoft VB program on a Linux computer to achieve a viable utility computing result. The problem is, that's virtually impossible, especially in an unattended, automated process.

lights, you have no awareness that your act of increasing the demand for electricity may impel your local power company to buy a few megawatts from a generator in Texas. It is invisible to you, as it should be. In utility computing, ideally, you are able to summon computer functionality without any concern for where the computing capacity necessary to fulfill your need is originating. More important, rather than forecast capacity needs in advance and overpurchase, you simply pay for what you consume with the assumption that a vast store of capacity—essentially an infinite amount of resources—is available to you at any instant.

In addition to flexible infrastructure allocation, the other key enabler of utility computing is the ability of some kind of controller application to achieve an overview of all available infrastructure resources and allocate demand among them in a sensible way. As shown in figure 12.3, a single user's request for functionality might be routed to available infrastructure resources in two data centers.

12.2 HOW OPEN STANDARDS ENABLE UTILITY COMPUTING

Now, if you've been paying attention for the last hundred or so pages, you should probably be thinking, "Okay, what's the catch?" You're right to ask; as with all utopian visions, reality is a bit different. Utility computing is a lot more easily said than done. The reason? Though utility computing is a hardware/infrastructure solution, it is primarily a software problem and hundreds of vendors are now introducing competing approaches, with none filling all the gaps.

The two key enablers of utility computing—the ability of resources to replicate their functionality on other resources and the ability of a central controller to allocate demand across different resources in separate data centers—are contingent on some kind of open interoperability of systems. If the resources in your data centers are heterogeneous in terms of operating systems, programming languages, platform, network protocols, and application integration (and let's face it, they are), you are going to have a heck of a time getting utility computing to work.

Of course, you could switch everything over to a single, unifying proprietary standard. But if you aren't ready for that reality and expense, then a utility computing architecture based on open standards begins to make a lot of sense. In fact, I believe it is going to be impossible for the major IT players to realize their utility computing goals without embracing a common set of standards. For this reason, utility computing is going to succeed in part by leveraging web services and an SOA approach.

Figure 12.3 illustrates the problem. If there is an overloaded Microsoft Visual Basic (VB) application running on a Windows box, and the available computer that the utility computing controller can replicate it on is a Linux machine, it will be complex, or even impossible, to make that transition. The matter gets messier if the other available machines are running yet more operating systems. If you aren't going to use open standards to solve this problem, you have several unappetizing alternatives. You could integrate with proprietary technology, rewrite your applications in an open language such as Java (which replicates easily on multiple platforms), or rewrite everything on a single proprietary standard and settle on that manufacturer as your basic source for all IT infrastructure needs. However, in addition to locking you to that company for life at great expense, this latter option requires that you undergo the slow torture of multiple application and data migration projects.

As shown in figure 12.4, if the application functionality has been exposed as a web service using SOAP XML, then it is possible to replicate that web service on alternative machines without concern for the operating system of the supplementary computer or the original programming language of the application itself. It is not a perfect solution, though. In a mainframe legacy environment, for example, load will most likely still have to flow to the mainframe regardless of whether it has been exposed as a web service.

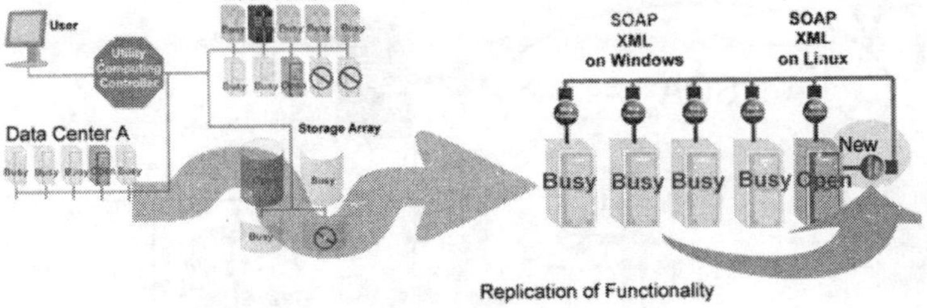

Figure 12.4 SOAP enables replication of functionality across multiple operating systems and languages.

12.3 UTILITY COMPUTING IN THE SOA

The concept of utility computing need not be limited to infrastructure. In an SOA, as we have seen, there are many load balancing and QoS issues that can be managed by using the ability to replicate web services on multiple computers on demand. As the idea of utility computing sweeps the major IT infrastructure vendors, the concept of the on-demand utility SOA is also taking hold. The vision that is being articulated is that of a self-managed, self-healing SOA that can automatically optimize performance by replicating web services as needed on multiple machines.

Figure 12.5 shows an SOA where one web service is being overloaded with demand. If this SOA were designed with a utility computing approach, then it would be able to replicate the overloaded web service on the most appropriate machine available. The result would be a balanced load and better overall QoS. However, as you may have predicted, creating such a utility computing SOA in the real world is a great deal more complicated than it might sound. Numerous management and security challenges spring to life when you try to implement a utility computing model in an SOA.

Message management becomes problematic when the web service that is being invoked continually jumps from one machine to another. The invoking computer has to keep track of where the intended web service is located. More specifically, it needs to know which instance of that web service to invoke—the one that is overloaded or the replicated replacement. How does the invoking computer know that the overloaded condition has calmed down and it is now okay to go back to invoking the old web service? If you throw in multiple versions of the web service as a factor to contend with, you'll be popping aspirin like candy.

Transport protocol and routing issues also get tricky when the location of the web service moves with little warning. The number and type of transport protocol transformations may change if the utility computing SOA moves the web service

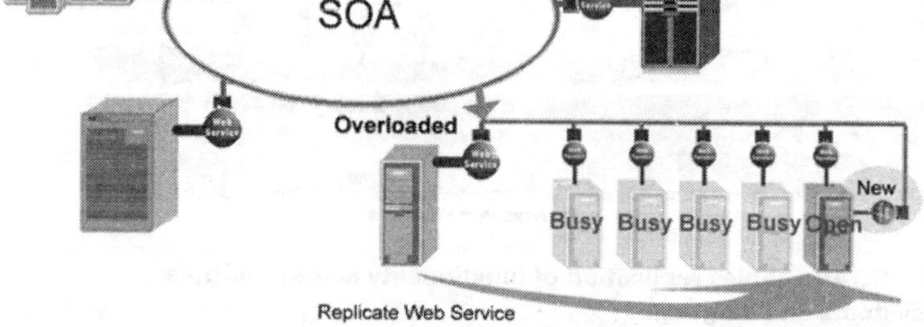

Figure 12.5 In an SOA utility computing scenario, an overloaded web service can bounce SOAP requests to a backup version of itself that has been replicated on another machine.

from one data center to another. And the definition of what constitutes the most reliable or fastest path to a web service will likely change along with that service's location on the network.

Security, too, becomes complicated under the utility computing SOA. If the web service replicates within the same domain, it is less of an issue. However, if the web service moves across the line between data centers and domains, the security policies that keep everyone safe have to be able to adapt on the fly to make the shifting web services respond securely to their invocations.

The question, though, is how you manage such a system so that it works the way you want it to. Answer: You need an SOA management and security application, whether you buy it, build it, or rent it. You will not be able to enjoy the benefits of the SOA—or in this specific case, the utility computing SOA—without a management application. Let's see how it works by examining some of the difficulties involved in creating a utility computing SOA.

By placing SOAP interceptors through the SOA and utility computing backup infrastructure, you can have an SOA that anticipates load and performance problems and acts to correct them before they occur or immediately after. Figure 12.6 provides a simplified view of what this means. As the web service in question becomes overloaded, the utility computing features of your SOA decide to replicate it on another computer. In order for the utility computing SOA to accomplish its goal of diverting demand from the overloaded service to the new, replicated instance of the web service, the fact of the replicated service's existence has to be instantly propagated throughout the SOA.

When the replicated web service comes into being, its location is sent to the SOA management solution's enhanced UDDI. When a computer in the SOA sends a SOAP

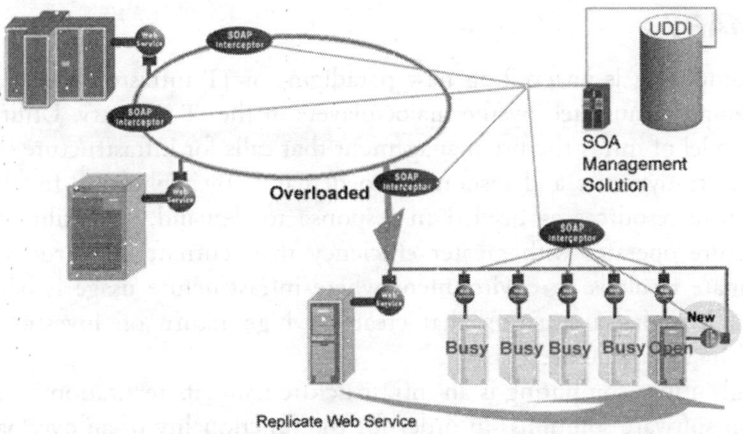

Figure 12.6 In an SOA utility computing scenario, an SOA management solution uses SOAP interceptors to measure load, trigger web service replication, and manage SOAP message flow to balance the load.

request to invoke that web service, the nearest SOAP interceptor stops the message and looks up the condition of the destination web service on the UDDI. The UDDI, which has been updated to know about the new instance of the web service, gives the SOAP interceptor the correct location, routing, transport, versioning, and security information it needs to forward the SOAP request to the replicated web service.

The SOA management solution also conveys whatever QoS, SLA, or contract terms applied to the overloaded web service to the replicated version. The SOA management solution measures response times and other performance criteria to ensure that the replicated version of the web service is acting as it was meant to. Overall, the SOA remains "aware" and "intelligent" about the existence, location, and performance of all its web services. If and when the replicated web service is decommissioned, the fact of its closure is also posted to the enhanced UDDI, which in turn has the ability to inform the SOAP interceptors to stop sending SOAP messages to the now defunct replicated service.

12.4 THE SAVVY MANAGER CAUTIONS: SECURE YOUR UTILITY COMPUTING

At the risk of contradicting myself, you may need to get a little overly hung up on security when it comes to utility computing. Why? Unlike traditional models of computing, utility computing is big on sharing of resources. Where there's sharing, there are increased security risks. In addition, many utility models include outsourcing of IT operations and hosting arrangements—which means more security worries. If you are looking into utility computing, have your team work out a detailed and highly flexible approach to securing your utility computing solution. Your security solution will have to adapt to the essentially fluid nature of utility computing.

12.5 SUMMARY

Utility computing is an exciting new paradigm for IT infrastructure management that is being promulgated by the major players in the IT industry. Utility computing is a model of infrastructure management that calls for infrastructure resources to become more dynamic and responsive to demand. By replicating functionality of infrastructure resources as needed in response to demand, the utility computing infrastructure operates with greater efficiency than current infrastructure models. The ultimate result is an environment where infrastructure usage is balanced and utilization is high—a situation that creates a high return on investment for the owner of the infrastructure.

Though utility computing is an infrastructure issue, its realization is largely contingent on software solutions. In order for the functionality of an overloaded infrastructure resource to be replicated, the software on the replicated resource must be compatible with that of the original resource. Heterogeneous operating systems and programming languages make for complexity in replicating infrastructure resources.

Open standards simplify the required replication of infrastructure resources in the utility computing model. An SOA can also run on a utility computing basis, with overloaded web services replicating themselves on underutilized machines in response to need. However, many management challenges result from implementing this concept.

SOA management solutions that rely on SOAP interception can manage and secure a utility computing SOA hub by tracking the constant shifting of available web services and ensuring that SOAP messages travel to their intended destinations securely and in keeping with the performance parameters expected by the users of the SOA.

PART 2

Understanding the people and process of enterprise SOA

We turn exclusively to Titan Insurance in part 2, with the goal of exposing you to the full depth of personal and process issues that can arise in the implementation of an enterprise SOA at a real company. Part 2 is the personal and political complement to part 1, which focuses on the technology of enterprise SOA. In my view, you need to have a deep appreciation for both the technological and human sides of the SOA puzzle in order to enjoy success with enterprise SOA.

CHAPTER 13

Exploring an SOA for Titan

"Okay!" I begin enthusiastically. "Now, let's talk about an SOA for Titan."

After all this, though, Jay is suddenly uncertain: "Can adopting our plans for an SOA now really make a difference for our situation?"

"Yes," I assure him, and go on to explain that adopting SOA standards will provide an approach to the integration headaches and set Titan on a path to lower the cost of future projects. With an SOA approach, the company can use XML and web services to replace the proprietary and custom interfaces that currently connect its various systems. The result will be a marked reduction in Titan's dependence on vendors to maintain those connections. In addition, I tell Jay, the SOA will be less expensive to operate once it is implemented.

Looking forward, an SOA will simplify the tricky legacy integration and legacy system replacement problems that Titan faces. For example, I explain to Jay, if Titan were to create SOAP interfaces between the InsurTech mainframe and each of the secondary systems that connect to it, then the InsurTech solution can be replaced piece by piece without having to rewrite any of those connectors. Dependent applications will simply be redirected over time (via a simple change in the UDDI registry) as incremental legacy functionality becomes available on newer systems.

In operational terms, the SOA will pave the way to eliminating the troublesome "fat clients" that are creating bottlenecks in customer service, claims management, and agency business. The SOA will provide the basis for extending the core functionality of Titan's critical systems out onto the Internet, a portal, and interactive voice response (IVR) phone links with customers and agents. We discuss this concept in depth. Although a fat client may not be a problem per se in Titan's case, the client is not desirable for a number of reasons. The company has a heterogeneous operating system environment, for one thing, and there is also a plan to enable possible outsourcing of call center functions and related tasks. To succeed, Titan wants to distance itself from having to rely on maintaining any kind of consistent desktop environment. Browsers are a solution, as you'll see as we continue with this story.

NOTE Also known as "thick clients," *fat clients* contain specialized code on the client side of a client-server architecture to handle data processing. In contrast, a *thin* client, for instance a web browser, places almost no dedicated code on the client side. The data processing is performed on the server. As a result, client-server applications based on thin clients are far easier to update than those based on fat clients, in which every client must be modified in order to accomplish an update of the program.

At the corporate level, an SOA enables upper management to gain great visibility into operations. An SOA provides the structure needed to deliver fast, flexible, and near real-time reporting on business operations. I explain that Titan will be able to create a "virtual data warehouse" and focus on managing business processes, rather than the underlying IT systems that support them.

In financial terms, while I can't give Jay an estimate off the top of my head, I feel fairly confident that the SOA represents the lowest overall expense of any of the options Titan is considering, factoring in the effects of long-term software maintenance, staffing levels, and infrastructure. I say that, ultimately, an SOA is the most effective way for Titan to bring its IT division purpose into alignment with its overall corporate goals. The company's IT problems are indirectly causing problems in the financial success of the whole merger between Apollo and Hermes. The SOA is, in my opinion, the most cost-effective way of bringing those problems under control.

I'm about to add, "And wait, you also get the bamboo steamer, too…" such was my dizzying pro-SOA spiel. Instead, though, I continue, "The SOA is a long-range vision. It's not a panacea or a magic bullet. Some parts of the SOA vision aren't ready for prime time, though standards and software packages are developing rapidly for the full realization of the promise. Many of the benefits depend on how the SOA is implemented and utilized. And, of course, the success of the SOA all depends on whether or not you do it right. Best practices are absolutely key in creating an SOA."

Jay is somewhat stunned by this whole discussion, but I can tell that I had given him some hope. He sees that I'm not trying to sell him on anything, that I'm merely trying to advise him on relatively new options. When we part, he thanks me for all of my help and tells me he'll think about what I've said and get back to me. A week later, I am invited to a meeting with Jay, H.P. Wei, and Dot Bartlett to discuss creating an SOA for Titan Insurance.

13.1 MEETING WITH TITAN'S PEOPLE

When I walk into Titan's third-floor conference room, I can sense the tension that is consuming the people sitting around the table. I recognize this tension, having been there myself many times. The IT executives who greet me are under tremendous pressure to perform but feel trapped by their circumstances. Many of them, it's clear, are worried that they might even lose their jobs if the IT problems aren't solved, or on a path to being solved, soon.

H.P. Wei leads off the meeting by saying, "I don't have a lot of time to meet today. Can we get right into it? What are you proposing? What will it cost? And how long will it take?" Skipping the small talk, I launch right into a summarized overview of the SOA that I'd given Jay at the restaurant the week before. Then, I outline an example of how this approach might impact Titan in a hypothetical implementation in the policy area.

Drawing an enterprise architecture diagram that resembles figure 13.1, I begin to explain how employing web services can be a good IT and business move for the company. Given that there is now a connection between the InsurTech policy database and the old Apollo policy database, I explain, we know that the old Apollo database is always up to date on the latest policy information. Let's assume, I continue, that we prefer to migrate policy information from the InsurTech mainframe over time, with all policy information eventually residing on the newer Apollo system. I can see that half the people in the room are about to object. I assume these folks are part of the former Hermes staff and have a vested interest in maintaining the mainframe, no matter how much of a hassle it has become. I cut short their objections by explaining, "This is an exercise. I don't really know what the best policy system is for Titan. Just work with me on this." They agree to let me go through my presentation without voicing their concerns until the end.

Let's assume, I continue, that we expose the functionality of the old Apollo policy system as a set of web service. That way, SOAP-based web services consumer applications at the user end can interact with the policy system by sending and receiving SOAP messages. If this were to be set up, the following would be possible:

- The former Hermes agents and staff, including customer service, could access one up-to-date policy database that contained both old Hermes and Apollo policies using a browser-based client that served as the user interface for the SOAP-consuming application. The fat clients and customer interfaces that are now in use to connect Hermes agents and staff to policy data could be eliminated, along with their upkeep costs.
- The Hermes IVR system could now tap directly into the combined Hermes/Apollo database using a SOAP-consuming application. This would eliminate

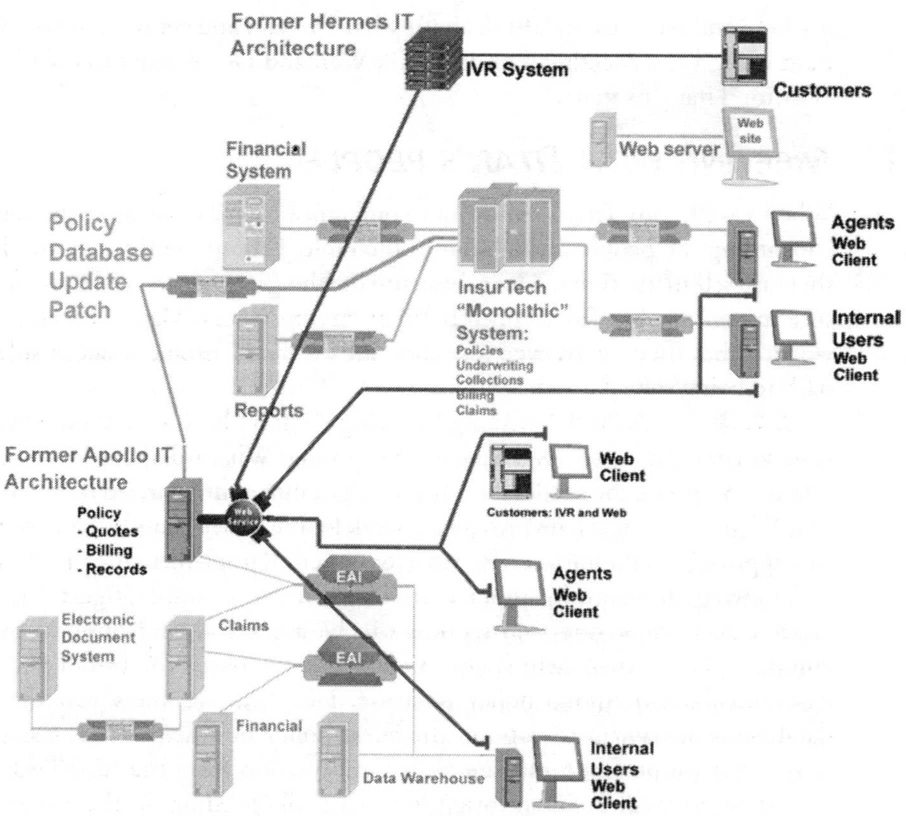

Figure 13.1 Hypothetical conversion of policy systems to web services

the interface that now connects the IVR system to the InsurTech mainframe. In addition to simplifying the architecture and reducing the complexity and cost of the maintenance of that interface, the IVR system could now access both Hermes and Apollo policy data. This way, both sets of customers, not just former Hermes customers, could use the IVR system.

- Former Apollo staff and agents could access the combined Hermes/Apollo policy database using a "thin" browser-based client instead of a fat client. Titan could eliminate the application server that it now uses to support the agent website and IVR system.
- Once the web services are in place, it becomes simpler to replace legacy systems. As shown in figure 13.2, if Titan wants to replace the old Apollo policy system with a newer one, the web services consumer applications that connect to it would not have to be changed.

I finish my presentation and prepare to have everyone in the room give me a standing ovation. In actuality, though, I am greeted by a few nods of interest and approval, a

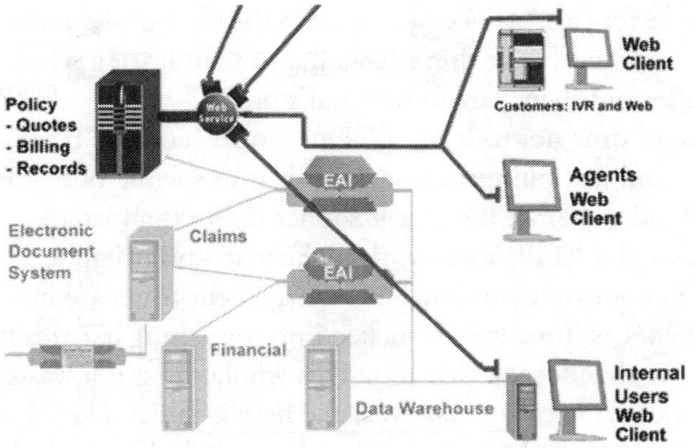

Figure 13.2
Legacy replacement

few blank stares, and more than a few defiant, doubtful looks by people sitting back in their chairs with their arms crossed. H.P. Wei, in particular, looks pretty dubious, and I quickly realize that I have made a mistake in presenting the example I selected.

By suggesting that it would be wisest for Titan to migrate its systems away from the InsurTech mainframe, I have inadvertently cast aspersions on the former Hermes staff and left them worried that they will lose their influence, jobs, or both. I can tell by the vibe in the room that the Hermes people, including H.P., are concerned that an SOA might mean the abandonment of a type of IT they are familiar with, coupled with the migration to a type of software architecture that they know very little about. Or, at least, they think they know very little about.

No one in the room says anything, and we're obviously waiting for H.P. to speak. I am about interrupt the silence, but H.P. beats me to it. "This is definitely of interest to us," he says, surprising me. "But my understanding is that this technology is immature, and that it will be quite a long time before it will be ready for prime time. We can't risk migrating our systems to an unproven technology."

"True," I agree. "And also not quite true. Web services and the SOA are definitely new, and there are many more standards that need to be ratified, and pieces of software that need to be created and improved before the whole world can create SOAs with ease. However, the SOA is certainly ready right now for adoption. And, of course, it would not be wise, or even possible, really, to migrate everything to an SOA framework right away. It has to be a phased process, like any large-scale IT migration plan. SOA is a target, a vision, not a project. The idea is to use standards for projects that have to be done anyway, but now will be done in the context of a more flexible organization principle."

"I like it," says Dot Bartlett from her side of the table. "We've either been paying software license and maintenance fees as if we're held for ransom, battling out-of-date software packages that the vendors can't or won't update, or wrangling with difficult custom interfaces. I would love to see us embrace an open standard and build from there."

"We don't have time for this," spoke up a man in the back of the room. "We have to move on this stuff right now. We don't have the time to learn a whole new set of protocols and languages and then start to fix what's broke."

"We may not have to time not to learn it," Dot replies tensely. "If we don't think this through carefully and just plunge ass-backwards into solving our problems with little Band-Aids here and there, we'll regret it sooner rather than later."

"The guy just admitted it hardly even works," the man says irritably. "The security issues are not solvable in our time frames. The management issues are unknown. The standards are half-baked. Last time we got sucked into something like this it was called CORBA, and we're now abandoning that too. This whole thing is a waste of time."

"Okay," H.P. interjects. "I realize that everyone here is under a lot of stress. I certainly am, but we need to remain open-minded and approach things calmly and rationally. This is what is I suggest: Let's get a proposal on the table so we can see how this plays out against our budgets and timelines. We can all agree our long-term plans are aligned with an SOA—the question is can we afford to get into this now?"

13.2 CONVERTING TITAN'S WISH LIST INTO AN SOA

When Jay and I meet to discuss doing the proposal on converting the items on Titan's "wish list" to web services, he has already started highlighting items on the list that he feels are the most urgent to complete right away. I stop him and explain that we need to step back, take a deep breath, and review the overall purpose of converting the wish list into an SOA before we get into specific SOA recommendations.

13.2.1 Matching the wish list to services and processes

"Why don't we forget the wish list?" Jay asks. "If it doesn't matter, then let's start with the important stuff first."

"No," I reply. "The wish list represents the most pressing issues for Titan at this time. Unless we respond to it, we may never get a second hearing there. If we go in there with a lot of theory, we'll be thrown out for good. So, let's go through the wish list and show H.P. Wei and Dot Bartlett just how an SOA could work for Titan. And," I add with a wink, "we may just find a good pilot project idea while we're at it. Let's take a look."

Titan's wish list currently looks like this:

1. Lower the IT budget.
2. Enable telephone and web access to all policy information for both agents and policyholders.
3. Develop a single application through which any employee or agent can access any claim or policy information from any location.
4. Implement a seamless, unified claims-processing system.
5. Develop a single claims payment check-printing system.
6. Implement a single bill-printing system.

7 Create a single payment and credit card processing system.

8 Develop a company portal.

9 Develop an agent portal.

"Okay," I say. "Number one is obvious. Let's take that off the list."

"Right," Jay responds. "Number two: 'Enable telephone and web access to all policy information for both agents and policyholders.' Well, we have two separate IVR systems and two websites, neither of which do it all." He springs up from the table and starts diagramming the systems on the whiteboard.

"Stop," I say. "Let's hold off on the systemic diagrams for now. We need to look at the processes involved in each wish list item. I want to know what the processes are and who the users of those processes are. Then, we'll see where they overlap. From there, we can start to map out a basic SOA." Together, we go to work and spend several long hours starting to draw out a chart, the final version of which is shown in table 13.1

Table 13.1 Titan's Wish List, the Business Processes Involved, and the System Services Required

Item	Process	System Services Used	Users
1: Enable telephone and web access to all policy information for both agents and policyholders, including rate quotes for new policies.	1. Submit policy number or policyholder ID. 2. Receive policy information (different data set for agents vs. policyholders; agents can see more business data than policyholders). Problems with current situation: Inefficient operations due to overlap and lack of coordination between two legacy systems; "fat client" incompatibility.	• Generate agent's view of policy information in response to request. • Generate policyholder's view of policy information in response to request. • Issue rate quote.	• Agents • Policyholder
2: Develop a single application through which any employee or agent can access any claim or policy information from any location. (Include rate quotes.)	1. Submit policy number or policyholder ID. 1a. Submit claim number or policy ID. 2. Receive policy information (different for agents vs. staff). 2a. Receive claim information (different for agents vs. staff). Problems with current situation: Inefficient operations due to overlap and lack of coordination between two sets of legacy systems; "fat client" incompatibility.	• Generate agent's view of policy information in response to request. • Generate agent's claim information in response to request. • Generate staff view of policy information in response to request. • Generate staff claim information in response to request. • Issue rate quote.	• Agents • Staff

continued on next page

Table 13.1 Titan's Wish List, the Business Processes Involved, and the System Services Required *(continued)*

Item	Process	System Services Used	Users
3: Implement a seamless, unified claims-processing system.	1. Titan receives notification of claim. 2. Titan initiates claim file on system. 3. Titan investigates claim. 4. Titan receives information from claims investigation. 5. Titan reviews claim. 6. Titan sends and receives numerous documents and letters related to the claim. 7. File paper documents (Hermes). 7a. Scan documents into system (Apollo). 8. Titan settles claim or litigates. (Must be approved by head of claims department.) 9. Close claim and archive. Problems with current situation: Two claims systems cause confusion and lack of quick reporting; redundancy in staffing and resources.	• Generate staff view of policy information in response to request. • Generate staff claim information in response to request. • Open system claim file. • Enter claim information in system. • Request and receive electronic documents. • Request approval of claim. • Receive approval of claim. • Transmit request for claim payment to financial system. • Archive claim.	• Staff • Agents • Policyholders • Third parties (doctors, lawyers) • Senior management
4: Develop a single claims payment check-printing system.	1. Head of claims department approves a claim. 2. Claim staff requests claim check from financial department system. 3. Financial system writes check. Problem with current situation: Two claims payment systems cause confusion and lack of quick reporting.	• Transmit request for claim payment to financial system. • Print check.	• Staff • Senior management
5: Implement a single bill-printing system.	1. Policy system generates billing information for policyholder: name, address, policy number, amount due, due date, past due balance (if any). 2. Policy system routes billing information to the printer farm, which prints the bill. 3. Bills are mailed to policyholders. Problem with current situation: Two billing (policy) systems and printer farms cause confusion and errors. Also, Titan wants to be able to do electronic, web-based billing.	• Generate policy premium due in response to request. • Transmit billing information to the printer farm.	• Staff

continued on next page

Table 13.1 Titan's Wish List, the Business Processes Involved, and the System Services Required *(continued)*

Item	Process	System Services Used	Users
6: Create a single payment and credit card processing system.	1. Request premium due for a specific policy. 2. Tender payment by credit card. 3. Process credit card with financial institution. 4. Update financial records. 5. Update policy system to reflect premium payment.	• Generate policy premium due in response to request. • Receive credit card information. • Process credit card transaction. • Update financial system. • Update policy system.	• Policyholders • Staff
7: Develop a company portal.	Request and receive any available policy, claim, policyholder, or financial information in a "company view" that includes any information required for company use, such as rate quotes.	• Generate staff view of policy information in response to request. • Generate policy premium due in response to request. • Issue rate quote. • Generate staff claim information in response to request.	• Staff • Senior management
8: Develop an agent portal.	Request and receive any available policy, claim, policyholder, or financial information in an "agent view" that includes any information required for agent use, such as rate quotes.	• Generate agent view of policy information in response to request. • Generate policy premium due in response to request. • Issue rate quote. • Generate agent claim information in response to request.	• Agents

"So, Jay, are you seeing what I'm seeing?" I ask.

"I only see a more detailed description of just how serious our problems are," he replies. "We'll never get all of these things done, at least not within any reasonable time and budget. And, the complexities of the interconnections between the legacy systems will drive us broke and insane at the same time."

"Really? Let's see which services are shared by the items on your wish list" (see table 13.2).

Table 13.2 Each Service, Matched with the Wish List Items It Supports

System Service	Shared These Wish List Items
A. Generate agent view of policy information in response to request.	1: Enable telephone and web access to all policy information for both agents and policyholders. 2: Develop a single application through which any employee or agent can access any claim or policy information from any location. 8: Develop an agent portal.
B. Generate policyholder's view of policy information in response.	1: Enable telephone and web access to all policy information for both agents and policyholders.
C. Issue rate quote.	1: Enable telephone and web access to all policy information for both agents and policyholders. 2: Develop a single application through which any employee or agent can access any claim or policy information from any location. 7: Develop a company portal. 8: Develop an agent portal.
D. Generate agent's claim information in response to request.	2: Develop a single application through which any employee or agent can access any claim or policy information from any location. 8: Develop an agent portal.
E. Generate staff view of policy information in response to request.	2: Develop a single application through which any employee or agent can access any claim or policy information from any location. 3: Implement a seamless, unified claims-processing system. 7: Develop a company portal.
F. Generate staff claim information in response to request.	2: Develop a single application through which any employee or agent can access any claim or policy information from any location. 3: Implement a seamless, unified claims-processing system. 7: Develop a company portal.
G. Open system claim file.	3: Implement a seamless, unified claims-processing system.
H. Enter claim information in system.	3: Implement a seamless, unified claims-processing system.
I. Request and receive electronic documents.	3: Implement a seamless, unified claims-processing system.
J. Request approval of claim.	3: Implement a seamless, unified claims-processing system.
K. Receive approval of claim.	3: Implement a seamless, unified claims-processing system.
L. Transmit request for claim payment to financial system.	3: Implement a seamless, unified claims-processing system. 4: Develop a single claims payment check-printing system.
M. Archive claim.	3: Implement a seamless, unified claims-processing system.
N. Print claim check.	4: Develop a single claims payment check-printing system.
O. Generate policy premium due in response to request.	5: Implement a single bill-printing system. 6: Create a single payment and credit card processing system. 7: Develop a company portal. 8: Develop an agent portal.

continued on next page

Table 13.2 Each Service, Matched with the Wish List Items It Supports *(continued)*

System Service	Shared These Wish List Items
P. Transmit billing information to the printer farm.	5: Implement a single bill-printing system.
Q. Receive credit card information.	6: Create a single payment and credit card processing system.
R. Process credit card transaction.	6: Create a single payment and credit card processing system.
S. Update financial system (with credit card transaction detail).	6: Create a single payment and credit card processing system.
T. Update policy system (with credit card transaction detail).	6: Create a single payment and credit card processing system.

13.2.2 Translating the wish list into a service map

"I'm still a little stuck on the concept of services," Jay admits. "What do you mean by a service?"

I explain: "With web services and the SOA, you can abstract the software from the service it provides. For a moment, let's forget all about how all the various systems need to work in order to, say, give you a policy premium when provided with a policy number. All we need to know is that the policy premium software is available as a service. Because the SOA is based on SOAP and open standards, any web service consumer application can request the functionality of a web service no matter where it is located or what software it uses to operate. Let's look at it this way." I sketch a diagram that resembles figure 13.3. "This is a service map. Imagine that each piece of software functionality required to realize the wish list items were a 'black box' that performed the required task magically. You don't need to know what systems are supporting it. You just know that the function is performed when you want it performed. Do you see how each wish list item can just reach out and grab the functionality it wants by accessing a web service?"

"Yes," he says. "I see that."

"So, in that sense, it's quite simple. Each service is available upon request, regardless of how the underlying IT system actually does the work. So, if an agent calls the IVR system and types in a policy number on the phone, the system requests the policy information from Service A. Service A responds by sending the IVR system the policy information.

"Okay," I continue. "Let's simplify. Here's a question: Do you really need eight separate applications to realize your wish list? If you can connect to any piece of software you need through XML web services, then all of your wish list applications could theoretically be browser based. What if you created a couple of high-functioning

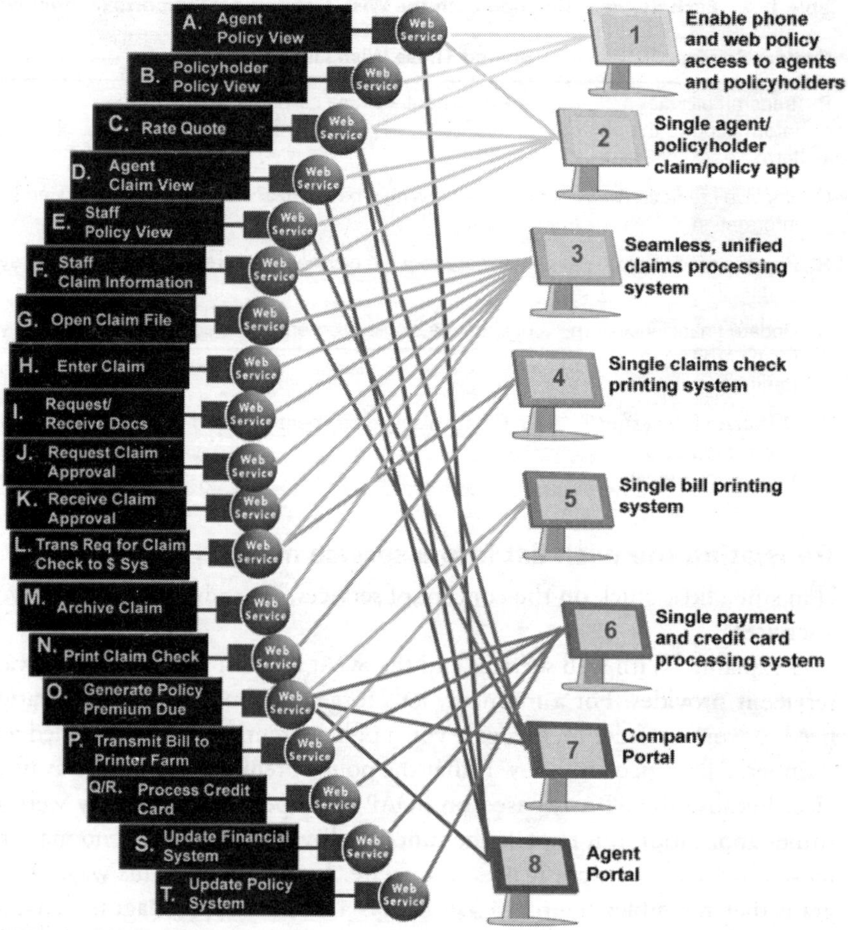

Figure 13.3 This raw service map shows how each application on the wish list interacts with a set of services. Each piece of software functionality required to realize Titan's wish list is expressed as a "black box" fronted by a web service.

portals to manage the work processes that you are trying to tackle with the wish list? Let's suppose, for example, that you devised a customer portal, agent portal, and company portal. And then you created two IVR systems, one for agents and the other for customers. That would look like this." I draw a crude approximation of figure 13.4 on the whiteboard. "Now, you have five front-end systems instead of eight. The three portals replace a whole host of cumbersome fat clients and specialized applications. All the user needs is a browser and they can perform any of the tasks on your wish list. The IVR systems are really just stripped-down versions of the portals that can be accessed over the phone."

"There are still a lot of lines. I can hardly follow them all," Jay says.

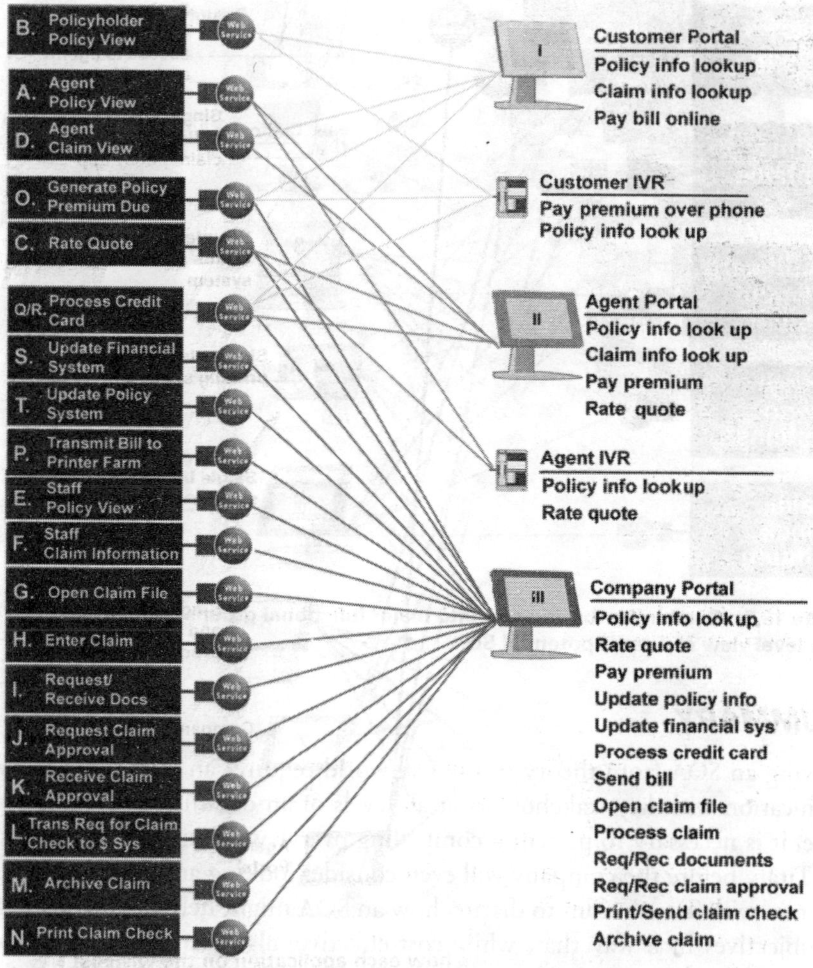

Figure 13.4 Simplifying the service map so the wish list has been condensed down to three portals and two IVR systems shows how the SOA can greatly reduce the complexity of the front-end. All fat clients and specialized applications are gone, replaced by browser-based portals and phone IVR systems that send requests for information and functionality to the SOA.

"True," I reply, "so let's simplify the service map once more." I re-sketch the diagram on the whiteboard. "Imagine," I say, "that we can gather the services into clusters that perform the tasks associated with each major functional area. This is the high-level view of your SOA. You have three portals and two IVR systems accessing five basic groupings of web services." The simplified service map shown in figure 13.5 becomes the basis for the proposal we present to Titan the following week.

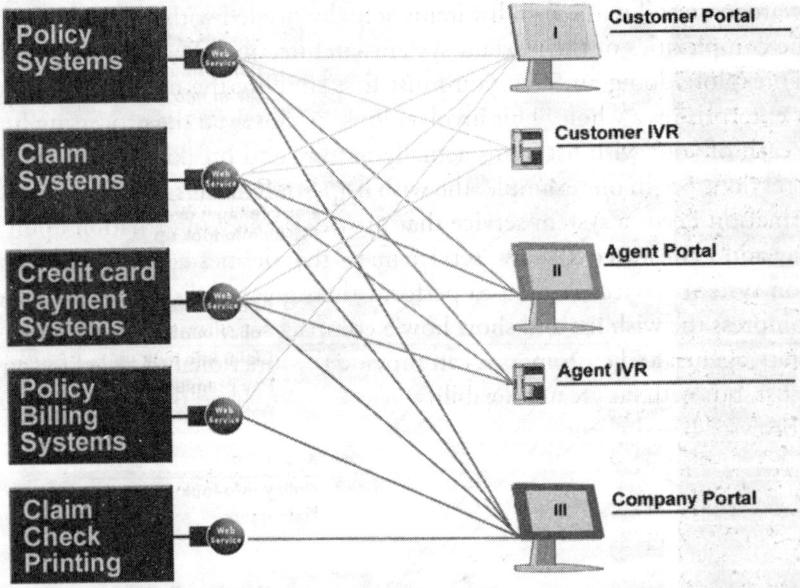

Figure 13.5 Combining the services into major functional groups creates a high-level view of Titan's potential SOA.

13.3 SUMMARY

Moving an SOA from theory to the real world requires an intensive process of communication with key stakeholders at all levels of an organization. With Titan Insurance, it is necessary to present a compelling overview of an SOA, and what it can do for Titan, before the company will even consider looking at a real proposal.

We met with Titan's team to discuss how an SOA might help the company achieve its IT objectives in a way that, while cost-effective, also guarantees them the greatest degree of flexibility in the future. In the meeting, we used the example of the insurance policy database to illustrate how an SOA at Titan could actually work. By replacing the existing proprietary interfaces and fat clients that connected staff, agents, and customers to the system with browser-based applications that communicate with the policy database through web services, Titan can eliminate a number of troublesome, expensive IT burdens. In addition, the SOA will ease the process of replacing legacy systems as they became obsolete.

The first step in exploring an SOA for Titan is to examine the company's IT "wish list" and determine how the items on the list, which represented the IT department's vision of ideal functioning, can be matched with business processes and the system services that support those processes. For this purpose, a service is a "black box" piece of software that performs a task without any regard for the underlying IT systems that may actually be involved. The point of the exercise is to gain insight into what software services Titan's wish list items actually needed without getting bogged down in the complexities of their extant systems architecture. That could come later.

To explore doing an SOA, you must first simplify the needs and requirements of your enterprise as a whole. This involves looking closely at the processing functionality that each of your wish list items actually require and breaking down those functions into services. So, in our example, the wish list item that calls for phone access to policy information needs a system service that provides policy information upon request.

Jay and I constructed a raw "service map" that defines how each wish list item can call on system services needed to perform their given tasks. From there, we decided to compress the wish list and show how a compact set of enterprise portals—one each for staff, agents, and customers—can provide the functionality called for on the entire wish list, but with far greater flexibility in architecture and the low-maintenance effect of a browser-based client.

CHAPTER 14

Achieving consensus at Titan

Having worked out with Jay a basic idea of what Titan's SOA solution might look like, we prepare to present our findings to the IT team. The purpose of the meeting is to achieve consensus in the group regarding the decision to move forward with an SOA. As I explain to Jay, this is one of the most critical steps in the whole process. Having lived through several comparable efforts in recent years, I can attest to the fact that many troubled SOA projects can trace their problems to a lack of consensus at the outset. It is absolutely essential that Titan's IT team be in agreement that a) an SOA is the right direction for them; and b) the approach outlined for their immediate needs is the right one.

14.1 THE SECOND MEETING

Before I can even begin to describe the potential pitfall of a poorly planned SOA project at the second meeting, trouble comes in the disarming disguise of an overzealous supporter. At the very beginning of the meeting, one of the Hermes developers spins a PC screen around to me and announces that he has already written Titan's first web service. Using a popular off-the-shelf web services development package, the developer has created a simple service that looks up the e-mail address of a Titan employee based on a simple query.

This situation presents me with a dilemma. While I am impressed that someone at Titan has taken the initiative to plunge into web services, I am also concerned that this kind of unplanned, unsupervised approach to creating an SOA will almost guarantee the failure of a serious SOA for Titan. I know from experience that the new web service cannot be managed or audited properly and cannot be secured. Inevitably, the team will barrel down this path and end up ultimately hitting a wall that can derail their entire SOA program.

I carefully say, "This is a great way to get started learning about web services, and you deserve a lot of credit for taking the initiative. However, may I ask that you not try to deploy this experimental web service until we've all reached agreement on how we're going to proceed?"

I go to the whiteboard and ask the team members to call out their ideas for what they envision achieving through the SOA. No one says anything, so I change my approach. I ask what they *want* to accomplish through the enterprise architecture, regardless of how it is actually built. This time I get some answers:

- A high degree of vendor neutrality/agnosticism
- Best-of-breed solutions in each area of insurance IT: policy, claims, billing, IVR, and so on
- Architectural elements that are easy-to-change
- Lowest cost
- Adaptability to current and changing business processes
- Real-time or near-real-time reporting
- High management visibility into operations
- The leveraging of existing investments in IT assets so as to minimize new purchases
- Reusability of interfaces among internal applications and the ability to share these applications with partners

14.1.1 Replacing the front-end

I then show figure 14.1 as a PowerPoint slide and begin a lengthy explanation of how Jay and I arrived at the service map shown on the right side. One of the first orders of business is to better separate the "presentation layer" from the business logic and begin to expose this logic as web services. In this way, the user experience becomes simply a matter of consuming services and displaying results, opening the door for the underlying services to be used and reused in many ways across the enterprise. At Titan, the immediate results are as follows:

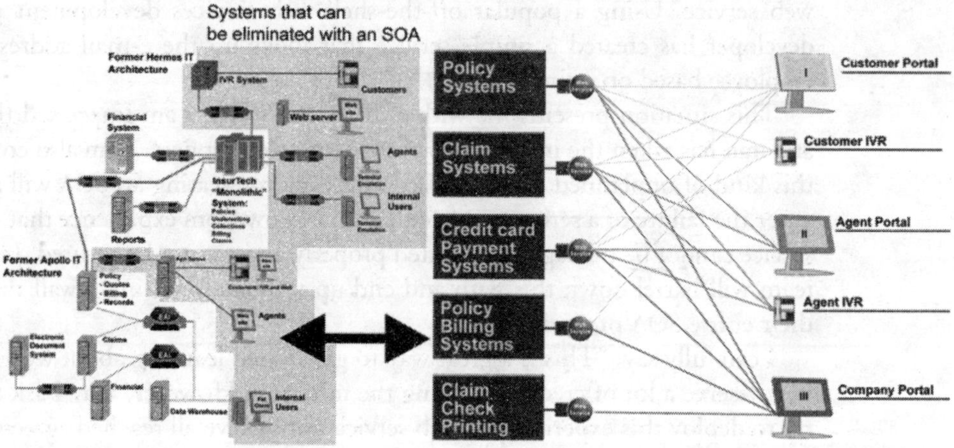

Figure 14.1 The proposed SOA and portals, on the right, replace most of the front-end interfaces of Titan's existing system architecture. By introducing the SOA, Titan can reduce or eliminate seven front-end systems and replace them with browser-based applications that use web services to access the functionality of the back-end systems for policy, claims, finance, and other areas.

- The Hermes legacy customer IVR system will be replaced by the customer IVR system in the new SOA.
- The Hermes legacy website will be replaced by the customer portal.
- The agent fat clients from both Hermes and Apollo will be replaced by the agent portal.
- The internal user fat clients from both Hermes and Apollo will be replaced by the company portal.

"Let's see how it would work," I continue. "Now, keeping in mind that this is a highly simplified view, see how each grouping of web services, such as policy systems, claims systems, and so on, access a different set of back-end systems. Take policy, for example. If a customer logs on to the customer portal and requests policy information, the customer portal will send the request to the web services we represent as a 'black box' called 'policy systems.' That black box is actually a bunch of different web services that have been exposed on the two policy systems in the Titan architecture" (see figure 14.2).

"And so on," I say, going through each of the next three slides (see figures 14.3, 14.4, and 14.5). "In each case, when the portals or IVR systems need information, they send a SOAP request to web services that have been exposed in the respective systems required to provide the information. To check on a claim, for example, an agent would use the agent portal to send a SOAP request to a web service on one of the two claims systems and receive his or her answer through the portal, as you can see in slide 14.3."

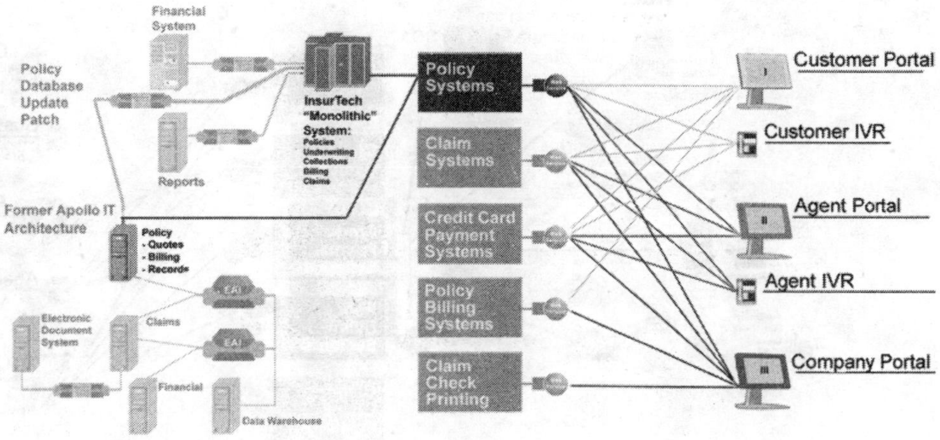

Figure 14.2 Policy-related queries from the portals and IVR systems flow to the web services that have been exposed on the two policy systems in the Titan architecture.

"I'm confused," Dot Bartlett speaks up. "If the customer wants to look up a past balance on an auto policy, versus an upcoming bill on a homeowners' policy, how does the policy systems 'black box' that you are showing know how to figure that out?"

"Well," I say, "this is a highly simplified diagram meant to give you an overview. Here's what it might actually look like." I click onto slide (figure) 14.6. "On each legacy system, we expose as many web services as it will take to deliver the functionality of that legacy system through to the portals and IVR systems. We may end up exposing a dozen web services on each system—for rate quotes, balance updates, underwriting, and on and on."

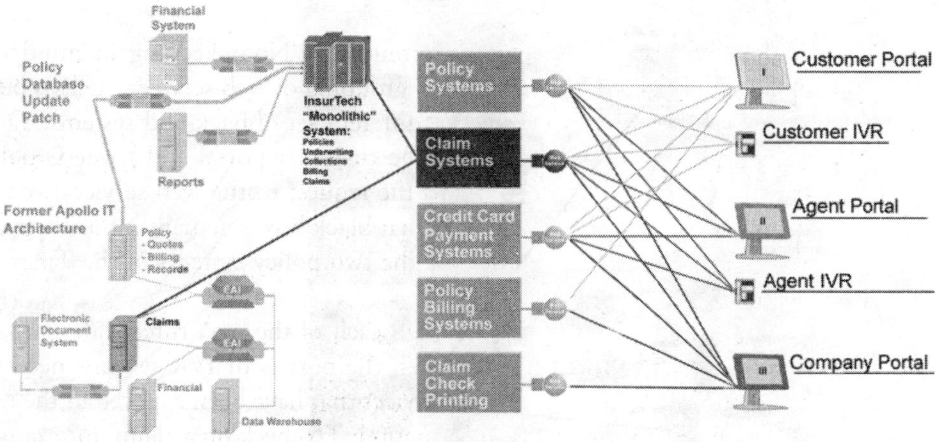

Figure 14.3 Requests for claim-related information flow from the portals and IVR systems to the designated web services exposed on the claims systems.

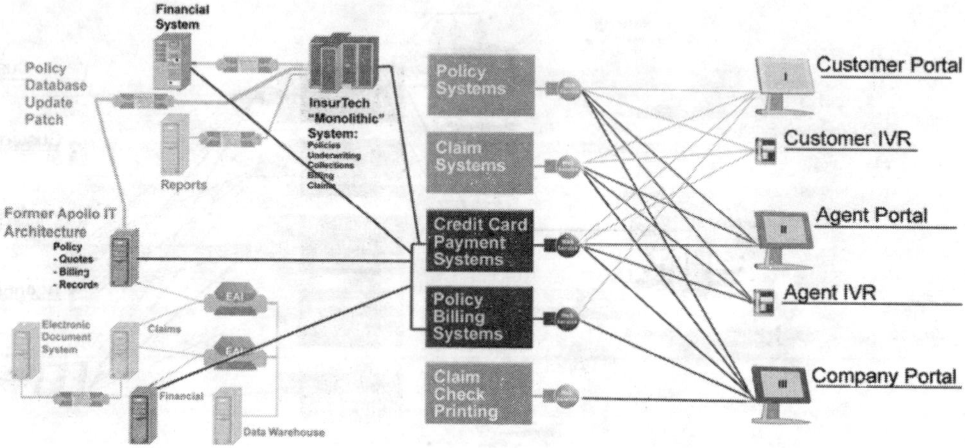

Figure 14.4 Credit card payment processing and policy billing requests flow from the portals and IVR systems to the designated web services exposed on the policy and financial systems.

"That's a huge amount of work," H.P. Wei chimes in. "Do we really want to do that?" "Well," I reply, "it looks like you're going to be doing a lot of work no matter what option you choose. If you go with a global IT supplier, InsurTech, or one of the EAI players, there will be a huge slate of work to do. The advantage of doing it this way is you give yourself the ability to expose these capabilities via standards now and reap the benefits over the coming years as future applications and processes emerge that need the same capabilities. It solves your immediate problem with no less, but no more, labor but at the same time you lay down a critical foundation of your SOA strategy for the future."

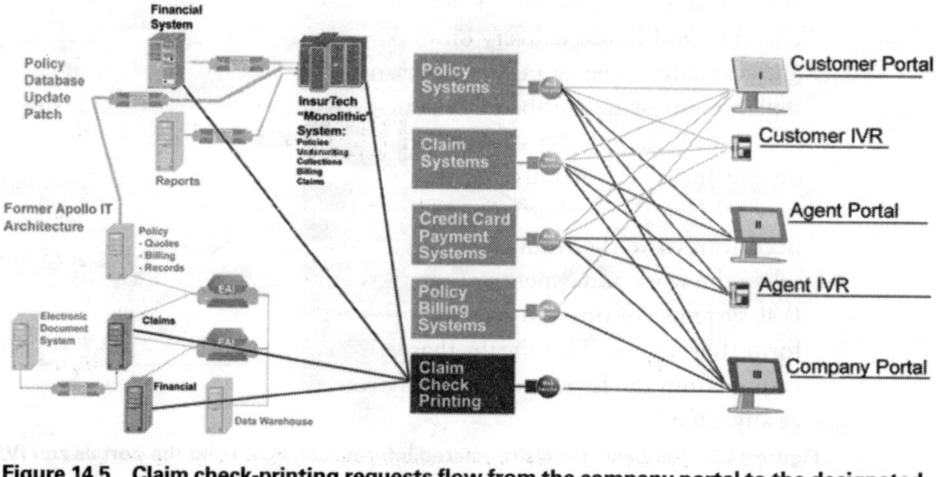

Figure 14.5 Claim check-printing requests flow from the company portal to the designated web services exposed on the claims and finance systems.

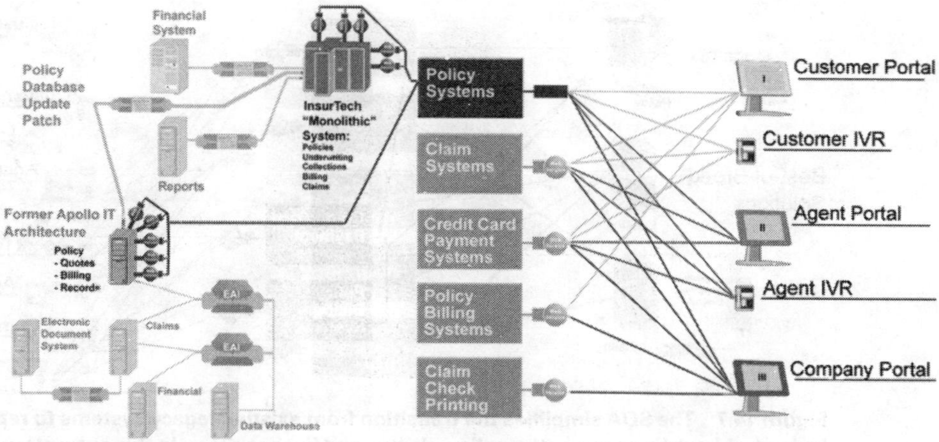

Figure 14.6 Digging down a layer beyond the highly simplified SOA diagram, this figure shows how the portals and IVR systems will consume a large number of web services that have been exposed on the legacy systems. Titan will have to expose as many web services as are needed to deliver the functionality of the legacy systems through to the portals and IVR systems. The justification for undertaking that degree of work is the ability that Titan then has to eliminate the complex and costly interfaces it currently maintains at the front-end.

"True," H.P. agrees, "but we are going to replace most of those interfaces if we go with InsurTech or IBM or whoever. What does the SOA get us that we can't get from them?"

"That's the key question," I say, "and it is absolutely the question you should be asking. Here's an answer…"

14.1.2 Transitioning to best of breed

"If your goal is to transition to an enterprise architecture consisting of best-of-breed systems across the board," I say, "then the SOA gives you the simplest, most cost-effective, and fastest delivery on making that transition." I click on slide (figure) 14.7 and explain: "The SOA simplifies the transition from existing legacy systems to replacement by best-of-breed systems in the policy, claims, and finance areas.

"In this example, let's assume that Titan will keep its policy data and functionality on the InsurTech mainframe but will replace the finance and claim systems with a new J2EE or .NET alternative. The SOA streamlines this process by eliminating the need to rewrite the front-end. We can swap out the back-end systems but save ourselves the work and expense of rewriting the consuming applications. The portals and IVR systems continue to consume the web services, blissfully unaware of what platform they are on. This means that you have 'loosely coupled' your consuming applications from the legacy system itself and are ready to swap out one service for another at any time."

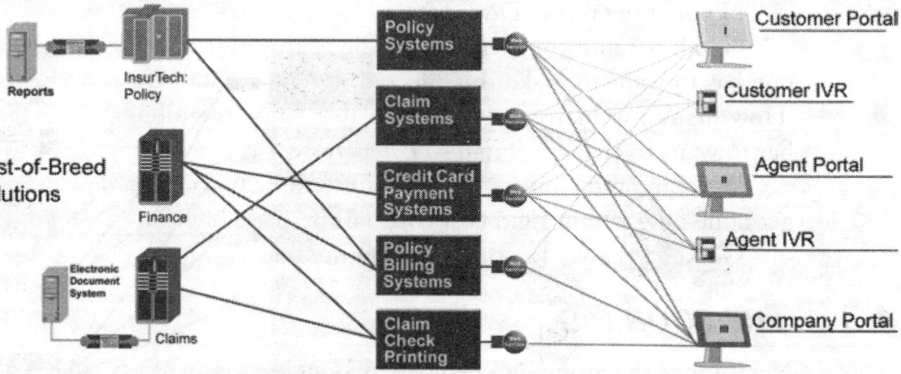

Figure 14.7 The SOA simplifies the transition from existing legacy systems to replacement by best-of-breed systems in the policy, claims, and finance areas. In this example, we assume that Titan will keep its policy data and functionality on the InsurTech mainframe but will replace the finance and claim systems with newer systems. The SOA streamlines this process by eliminating the need to rewrite the front-end portals and IVR systems, and corresponding web service consumer programs. The only piece of the puzzle that needs to be changed is the legacy system.

14.2 LEADERSHIP

After the initial presentation, Jay, Dot, and I adjourn to H.P.'s office. H.P. begins, "We want to do this. After listening to your presentation and discussing the alternatives ourselves, we have decided to move forward. What we need now is a good guide to best practices in implementing an SOA. That's why you're here, right?"

"I'll give you an overview of my SOA best practice recommendations," I reply, "but first I must stress the most significant best practice of all, the one that will determine the success or failure of your SOA."

"What's that?" Dot asks. "Choice of development environment or application server?"

"No," I answer. "Leadership. Leadership is the sine qua non of SOA development."

"I am going to appoint an excellent team leader for this project," H.P. says. "He's really one of our best people. You'll meet him the next time we get together."

"No, it has to be one of you," I say to H.P. and Dot. "One of you has to take direct charge of this program. You can delegate some of the work, but to keep web services work from falling into counterproductive mayhem, as opposed to constructive steps toward an SOA, we would do well to maintain active involvement from top IT management. Otherwise, it won't work. This is perhaps the most important best practice at the outset." This remark is greeted with surprised silence. "And," I continue, "no offense to you, Dot, but it should really be H.P. He's coming in from the IT legacy organization. If his old team perceives that he isn't behind the effort 100 percent, they might find excuses to sabotage the project if they run into problems, or to fall back on their standard proprietary interface work."

"No offense taken," Dot says.

"Good, because your team has to be in this in this wholeheartedly as well. Everyone has to want to make this succeed. Doing an SOA reminds me of that old joke, 'How many psychiatrists does it take to change a lightbulb? One, but the lightbulb has to want to change.' Titan's IT department is like that lightbulb."

"We're in on the bigger picture, but we have practical budget projects that have to get done now within rigid cost constraints," H.P. says.

"Good," I reply. "Let's move on to the four P's."

14.3 THE FOUR P'S

Next, I give the group an overview of SOA development best practices that I call the "four P's":

- **People**—Everyone in Titan's IT department is going to have to learn about XML, web services, and the principles of an SOA.
- **Pilot**—To help train people, and to prove the concept of web services at the same time, we will work with the Titan team to select a small web services project and execute it under our guidance.
- **Plan**—After the people have been trained in XML and web services and have had the experience of developing a web service in the pilot project, it will then be time to begin planning Titan's SOA in earnest. The SOA plan will include evaluations of possible applications that can be exposed as web services based on a "web services scorecard" process. In addition, the plan will include a flexible approach to a multiphased project plan over a period of years.
- **Proceed**—Finally, it will be time to begin the actual development of the SOA based on the plan.

These four steps form the foundation of best practices in SOA development. The remainder of this book summarizes how Titan goes through the four P's and starts on the road toward a successful SOA.

"Are we getting closer to consensus on how we are going to approach this SOA?" I ask. "We have a basic idea of what we want to accomplish with the SOA, how it can be structured, who is going to lead the effort, and the steps we are going to take." There are nods around the room.

"Any questions?" Everyone breaks out laughing—they have so many questions they don't even know where to begin. H.P., however, has one question that is uppermost in his thoughts:

"What if we change our minds about this once we start?"

"I think you'll like the answer," I say. "Unlike many large-scale IT architecture decisions, a path to utilize standards is flexible and reversible. You may decide, a few months into this, that you do indeed want to go with a proprietary EAI system, or a customer interface, etc. At that time, the work you have done exposing web services and front-end interfaces such as your portals and IVR systems can be plugged right into whatever new solution you adopt. The reason? Most of the major companies in the industry are moving toward web services and XML right now as we speak. For example, if you decide to extend your EAI system instead of replacing it, you will almost surely discover that the EAI module you get will have XML and web services interfaces as part of the package."

"Do we have consensus?" I check again. "Yes," everyone responds. We are ready to begin.

14.4 Summary

In order for the SOA to come to life without major problems, it is critically important to achieve consensus among the key stakeholders in the effort before you begin. For Titan Insurance, it is essential that its team be in agreement that a) an SOA is the right direction for them; and b) the approach outlined for them is the right one. And, while the team members could change their minds about virtually any aspect of the SOA as they proceed with its development, it is necessary for them to begin "on the same page."

We held a second meeting of Titan's IT staff and reviewed the organization's goals for an SOA, including the realization of the wish list items, a high degree of vendor neutrality, the ability to implement best-of-breed solutions as needed, simple change processes, low cost, and high management visibility into operations. Then, we presented and discussed the simplified SOA map that we had developed in the previous chapter. This time, however, we included Titan's legacy architecture in the diagrams and showed how the new portals and IVR systems that we envisioned implementing would effectively replace most of the existing front-end interfaces that were causing so much trouble for Titan.

The next part of the presentation illustrated how the SOA will simplify the process of changing the back-end systems from its current legacy configuration to that of a best-of-breed approach. Once the web service consumer applications of the portals and IVR systems have been created, they won't need to be rewritten in order to access new best-of-breed systems that replace the legacy systems on the back-end.

We then addressed leadership, a crucial aspect of the consensus-building process. After some discussion, it was agreed that H.P. Wei, the former CIO of Hermes and now the CIO of Titan, the most senior person in the company's IT organization and the leader of the dominant IT team, would take charge of the SOA vision personally. If he did, I cautioned, there were many ways the project could potentially unravel, including a lack of backing from the top as well as a perception among the rank-and-file members of the IT department that the SOA was not important enough to justify the challenges that it would inevitably bring. Top leadership is necessary to assure everyone involved in the project that the SOA requires the highest level of professional discipline and commitment.

Finally, we outlined what I call the "four P's," the steps that form the foundation of best practices in the SOA development process: people, pilot, plan, and proceed. To make the SOA work, Titan's people will have to be trained in XML and web services. We will select a web services pilot project and use it as part of the staff's practical training process. At that point, we will be ready to begin planning Titan's SOA for real using a "web services scorecard" approach that would help the staff evaluate which legacy system functionality is best suited to exposure as a web service. Only then, after the people, pilot, and plan are ready, will we be ready to begin implementing the SOA.

CHAPTER 15

People: starting the training

After the top leadership has been selected, staff training is the most critical factor in ensuring success in developing an SOA. It is essential that you achieve "buy-in" from all of the IT personnel who will be involved or affected by the new architecture. Though it may sound obvious, you have to be constantly aware that an SOA is a human undertaking. It is not a single project or a software package that you buy from a vendor. If you get your people involved in a positive, continuous learning–based approach to SOA development, you will find that they will be able to overcome the inevitable challenges that arise in such a massive transitional undertaking. If you do not succeed in this vital human dimension, your SOA is likely doomed to failure, probably at the hands of the very people trusted with its creation.

15.1 Grouping for SOA training success

While there will be a training period as you set up your SOA, it helps to bear in mind that you will be trying to encourage an atmosphere of continuous learning that will not stop when the official training period is over.

The first thing I notice at the big kickoff meeting for the SOA project at Titan is that there are two sets of chairs divided by an aisle in the middle. On one side sits the former Hermes team and on the other are the Apollo people. This is not a good sign. These two groups of people must learn to work together if this project is going to succeed. Indeed, many of the problems they are facing had been caused by a lack of cooperation between the two groups over the last two years.

I don't say or do anything about this division right away. Instead, after an introductory speech where I emphasize the importance of getting everyone in the room involved in developing an SOA for Titan, I ask for a volunteer to go to the whiteboard and draw a detailed organizational chart of the Titan IT department (see figure 15.1).

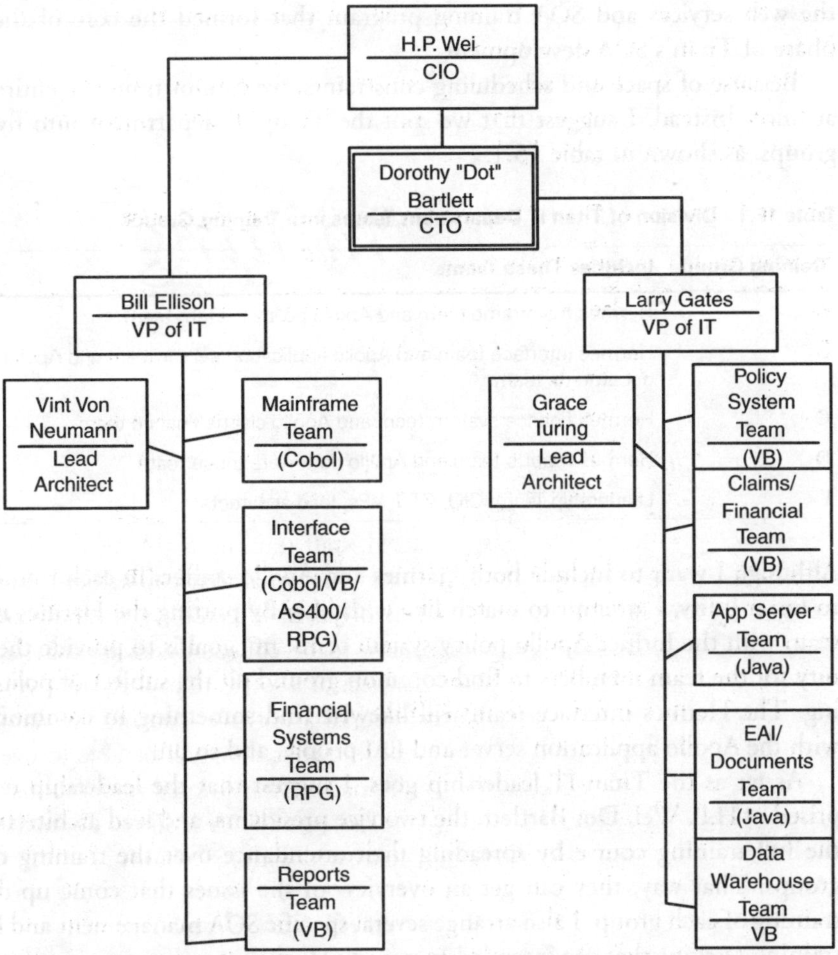

Figure 15.1 Organizational chart of the Titan IT department showing team groupings and skill sets

The chart our volunteer draws includes the team groupings and major skill sets of each group. There are no big surprises here. The former Hermes team, which mostly tended to the monolith InsurTech system, is skilled in Common Business-Oriented Language (COBOL) and Report Program Generator (RPG.) The old Apollo team, which relied mostly on Microsoft-based systems and an EAI platform, has heavy experience in Visual Basic (VB) and Java.

What is it going to take for this fragmented, technologically heterogeneous group to come together and collaborate on a cohesive SOA? Now, there are books and consulting practices that focus on "change management," and I am surely no expert on the subject, but I know IT. For Titan, web services and the SOA are a new paradigm and must be treated as such. My instinct is to mix the groups up as we proceed with the web services and SOA training program that formed the core of the "people" phase of Titan's SOA development.

Because of space and scheduling constraints, we cannot train the entire group all at once. Instead, I suggest that we split the Titan IT department into five training groups, as shown in table 15.1.

Table 15.1 Division of Titan IT Department Teams into Training Groups

Training Group	Includes These Teams
A	Hermes mainframe team and Apollo policy system team
B	Hermes interface team and Apollo application server team and Apollo EAI/ documents team
C	Hermes finance system team and Apollo claims/finance team
D	Hermes reports team and Apollo data warehouse team
E	Leadership Team: CIO, CTO, VPs, lead architects

Although I want to include both Hermes and Apollo staffers in each training group, to foster unity, I attempt to match like with like. By putting the Hermes mainframe team with the former Apollo policy system team, my goal is to provide the opportunity for the team members to find common ground on the subject of policy processing. The Hermes interface team will likewise find something in common (I hope) with the Apollo application server and EAI people, and so on.

As far as the Titan IT leadership goes, I suggest that the leadership team, comprised of H.P. Wei, Dot Bartlett, the two vice presidents, and lead architects, sit in on the full training course by spreading their attendance over the training of all four groups. That way, they can get an overview of the issues that come up during the training of each group. I also arrange several specific SOA management and leadership training sessions that are intended to convey IT change management information as well as serve as forums for issues that come up during the whole process.

When I lay out the training groups and schedules to the Titan people, I hear a vast and diverse amount of grumbling about the difficulties I'm creating in their lives.

Don't I know that they are busy and overworked as it is? Don't I realize that the old Hermes and Apollo offices are five miles apart? This kind of reaction is typical of a group that is resisting change, and let's face it, most of us don't like change. However, with their top leadership on board explaining that this is going to happen no matter what, people begin to cooperate.

The training process calls for each group to meet one day a week for ten weeks. That way, the four groups will meet on each successive Monday, Tuesday, Wednesday, and Thursday. The group members can attend to their ongoing IT department duties on the other four days of the week. Given the rigors of their current jobs, it's not realistic to expect to pull people out of work for two weeks. A further benefit of spreading the course out over ten weeks is the opportunity it affords group members to read, experiment, and explore web services during the other days of the week.

To facilitate cooperation and a smooth training program, I make a few suggestions to H.P. Wei and Dot Bartlett. First, I recommend establishing a web conference link between the two sites, so that the training groups can share applications and virtual whiteboards at any time. In addition, I encourage them to make the training fun by springing for a good lunch on each training day and/or an evening activity such as bowling or darts after class. It might cost a little, I explain, but breaking down barriers between the old Hermes and Apollo teams is worth every penny.

15.2 GOING BEYOND THE BASICS

Our approach to SOA best practices training stresses practical experience over classroom learning. Any experienced software developer can easily pick up the syntax and nuances of XML, so after we conduct two initial sessions on SOAP, XML, UDDI, and WSDL, we commence a session meant to introduce the groups to the paradigm shift from developing software for specific business requirements to developing web services to be part of an SOA.

There is a massive cultural difference between what web services developers do today and what they have to do in the context of an SOA. To get developers working well in an SOA program, you have to change the way they think about software. With an SOA, developers can no longer consider just the specific requirements they have to meet in a given assignment. Instead, they have to focus on the good of the enterprise as a whole, and take into account reusability and abstraction.

In SOA best practices training, we emphasize the need to include steps in that design process that make the developers ask themselves:

- What are the reusable services within this application I'm building today?
- What services are obtainable in this design process (or in this application)?

To help the groups see the best practices difference in an actual example, I ask for a description of the process they went through to create a new agent policy rate quote application. Both the Hermes and Apollo teams had followed a similar method:

1 Gather the business requirements.

2 Create a software requirements document and get approval from the business "customer."

3 Create a project plan.

4 Execute code in the development environment.

5 Test the code.

6 Release to production.

Hermes and Apollo had always followed a proven, professionally sound approach to application development, and the results in each specific company case were good. Figure 15.2 shows what the finished product of a policy rate quote application development project would have looked like. The business process, shown at the top of the figure, captures the specific steps used by agents in requesting and receiving policy rate quotes. The client-server application that the team would develop matched those business process steps.

This narrowly focused process is by far the most cost-effective and time-efficient way to develop a specific piece of software, but it does not work well for an SOA. In the case of the agent policy rate quote application, the conventional process results in an effective client-server setup that sends a request containing policy application data to the mainframe, and then receives a response that contains the policy rate quote and some information relating to the agent's commission on that particular insurance product.

Here's the best practices challenge: With the SOA, Titan's developers and their managers must learn to think in terms of building web service applications with the

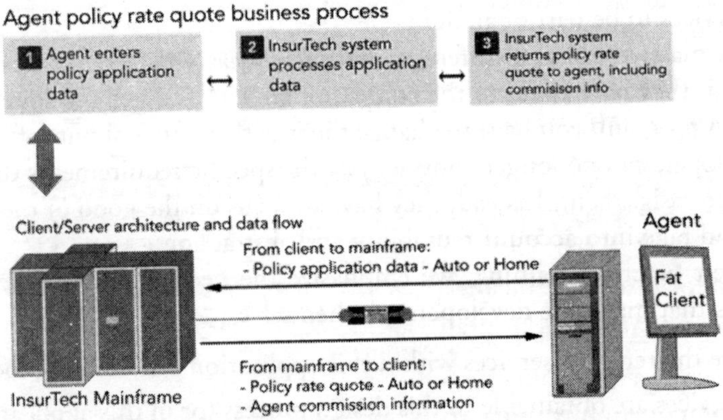

Figure 15.2 Prior to the SOA training, the development team at Hermes would create a client-server agent policy rate quote application that met the specific business requirements laid out for the agent policy rate quote business process.

potential for reuse in multiple use cases. In contrast to traditional software development, where developers do not necessarily have to consider eventual reuse of application components, with web services, developers have to learn to build a step or two further into the application development process. They need to think through the systems that may want to use the same web service, or some part of it, subsequently. How do you design a piece of software for future requirements that you cannot be sure about today? Of course, developers can't dream up every single requirement that exists for possible future services, but they have to take the design a little bit further than their own limited sphere of influence. Developers working on a policy rate quote application, for example, must have a slightly larger view of the world than they have today, as shown by the following amended development process steps:

1. Gather the business requirements.
2. Create a software requirements document and get approval from the business "customer."
3. Brainstorm alternative use cases and discuss with potential stakeholders.
4. Develop design specifications for a web service application that can meet some or all of the potential use cases.
5. Create a project plan.
6. Execute code in the development environment.
7. Test the code.
8. Release to production.

For our policy rate quote example, the groups came up with five use cases for the application:

- **Agents:** A rate quote function that returns the policy rate quote and commission information
- **Customers:** A rate quote function that returns just the policy rate quote
- **Underwriting staff:** A rate quote function that returns the policy rate quote and underwriting information
- **Actuarial:** A rate quote function that returns the policy rate quote and actuarial data
- **New line of insurance business:** A rate quote function that returns policy rate quotes for a new line of insurance products, such as earthquake coverage

The resulting web service would resemble the one shown in figure 15.3. The web service, and its component functional parts, will be able to serve the needs of the multiple use cases. In this case, the policy rate quote web service can respond to SOAP requests that invoke it to deliver policy rate quotes with additional information for agents, underwriting staff, and actuaries. In addition, the web service could be designed to

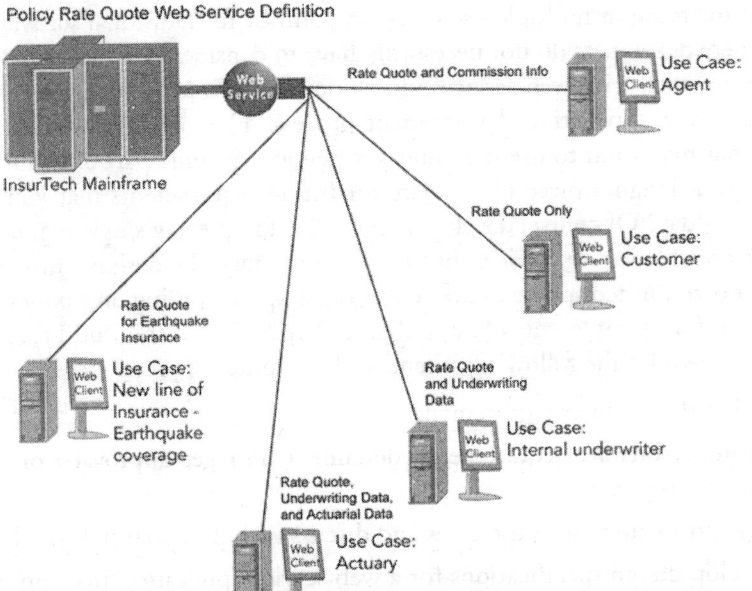

Figure 15.3 The best practices application development process to develop a policy rate quote web service will take multiple use cases into consideration in the design phase. The result will be a web service that can be reused across a reasonable number of different use cases, including those that have not been implemented yet.

handle future insurance policy needs, such as those required for the underwriting of earthquake coverage, which Titan currently does not offer but is considering for the following year.

In training, we point out that, while the development process required for the policy rate quote web service is more involved, time-consuming, and expensive than that needed for the agent policy rate quote client/server application depicted earlier, the end result has far higher utility. The web service can provide data to four existing use cases and one future use case. In contrast, the proprietary application-specific approach would solve the problem at hand but would have to be rewritten for each use case. As we explain to our training groups, this is the essence of the SOA. The policy rate quote is a service that is available in multiple user scenarios. How it is created is of secondary importance. At this point, what it does and who can use it are the prime considerations. We emphasize this many times in training: an SOA views software applications as services that can be used at will.

Then, even though it is a sort of "cart before the horse" problem, you have to get developers thinking in terms of using already existing web services in their designs. As we know, with web services you can reuse code quite efficiently. Instead of coding everything from scratch, we can use previously written web services in the software we are developing. In the SOA training, we encourage a development process that asks, early on, what existing web services can be used.

A big part of changing the way developers think, too, has to do with letting them imagine a different IT department as well. One of the main reasons that developers have traditionally had a narrow, requirement-centric focus has been due to budget. Developing web services takes longer than developing traditional software. There is simply no way around that. The kind of enterprise-level thinking that is required to implement web services makes them more costly to develop. The savings result from efficiencies that occur *after* the web services have been developed. The potential efficiencies of web services are so great that most organizations in the world are shifting to this model. What is less understood is that a shift to this model without proper governance and foresight actually adds inefficiency rather than solving anything. For this reason, I preach planning above all else and, barring that, I advise a company to run the other direction rather than fall into the trap of web services euphoria.

In a related area, we must work with the Titan team to rethink their infrastructure planning because an SOA can change the load characteristics and other requirements of an enterprise infrastructure. They might have to upgrade application servers, and/or put in bigger boxes and bigger database servers to support additional load from other applications that might be consuming that service.

As soon as you start offering services, you run into operational concerns over running shared applications. In addition to existing systems that may need attention, new systems, such as a UDDI server, should be considered in light of the need to govern and provide services in the enterprise. In the past, your operations management people understood DNS servers. They understood routers and firewalls. They understood (to varying degrees) application servers and the platforms they require. Now, you are bringing in a whole new set of services and problems for operations groups. These folks have to look at a service level that they have never seen before in their lives. Now you have service-level agreements (SLAs) that must be maintained between applications; now those SLAs are at the application level, not at the network level.

So, your systems management group (the operations management people) must be motivated to understand an SOA. They have to be able to maintain your UDDI servers as well as a web services management platform to abstract and enforce security, monitor performance, and ensure quality of service. In the past, they had to deal with a server being up or down, but now there's this almost abstract concept of a service, which could be up or down or in violation of an SLA. The state of the service may have no correlation whatsoever to the underlying hardware platform, which is what they've always dealt with in the past. With the SOA, a whole new level of complexity is inflicted upon operations management.

During the training one of our most important goals is to get the Titan team to rethink their basic assumptions and attitudes about working in IT, working with each other, and working with upper management. In addition to communicating the specific kinds of changes that might occur when the group starts to deploy the SOA, we work with the Titan people to get over a defeatist, "we can't afford it" attitude. The Titan group, like so many other developers, has been conditioned by years of budget wars to reject any idea that might be perceived to cost more than the minimum required to get the basic job done. And, while I admire cost-effective IT processes, it is necessary to transcend that approach when rolling out an SOA. By showing that top management is committed to making the SOA work, we convinced the team that increased infrastructure resources will be provided, within reason. It is clear to all involved that this approach will ultimately result in considerable savings—and that doing it right now is critical.

15.3 ADDING AN "ARCHITECTS' COUNCIL"

The last significant piece of the "people" puzzle is the organizational structure of Titan's IT department. It's not my business to tell Titan who should report to whom, so I suggest to upper management that they organize themselves for the purpose of implementing the SOA. I recommend they create an "architects' council" that will serve as a steering body for the SOA.

The council will review the various design suggestions that come from the project teams, suggest modifications, and ratify the final SOA plans. The council will serve as a governing body for the SOA, one that can resolve disputes and set a clear direction for the whole effort. It won't detract from the power of the top executives, but it will provide an organized forum for discussing different points of view on any matter that might affect the quality or cost of the SOA.

I suggested that the council consist of H.P. Wei, Dot Bartlett, the two vice presidents, and lead architects, and one representative from each of the Hermes and Apollo teams. That way, everyone will feel that they have a voice in the SOA development process. H.P. decides to follow this suggestion. The first meeting of the architects' council is held in the final week of the training period, which turns out to be a good thing because there are numerous grievances and comments from almost every party. The council provides an arena where each stakeholder in the process can air his or her feelings or ideas and achieve some resolution. Over the next few months, the council will serve this purpose again and again.

15.4 SUMMARY

An SOA is a human creation that must serve the needs of a variety of individuals' needs. As a result, an organization planning to develop an SOA should devote substantial attention and resources to the people side of the SOA development process at the outset.

SOA best practices training is a necessary first step in getting your organization's people on board and up to speed with the SOA. If your organization is fragmented, as was Titan Insurance, I recommend you "mix and match" people from different backgrounds into heterogeneous training groups that will encourage people to work together.

After you cover basic SOA information such as SOAP and UDDI, I recommend that SOA best practices training emphasize the cultural differences between conventional application development and SOA development. This means focusing on the changes in the software development process that are required to develop web services in an SOA that will satisfy multiple use cases. This includes those services that don't exist yet. The goal is to reduce the need for rewriting the web service in each successive use case. Getting developers to think more broadly than they have in the past and focus on the reuse potential of each web service they develop is a major shift. It is necessary to spend time and money to ensure that your SOA developers master the new multiuse SOA development paradigm.

To ensure a smooth transition to an SOA, your organization must establish a governing body for the SOA development process. In Titan's case, the IT department created an "architects' council," with representatives from top management of each major application development team. The council will serve as a steering group for the SOA development effort and as a forum for the discussion of issues that arise in the process.

CHAPTER 16

People: establishing best practices

Having formed the training groups and taken them through the basics of SOA design and development, it's now time to delve deeply into best practices in SOA development. As I explain to the training groups, these best practices break down into two major phases:

- **Service discovery**—Service discovery begins with an analysis of the complete corporate environment that identifies viable business initiatives that can be realized by an SOA. The business initiatives are then broken down into their component business processes and supporting web services.
- **Service creation**—In the service creation phase, developers use a "web services scorecard" that evaluates which web services are the best candidates for development according to a set of criteria that attempt to balance complexity with reuse potential. In tandem with web service development, the team will finalize the supporting architecture required to make the SOA a reality. In addition, this phase establishes mechanisms to manage, measure, and refine web service performance upon deployment.

16.1 SERVICE DISCOVERY

As I explain to Jay, building effective services probably has more to do with business processes than it does with technology. Good service design is about developing resuable capabilities that serve the needs of processes that could vary widely in their function, ranging from internal departmental needs to external supply chain and partner relationship management. The service itself will exist independently of the context in which it is used, independently of the processes that invoke it. For that reason, services must be defined with extreme care; if they are too granular and specific to a particular business case, the primary value to the organization over time will be lost.

16.1.1 Modeling the business

In the Titan example, the business modeling process requires that we revisit the "wish list" that the developers have been fussing over for the last few months. To do this effectively, I set up a number of parallel SOA training sessions with Titan's business management executives. After giving them an abbreviated lesson on web services and the SOA, I ask them to return to the original wish list—which they had created, incidentally—and to look at it again in the context of an SOA. I ask them to break the wish list down into major business initiatives and component processes that can be well served by access to various systems. After a lot of discussion, we boil the wish list down into two essential tasks, shown in table 16.1. For all of the complexity of the situation, Titan's management has two basic objectives: reduce the cost of selling insurance and lower the cost of processing claims. All IT requirements necessarily flowed from these two mandates.

Table 16.1 Titan's IT Wish List

Initiative	Objectives	Component Processes
Cost reduction in policy underwriting	**Use IT to cut costs associated with selling insurance:** • Reduce customer service representative overhead • Streamline communications with Titan's agent • Improve efficiency of billing process • Improve efficiency of payment processing	• Policy underwriting • Billing • Payment processing
Cost reduction in claims processing	**Use IT to cut costs associated processing claims:** • Streamline communication between multiple parties involved in claims processing • Improve efficiency of claims payment process	• Claims processing • Claims payment process

Once you identify the major business initiatives that will drive the direction of your SOA, evaluate each initiative to determine those that should receive the highest priority consideration for SOA development. A variety of methods are available for conducting such an evaluation, some that are simple and others that are quite complex. In general, the most effective way to identify the types of business initiatives that a service should accommodate is to look at the most pressing business needs and prioritze from there. In other words, SOA is not a sweeping companywide initiative, but more of a beacon in the distance that is achieved by navigating through small, practical projects one by one. In this way, services are defined in relation to immediate business needs and are then reused as additional business needs arise in the future. To ensure that these future business needs are acommodated in the design of the service, it is imperative that, to the greatest extent possible, other departments within the organization are queried early regarding how and why they might need the same service in the future. It is important to ensure that the tyranny of immediate deadlines and pressures do not ride roughshod over the opportunity to deploy services in the context of best practices, moving the SOA goals of the company forward. Similarly, when deciding which applications to expose as services and when, the clear path will always be based on which business case is stronger and more immediate rather than any particular technological imperative. At Titan, the analysis progresses as shown in table 16.2.

In Titan's case, we evaluate the two inititiaves using strategic, operational, and finance factors. As summarized in table 16.2, we've listed the benefits and challenges attendant with each initiative and assigned each factor a score on a scale of 1 through 10, with 10 representing the highest level of benefit to Titan. The policy-related initiative is the clear winner. As a result, we decide to table the claims-related initiative for the time being and concentrate our SOA development on the policy matters.

16.1.2 Process definition

Now that the Titan management team has identified these business initiatives, I invite them to meet with the IT training groups for a "meeting of the minds." Working together, the two groups model the business processes that are at the center of the business initiatives. Figure 16.1 shows the business process model for policy underwriting. In the business process models shown in the figures, the ⏷-shaped box indicates a

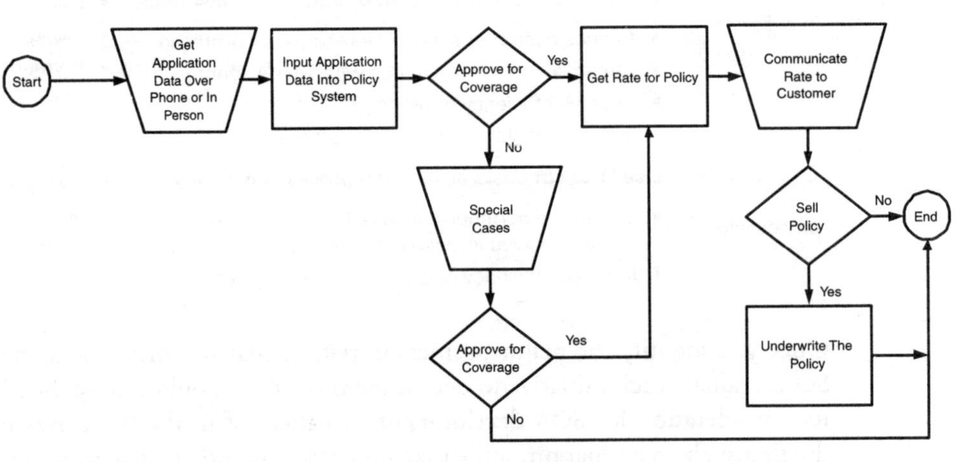

Figure 16.1 Business process model for policy underwriting

Table 16.2 Evaluation of Titan's Business Initiatives

Initiative	Strategic Factors	Operational Factors	Financial Factors	Evaluation
Cost reduction in policy underwriting	Simplifying agent sales process will help increase policy sales: • Agents will remain loyal to the insurance company that makes their lives easier. • Policyholders are sensitive to customer service issues. Improving customer service will help customer retention rates.	The customer service department is already set up to handle agent sales issues. The cost reduction plan will represent an incremental change in procedure.	Titan spends $20 million per year on customer service and policy underwriting expenses. A 5% improvement in efficiency translates to a $1 million savings.	The policy initiative presents the more compelling strategic, operational, and financial case.
Rating	7	3	8	Score: 18
Cost reduction in claims processing	Streamlining the claims payment process will benefit those policyholders who have claims. Better, faster claims payment will enhance Titan's brand image as a good insurance company to work with.	Claims management is currently handled by two completely separate departments using two completely different types of technology (paper based vs. electronic document). The implementation of an SOA will only be a small part of a large-scale reorganization of the claims unit.	Titan spends $5 million per year on claims processing overhead. To reach the $1 million savings likely to be realized by the policy sales initiative, the claims initiative would have to result in a 20% improvement, which is unlikely to occur. The probable savings from the claims initiative would be $500,000 per year.	The claims initiative, while worthwhile, is part of a bigger operational change program. In addition, the cost/benefit of the initiative is not as good as the policy initiative.
Rating	3	1	1	Score: 5

manual process, while the ▭-shaped box represents a computer process, or "service" provided to the business process by Titan's IT systems. (Diamonds are also services.)

While this may seem a little confusing (and I apologize for that), an important step in developing an SOA is to understand how business processes call on "services" from IT systems, regardless of whether the services are based on SOAP or some other standard. In the case of the business process model in figure 16.1, the services described are provided either by the InsurTech mainframe or the old Apollo policy systems.

Titan management has identified the first step—the acquisition of policy applicant information, either by hand, over the phone, or in person—to be the most time-consuming and inefficient step in the process. In addition, the communication of the policy rate quote to the customer over the phone or in person is also considered highly inefficient. The management team is interested in seeing how the SOA could help improve the efficiency of those tasks. The obvious answer, which we have already explored in a preliminary fashion, is to migrate some of those processes to a browser-based portal application.

We repeat the business process modeling exercise for the billing and credit card payment processes of the policy business initiative. As shown in figure 16.2, the payment and billing business process is complex. It's not hard to see why Titan's management feels that this is a good area to examine for simplification and cost containment. The billing process in particular relies on numerous manual steps and paper-based procedures. Titan management has a strong interest in encouraging their policyholders to migrate toward an online or phone-based billing process and phase out paper-based billing altogether over time. In the short run, though, the company knows it's going to have to continue with paper-based billing while making the process efficient and more cost-effective at the same time. The big question is, with these business goals in mind, which applications makes the most sense to expose as web services?

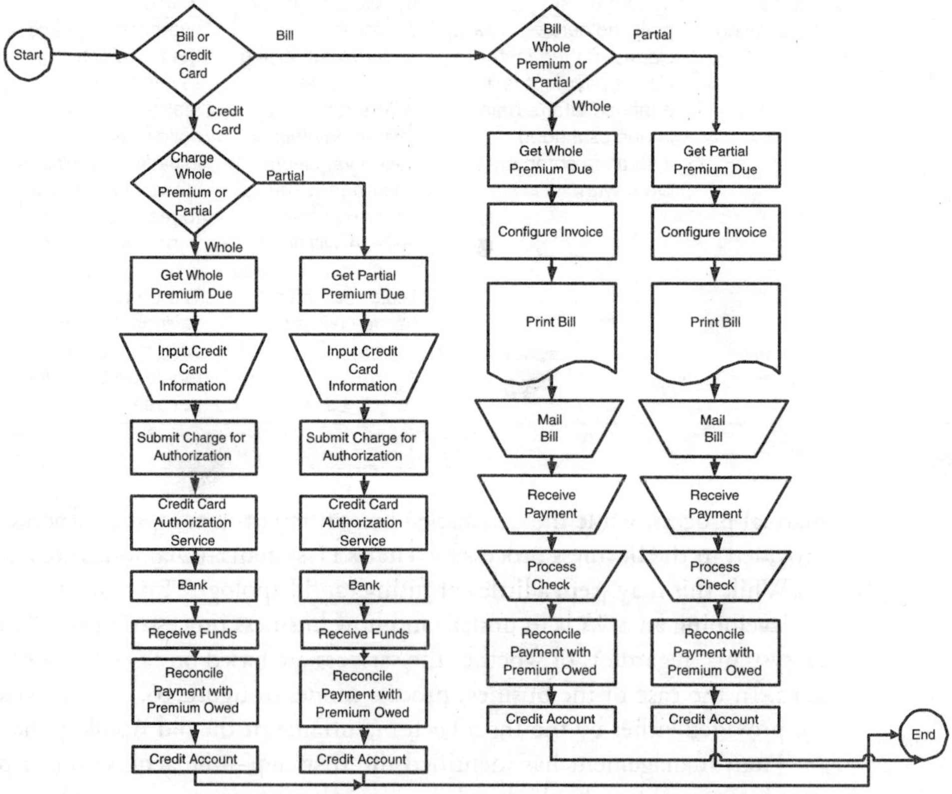

Figure 16.2 Business process model for policy premium payment and billing

Also, which ones make sense to implement earlier than others, and which one will make the most effective learning experience as a pilot web service project?

The goal of SOA development best practices is to identify the services that are used by a business process (ideally various different processes from multiple parties) and identify the best candidates for exposure as web services. The challenge for developers is to learn a methodology for evaluating which services will be the most feasible candidates. Before evaluation, we recommend compiling a service inventory, as depicted in table 16.3, from the business processes you have defined for possible SOA development.

Table 16.3 The Service Inventory

Process	Service	Current Location of Service
Policy underwriting	Input application data into policy system	Policy systems
	Approve for coverage (system-based decision)	Policy systems
	Get rate for coverage	Policy systems
	Underwrite the policy	Policy systems
Charge premium	Get whole premium due	Policy systems
	Get partial premium due	Policy systems
	Submit charge for authorization	Policy systems
	Credit card authorization	Authorization services (outside)
	Receive funds	Finance systems
	Reconcile payment with premium owed	Finance and policy systems
	Credit accounts	Finance and policy systems
Bill premium	Get whole premium due	Policy systems
	Get partial premium due	Policy systems
	Configure invoice	Policy systems
	Receive funds	Finance systems
	Reconcile payment with premium owed	Finance and policy systems
	Credit accounts	Finance and policy systems

16.2 SERVICE CREATION, PART I

Now that the groups have identified 16 services that supported the business processes under consideration in the policy business initiative, the time has come to begin part I of service creation. In this stage, we evaluate which services ought to be given priority for exposure as web services. In part II, which will take place after the pilot project, we go about planning the entire SOA.

How do you determine the priority for web service creation? Should you just go down your list starting at the top and begin exposing each software service needed to support the business processes as web services, or should you pick and choose? If so, how? The answers reflect how I recommend that you approach SOA development: using an incremental process based on methodical prioritization of services that need to be exposed. It is not advisable under any circumstances to try to convert an enterprise architecture to an SOA in one all-consuming sweep. Because of the still-evolving nature of web services, the human and organization transitional issues involved, and the inevitable time frame of such a conversion, attaching an SOA with a broad brush is ill advised. The most sensible approach is to examine each potential web service in the service inventory and determine which ones will be relatively simple to execute and create the highest utility in the emerging SOA.

16.2.1 Rating the services

To find the highest-priority services to be exposed as web services, I recommend that Titan use a web services "report card," a tool we consider one of the cornerstones of SOA best practices. The report card rates potential web services on the basis of four key factors:

- **Migration**—Will developing this web service simplify anticipated system migration plans?
- **Isolation**—Does this web service isolate the consuming application from performing complex business logic in order to use the web service?
- **Flexibility**—Can the web service handle multiple consumption scenarios?
- **Reusability**—Can the web service have multiple, diverse consumers?

The service that has the right mix of these qualities will be a good candidate for exposure as a web service. Services that do not meet these criteria should be given lower priority for web service exposure, or possibly never be exposed at all. To illustrate the process, we mentor the Titan training groups in the use of the report card to rate two web service candidates, "Underwrite the policy" and "Authorize credit card," and then compare the results. Working at the whiteboards, we come up with figures 16.3 and 16.4, which illustrate the logical flow of each service as it exists now in the Titan architecture.

As figure 16.3 shows, the "Underwrite the policy" service, while simple in its basic logical flow, is integrally tied to the functioning of the policy system. In reality, policy underwriting is a highly complex process with very detailed application logic that feeds off extensive actuarial databases and policyholder records contained in the policy system.

Credit card authorization, as depicted in figure 16.4, requires the finance system to format and send a customer's credit card information (card number, expiration date, and so on) to one of several credit card authorization services used by Titan. Each credit card authorization service requires its own custom interface. The "pain point" for Titan has been the cost and effort involved in maintaining these interfaces. Not only do the existing interfaces require constant maintenance and updating, they make it costly for Titan to replace authorization services, which the company occasionally wants to do.

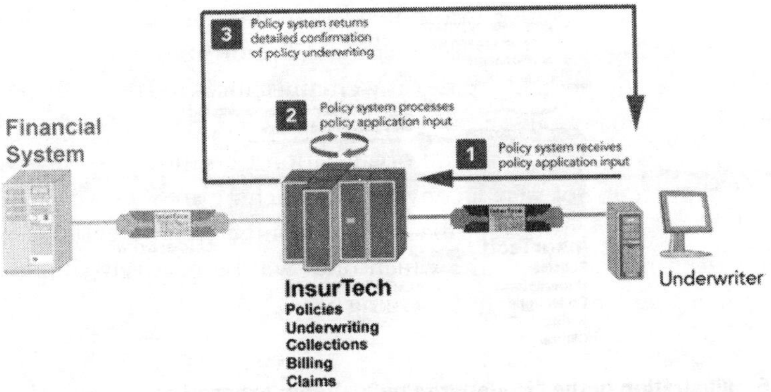

Figure 16.3 The "Underwrite the policy" service involves three steps that take place in the policy system: the system recieves policy application data, processes the data, and returns a detailed confirmation of the underwritten policy to either the agent or internal user who requested the underwriting.

When exposed as a web service, "Underwrite policy" will look like figure 16.5. The underwriter's system, which will most likely be the new company portal discussed earlier, will consume the web service by creating a SOAP request that contains the policy applicant's data. The web service, exposing the functionality of the policy system, will

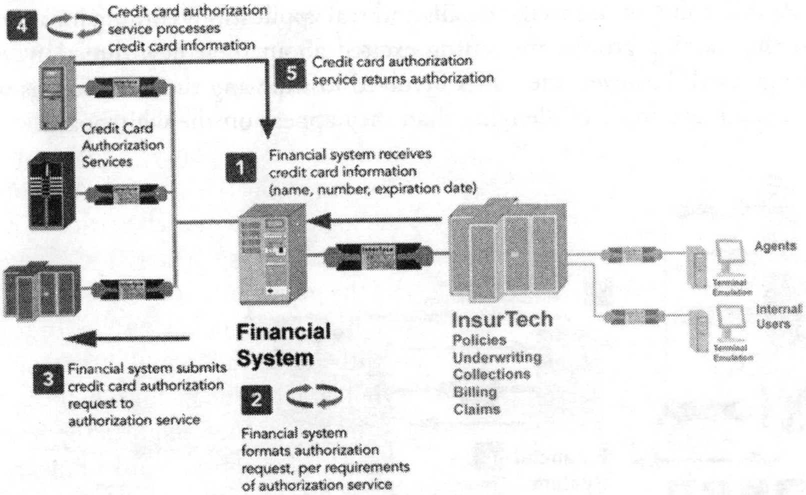

Figure 16.4 The "Authorize credit card" service involves five steps that originate and end with Titan's finance system. The finance system, which has received the customer's card information from the policy system, must format that information to suit the needs of one of three possible authorization services. One of Titan's big challenges has been the effort required to keep up with the ever-changing message formating needs of these authorization services.

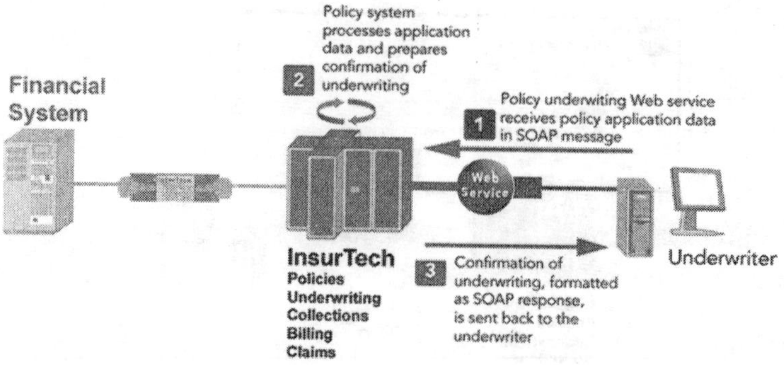

Figure 16.5 Illustration of the "Underwrite policy" step exposed as a web service

process the incoming SOAP request and return a detailed policy underwriting confirmation as a SOAP response.

The "Authorize credit card" service, exposed as a web service, will resemble figure 16.6. The web service will sit on the finance system, masking the complexity of formatting the credit card authorization requests to each outside credit card authorization service provider. Currently, Titan has to maintain highly complex, custom interfaces that manage the formatting of authorization requests that flow to each separate outside authorization service. The web service eliminates the need for these interfaces by standardizing the authorization request into SOAP format.

At this point, with specific details and real applications coming into view, I can tell that the training groups are getting excited about their new direction. As you may have guessed, however, the issues involved in exposing these services as web services are a good deal more challenging than they appear on the whiteboard.

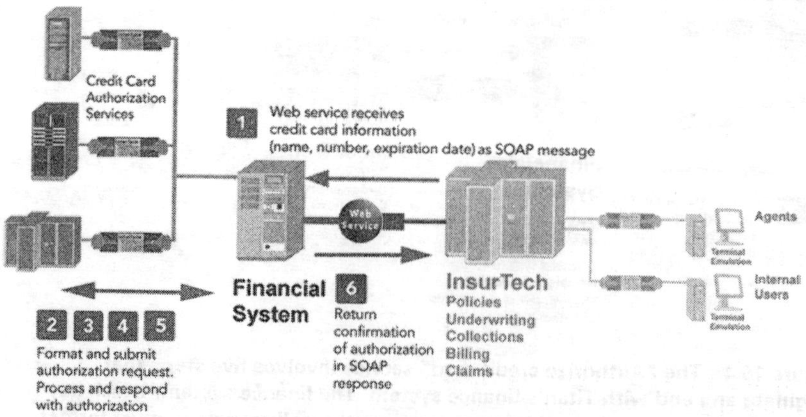

Figure 16.6 The "Authorize credit card" service exposed as a web service. The web service will expose the finance system's functionality and allow the policy system to create a SOAP response containing the customer's credit card information.

16.2.2 Migration

Migration refers to the transformation of enterprise architecture by the phasing out of old systems and the introduction of new ones. In terms of the web service report card evaluation, migration is an important factor because it is only worth creating a web service for a legacy system if it will either simplify migration plans or remove the need for those plans through its own existence. For each of the two services we're considering, the groups have to discuss several migration scenarios to see how the services will fare under such changes.

The "Underwrite policy" web service has a streamlined migration path that is deceptively appealing. As shown in figure 16.7, it appears to the training groups as if they can just swap out the old policy system and stick the "Underwrite policy" web service right onto it. Not quite, it turns out. As we discuss it in more detail, we begin to see that a web service exposed on the existing policy system will have to contain a lot of programming logic specific to that policy system's approach to policy underwriting. If Titan is to replace the policy system, it's likely that whatever "Underwrite policy" web service they have will either have to be scrapped and rewritten or revised so extensively as to make it not worth the effort.

In contrast, the simplicity of the "Authorize credit card" web service, and the near universality of credit cards in business and e-commerce, make it a good candidate for migration. As depicted in figure 16.8, migrating to a new policy system won't necessitate much change in the basic credit card authorization web service. The message requirements—name, credit card number, expiration date, and so on—won't change at all even if the policy system is completely replaced. If the finance system is migrated to a new platform (a step that is under consideration), again the credit card processing function won't be affected much. Ultimately, as is already being contemplated, the

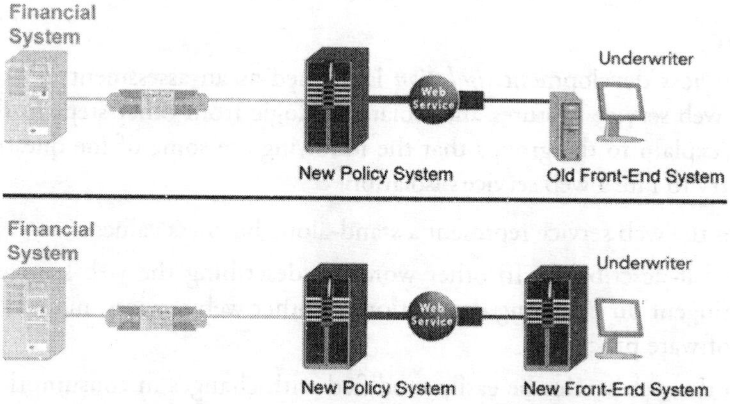

Figure 16.7 Possible migration scenarios for the "Underwrite policy" web service. Though simple in appearance, the process of migrating this service to new systems will likely require extensive reworking of the web service given the amount of specific programming logic it contains.

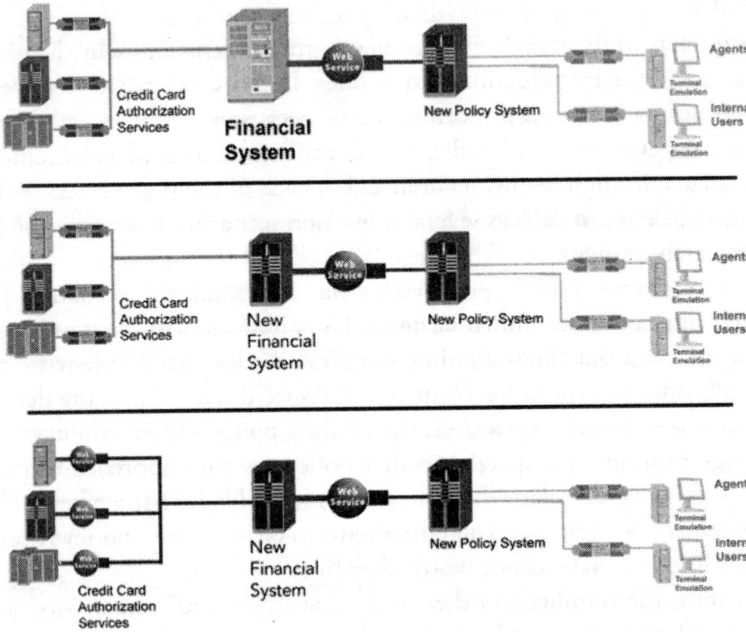

Figure 16.8 Possible migration scenarios for the "Authorize credit card" web service, including the possibility that the outside credit card authorization service providers might change their interfaces to web service standards

outside credit card authorization service providers themselves are going to convert their interfaces to web services. In all three migration scenarios, the "Authorize credit card" web service is seen by the training groups as a streamlined part of the process.

16.2.3 Isolation

In web services development, *isolation* is defined as an assessment of how well the proposed web service captures and isolates its logic from other steps in the business process. I explain to the groups that the following are some of the questions we ask when we try to rate a web service's isolation:

- Does the web service represent a stand-alone business value?
- Is it self-describable? In other words, is describing the web service accurately contingent on including descriptions of other web services, manual operations, or software processes?
- Can the web service be easily modified with changes in consumption use cases independently of other functions or services?

These factors help you see where you have defined a web service that is difficult to extricate from other services, and therefore not appropriately defined yet as a stand-alone service. For instance, if you have a poorly isolated service A that is interwoven with the functionality of service B, then a modification of B will likely necessitate a modification of A. Too many of these interdependencies can create a maintenance headache in an SOA.

The "Authorize credit card" web service scores fairly high marks for isolation, which means the service is quite distinct. It receives credit card information from a source, formats an authorization request, sends it, and responds with a confirmation of authorization. It is a stand-alone business process. It can self-describe—"Authorize credit card" pretty much says it all. It can be modified for different consumption use cases, such as telephone IVR input, and so on, independently of other services. In other words, you can add, remove, or modify the web service consumer applications that hit the "Credit card authorization" web service without having to modify any other service in the enterprise architecture.

The "Underwrite policy" web service is a different story and is far less isolated than the credit card example. If the web service were to be created, it would encompass a range of logical processes, such as actuarial calculations and customer database querying. As a result, it does not represent a stand-alone business value. It is part of other processes, so it cannot be fully self-describing. It is difficult, or nearly impossible, to modify its consumption use cases without having to alter other dependent processes within the policy system.

16.2.4 Flexibility and reusability

The degree to which a web service is flexible reflects its ability to handle multiple consumption cases and variations in use cases. In this context, the "Authorize credit card" web service is fairly flexible. It can handle Visa or Mastercard, for example, with virtually no modification to its interface. To handle an American Express card, which has more integers in its credit card number, a slight modification is required. And, as we discussed earlier, the "Authorize credit card" web service would work well with any number of potential web service consumers, such as web, IVR, and so on. In contrast, the "Underwrite policy" web service has one basic consumption case and must be extensively modified to handle different types of insurance policies.

Similarly, in terms of reusability, the "Authorize credit card" web service is far more versatile than the "Underwrite policy" web service. As Titan grows, it's likely that many different lines of business and systems, including those that do not even exist yet, will be able to use the credit card authorization service. Any line of Titan's business that needs to process credit cards—a business process that is unlikely to change substantially over time—can make use of the web service once it is operating. The "Underwrite policy" web service, in comparison, has virtually no reuse potential beyond its initial function.

16.2.5 Other factors

The fifth category on the report card covers other factors that may influence the decision to give a particular web service priority for development. Though these factors vary, it is usually worth looking into the implementation cost, development timeline, technical, and organizational challenges involved in bringing the proposed web service to life. Let's see how our training groups compare the two potential web services using these other factors.

The training groups evaluate the two web services and determine that the "Authorize credit card" web service will be somewhat less costly to develop and implement than the "Underwrite policy" web service. Technically, the mainframe "Underwrite policy" project is more challenging than the credit card web service, due in part to the fact that the "Underwrite policy" web service is part of a larger migration plan from the fat clients to the portals. Organizationally, too, the training groups realize that the policy-related web service is going to have to be part of a bigger picture of changing the way the two former companies are integrating in the policy area. For these reasons, the "Authorize credit card" web service looks better for priority development than the "Underwrite policy" web service.

16.2.6 Overall evaluation

In every evaluation category of the web service report card, the "Authorize credit card" web service ranked higher than the proposed "Underwrite policy" web service. This may not be a big surprise, given that I set up the comparison as a training exercise. In your organization, you may find the differences between proposed web services to be far subtler. Nonetheless, as we complete our evaluation, our report card, shown in table 16.4, presents the "Authorize credit card" web service as the clear winner.

Table 16.4 Web Service Report Card

Factor	Score for "Authorize credit card"	Score for "Underwrite policy"
Migration	7	2
Isolation	6	1
Flexibility	8	2
Reusability	7	2
Other Factors	5	3
Total	**33**	**10**

16.2.7 Next steps

Now that we've walked the training groups through the process of exploring business processes and evaluating the corresponding web services, it's time to select a pilot project. Though the training groups are eager to jump in with the "Authorize credit card" web service, Jay and I feel that it might be a little too complicated to use as a pilot. Instead, we suggest looking at one more web service before making the decision. That exploration is covered in the next chapter.

After the pilot, we'll enter the planning stage of Titan's SOA. At that point, we will delve deeply into the second part of service creation. We will look at the big infrastructure questions, target architecture, selection of platform, and other issues involved in starting the SOA project in earnest.

16.3 SUMMARY

Now that Titan's training groups are up on the basics of SOA design, they can begin to acquaint themselves with SOA best practices. We recommend a two-step approach: 1) service discovery, which is an analysis of the overall business initiatives that are driving SOA development, their component business processes, and supporting web services; and 2) service creation, which is an in-depth process of evaluating which potential web services are the most logical ones to give priority in development. The evaluation process is based on a web services "report card" that ranks the service's qualities in terms of system migration potential, logical isolation, flexibility, reusability, and more.

After reviewing Titan's wish list a second time in the service discovery phase, the training groups have determined that the company has two essential business initiatives: cost reduction in the policy arena and cost reduction in claims processing. An examination of the merits of each initiative has revealed that the policy area will be a more profitable place than claims processing to begin with SOA development. This is an important first step in best practices SOA development—start with the business initiative that makes more business sense, rather than wasting time and money on an initiative that would be better to defer until a later date.

Continuing with service discovery, the training groups have mapped out the business processes that are inherent in two representative business processes in the policy initiative: policy underwriting and credit card authorization. After mapping the policies, the groups have created a "service inventory" that lists the software services that each business process requires to be executed. Because Titan does not yet have an SOA, the "services" under discussion are provided by the various legacy systems operating at Titan. The challenge the groups faces in the first part of the service creation phase is to evaluate which of the services provided by Titan's legacy systems will be the most sensible to expose as a web service first.

The training groups have compared the potential "Authorize credit card" and "Underwrite policy" web services using a report card that rates the two services on these factors:

- **Migration**—How well the web service will serve Titan's system migration plans
- **Isolation**—How well the web service isolates the core business logic involved in its processing, an issue that has implications for change management and overall system updates
- **Flexibility**—A rating of the web service's ability to adapt to changes in consumption use cases

- **Reusability**—A rating of the web service's potential to be used by other, subsequent web service consumer applications
- Other factors, including implementation cost, timeline, technical, and organizational challenges

Based on these factors, the "Authorize credit card" web service has proven to be a far more practical, flexible choice than the "Underwrite policy" web service. A comparison between the two shows that the credit card web service has great potential to adapt and be reused throughout the SOA, whenever credit card processing is required. In contrast, the policy underwriting web service represents a deep but narrow piece of business logic for Titan, and one that won't migrate well or have much reuse potential as Titan continues to evolve.

CHAPTER 17

People: establishing best practices

After a few weeks of training, some amazing changes are taking place in the Titan IT department. The blending of former Hermes and Apollo people in the training groups has resulted in some new friendships (although the after-work margaritas with the team may have contributed to that as well) and a general sense of unity about the major work that looms ahead in creating an SOA. After mastering the principles of the SOA and web services, the time has come to execute a pilot project that will give everyone a practical opportunity to put their newly learned skills to the test.

17.1 SELECTING A PLATFORM

The newfound unity of the training teams threatens to dry up as soon as we began to discuss development platforms. As in so many other areas of IT, there are two basic camps: Java or Microsoft. The Apollo group is essentially a Microsoft shop. Most of their homegrown applications have been developed using Microsoft SQL, ASP, Visual Basic, COM, and so on. Many of their applications run on Windows products. They are eager to have Titan embrace the new .NET Framework for XML and web services. The former Hermes team, the ones who have more "clout," are expert in neither Java nor Microsoft. The Hermes team is a mix of old mainframe guys (COBOL aficionados primarily), IBM hardware specialists, and Java developers. As a group, though, they are more inclined to go with Java because they consider it more open and flexible.

In some ways, this argument is like trying to convince a Yankees fan that the Red Sox are a better team. There are valid points of view on both sides, but you risk bodily harm by introducing logic into the conversation. We discuss the issue in depth and come up with what I think is a pretty creative solution. We will develop our pilot web service using Java, but we will also experiment with creating a Microsoft-based web service consumer application using the Microsoft platform to learn about the subtle interoperability challenges that still manage to exist between the two platforms despite the agreement on the web services standards.

Our reasons for selecting Java are as follows: Both groups agree that it is likely that they will be deploying some of their new SOA applications on application servers from BEA or IBM in the future, and since that requires some organization knowledge of J2EE, they figure this is a good time to learn. On an interpersonal level, it is nearly impossible as well to convince anyone in the "anti-Microsoft" camp that they should agree to "cave in" to the giant from Redmond. To be honest, I am basically neutral myself. I see great strengths and challenges in both platforms. The important goal from my perspective is to convince the training groups to agree that they are going to work with one platform or the other.

17.2 CHOOSING A PILOT PROJECT

At first, we all just assume that we're going to develop the "Authorize credit card" web service as our pilot. However, as we begin to explore the issue in greater depth, we see that it is perhaps just a little too complex for a training exercise. Instead, we discuss a number of alternatives before circling back to a potential web service that we had examined earlier: "Get premium due." As we had seen previously, "Get premium due" was a step in several billing- and payment-related business processes. The "Get premium due" function was invoked by a wide range of consuming applications, including the IVR system as well as the agent, company, and customer portals.

The web service itself is quite simple in its essence. As shown in figure 17.1, the consuming application sends a SOAP request containing the policyholder's name and policy number to the web service. The web service then processes the request by retrieving the premium due from the policy database, which is contained in the InsurTech mainframe system. Then, the web service sends a SOAP response containing the premium due back to the consuming application.

Going to the whiteboard, the training groups demonstrate that the "Get premium due" web service has many potential consumers. As shown in figure 17.2, there are 12 potential use cases for the service because it is an integral part of many billing and customer service business processes. In some cases, the customer, agent, or staff member might want to process a payment. In other cases, the user is simply making an inquiry: "What do I owe on my policy right now?"

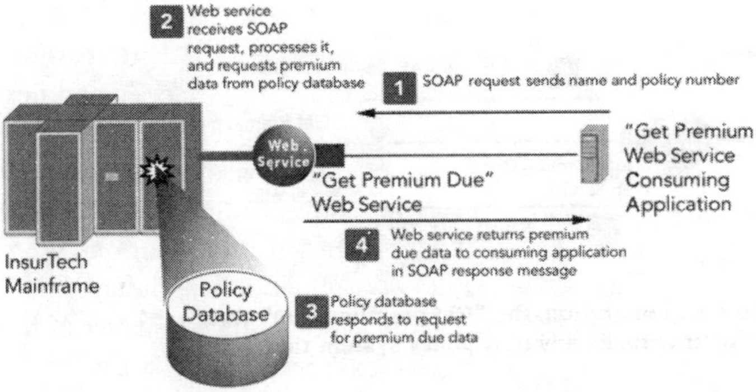

Figure 17.1 Proposed web service for "Get premium due." The web service responds to a SOAP request containing the policyholder's name and policy number with a SOAP response, derived from the InsurTech policy database, which contains the amount of the premium due.

While we can all "eyeball" the web service and see that it has great appeal as a pilot, we feel it is appropriate to put our best practices to work and evaluate the "Get premium due" web service according to the web service report card (see the previous chapter). So, the groups set out to evaluate the "Get premium due" web service for migration, isolation, flexibility, reusability, and other factors.

The web service seems to be a great enabler of migration. As depicted in figure 17.3, the simple business logic functionality of the web service—providing a policy name and number and receiving a premium due figure—can migrate to virtually any new policy system that Titan might install. Regardless of the type or software configuration of the new system, it's highly likely that it will function at the level of policyholder's name, policy number, and policy premium due.

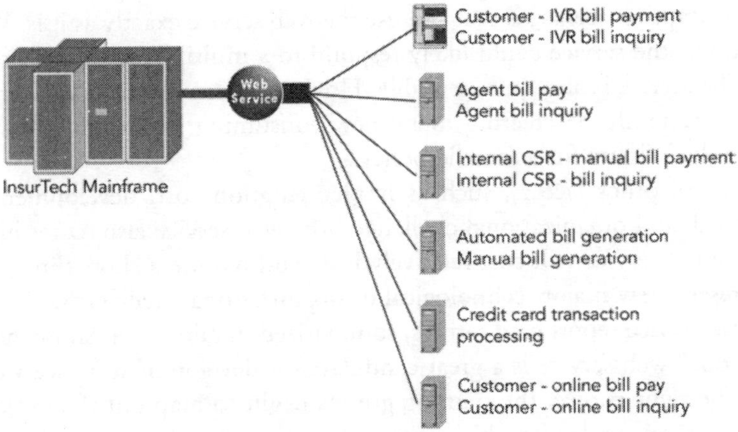

Figure 17.2 There are 12 possible use cases for the "Get premium due" web service, including billing, payment processing, and customer inquiries.

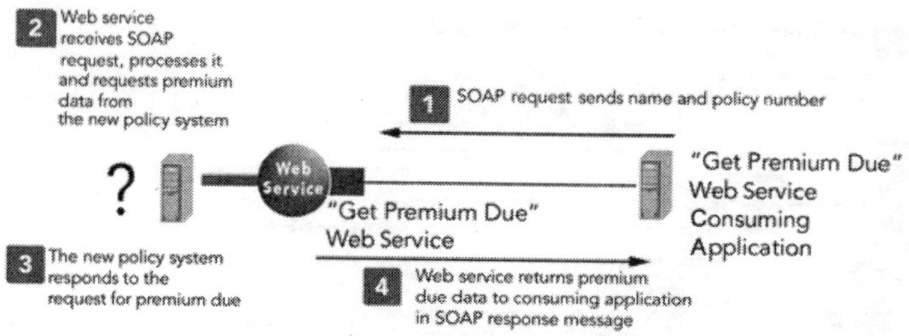

Figure 17.3 In terms of migration, the "Get premium due" web service can work with virtually any new policy system that Titan implements.

In terms of isolation, the web service rates a mixed score. On the request side, it is almost completely isolated. Regardless of the business logic involved in getting the premium due, the request parameters will almost always be the same: name and policy number. On the response side, the web service is less isolated. To answer the request, the service must be integrated into the logic of the policy system. It will be somewhat difficult to separate the response side of the service from the business logic of the policy system. If the business logic of the policy system changes, it might necessitate a change in the web service. However, given the simplicity of the service, it shouldn't be a very complex change.

In addition, the web service does not require the consuming application to perform any business logic. All the consumer has to do is provide the policy name and number in a request and, in return, it receives the premium due for that policy. There are virtually no calculation or logical steps to follow in order to consume the web service. In this sense, the "Get premium due" web service is extremely isolated and thus deserving of a high rating for isolation.

The web service is very flexible. As we showed in figure 17.2, there are at least a dozen consumption scenarios that can use the web service exactly as it is. With minor modifications, the service could likely respond to a multiplicity of consuming applications. The service is also quite reusable. However Titan modifies its architecture, it will almost certainly be creating many new consuming applications that require a "Premium due" figure for a specific policy.

In terms of other factors, such as implementation cost, development timeline, technological, and organizational challenges, the web service also scores high ratings. Developing the service will cost relatively little and require a short time period. The project presents few major technological or organizational challenges.

The web service report card ratings, summarized in table 17.1, show that the "Get premium due" web service is a great candidate for development. Once we've agreed we made the right choice, the training groups begin to map out the project and get busy. A very short while after this exciting start, though, I hear a lot of moaning and groaning from the groups. Now comes the fun part.

Table 17.1 Report card for "Get Premium Due"

Factor	Score for "Get Premium Due"
Migration	8
Isolation	6
Flexibility	8
Reusability	8
Other factors	5
Total	**35**

17.3 CONFRONTING A REAL ARCHITECTURE

When the training groups start to map out how a web service consumer application will actually get into the Titan domain, submit its SOAP request, and receive the SOAP response, they begin to see that there are a number of significant problems that they have not anticipated. With the working consumption use case of an insurance agent paying a premium bill, the groups use the whiteboard to look at the real architecture that will be required to make the web service work. As figure 17.4 shows, security and message protocol issues make the hypothetical "Get premium due" web service a great deal more complex than the groups had first thought.

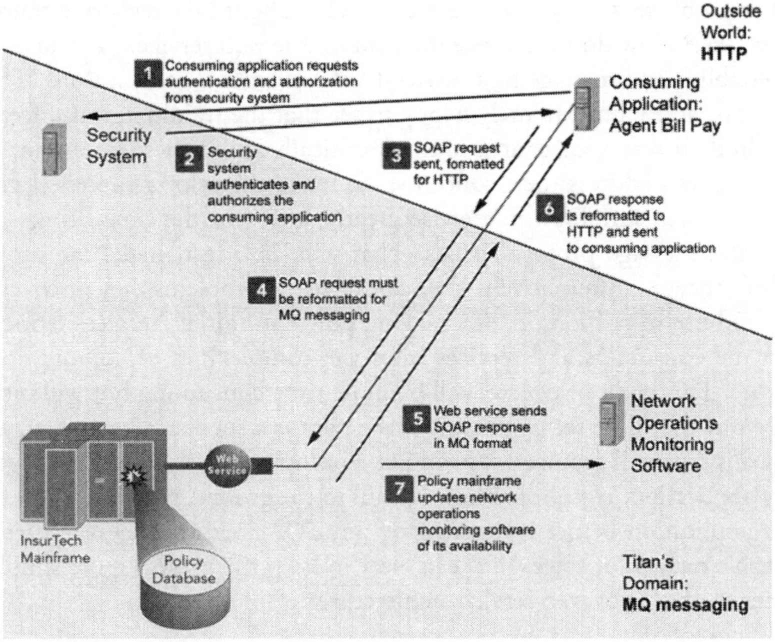

Figure 17.4 A more realistic look at the actual architecture that will be required to realize the "Get premium due" web service

Titan's security infrastructure, which has not been given much consideration until this point, now looms large. Before the consuming application can even send its SOAP request, it first has to be authenticated and authorized to do so by the Titan security system. Then, once a consuming application has established secure access to Titan's domain, it will send a SOAP request that is formatted to travel on an HTTP messaging protocol. That's fine, until it hits the Titan domain, which operates using the Message Queuing (MQ) messaging protocol. The SOAP message will have to be reformatted in order to reach the web service in recognizable form. To get the SOAP response back to the consuming application requires another message protocol transformation from MQ back to HTTP. Finally, Titan's network operations monitoring system, which ensures that all of Titan's systems are operating properly on their respective networks, has to be updated on the status of the policy system—an action that requires the web service to interface with the network operations monitoring system.

None of these problems is insurmountable, but they create a serious challenge. To satisfy Titan's security, message transformation, and network operations requirements, the training groups realize they will have to create so much custom code in both the web service and consuming application that it will literally defeat the entire purpose of the web service approach. The result will be yet another hard-coded, custom interface—not at all the intent of a web service and SOA. And each consumption scenario presents a slightly different set of unique security and messaging factors, which only makes the whole situation more complicated.

Other problems soon emerge as well. "What about failover?" one training group member asks. "How do we balance the load on the web service?" asks another. "How do we establish and manage to a service-level agreement?" asks a third. These are all good points, and I am extremely happy to see that the training groups feel confident enough in their new subject area to think critically about these important issues.

Here's how I address their concerns. To make the pilot a success, I give them a choice: They can simplify the exercise greatly and—for the time being—ignore the security and message protocol issues. That will, in effect, make the project into a "proof of concept." Alternatively, they can solve the problems they discover in a more generic and useful fashion, in effect laying down an initial "services fabric" that will abstract the consumers and services from the complexities of communicating with each other. This path, of course, will be more time consuming but will ultimately be the only way they'll be set up to scale if the pilot is a success. Creating an abstraction layer of this type will require procuring or developing a web service management and security application. It is probable, I explain to the groups, that Titan will have to get such an application before embarking on any SOA rollout process in earnest. However, at this early pilot stage, they can elect to keep the project quite simple in order to master the basics of web service architecture.

17.4 SETTING GOALS AND ACHIEVING SUCCESS

The training groups come back to me with their answer, which isn't quite what I've been expecting. They have elected to develop a proof of concept using a simplified set of assumptions. However, they also announce that they intend to go through the exercise of doing the architecture for the pilot web service using a hypothetical web service security and management application. Indeed, the architects' council at Titan is considering a number of competing products in that area at the time.

The architecture for the proof of concept is shown in figure 17.5. The architecture, which also serves as a development environment for the project, places the web service on a Sun box. The web service is developed using a Java web services development tool. To simplify the design and development process and maximize the learning aspects related to web services, the groups decide to create a test database of dummy policy and premium information that the web service can easily draw upon. The alternative—connecting the web service to the real, live policy database—would create a burdensome task that would detract from the web services education inherent in the proof of concept. The .NET and Java web service consumer applications are housed on a Windows and a Sun box, respectively. Finally, the groups have set up a third Sun box to house the UDDI.

To make the exercise interesting (though some think it's merely for torture purposes), I mandate that the groups follow a development process that mimics true service-oriented development. Each training group, with the exception of the top executives, has to develop both the "Get premium due" web service as well as a web service consumer application. However, the groups have to develop a consumer for another group's service, and a service for another group's consumer. So, Training Group A is to develop their version of the web service and call it Web Service A.

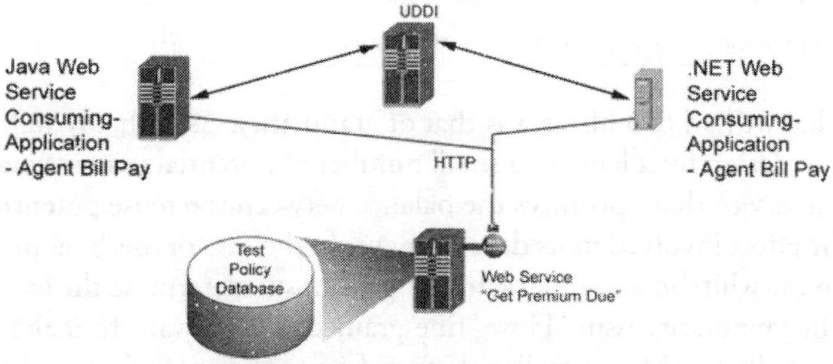

Figure 17.5 Architecture of the proof of concept. To simplify the design and development of the proof of concept, the training groups have set up a development environment with the web service housed on a Sun box. They've developed the web service using a Java tool, and connected the web service to a test database loaded with dummy data. The .NET and Java web service consumer applications are housed on a Windows and a Sun box, respectively. Finally, the groups have added a UDDI housed on a third Sun box.

Training Group B, in turn, has to develop a consumer application using only the WSDL and information posted on the UDDI. Group A, then, also has to develop a consumer for Web Service B, which is being developed by Group B. We force the groups to work "blind," without the ability to speak with the other groups about how they have designed their services and consumer applications. The idea here is to simulate the process by which Titan will be developing applications and web services as it grows into an extended SOA. We want to see how well the groups can create web services that work according to the standards and that do not require any information beyond the WSDL to enable the creation of consumer applications.

I don't know if the groups adhere to the "blind" policy completely, but Jay and I create some fun incentives to stick to the rules. At the end of the process, each group gets to evaluate the performance of another group that is different from the group for which they have had to develop a consumer application. Table 17.2 captures the "round-robin" style of development and evaluation that we follow. For example, Group A gets to test-drive the web service and consumer applications created by Group C, with whom they haven't worked directly during the development process. The evaluation consisted of two parts: a subjective look at how the development process has gone in terms of group cohesion, time to completion, and so on. Then, the groups put the new web services and consumer applications through some tests to see how well they work. The groups with the highest score get a free dinner.

Table 17.2 The "Round-Robin" Approach

Group	Develops	... Evaluates ...
Group A	Consumer for B	Group C's performance
Group B	Consumer for C	Group D's performance
Group C	Consumer for D	Group A's performance
Group D	Consumer for A	Group B's performance

One issue that we had to address was that of granularity. As with any web service, you can choose to design for a large or a small number of potential usage scenarios. Ideally, you design a service that optimizes the balance between the reuse potential of the service with the effort involved in its development. In the case of the "Get premium due," we return to the whiteboard with the training groups to determine the factors that contribute to the granularity issue. How "fine-grained" do we want to make the service?

After some discussion, we realize that we face three major factors that contribute to the issue of granularity in the "Get premium due" web service. They are shown in table 17.3. The first factor concerns the way the web service will accommodate differences in the policy-numbering protocol. At Apollo, policy numbers have been eight digits long, with an A at the beginning for auto policies and an H for homeowners' policies. Hermes has used a nine-digit number for auto policies and a ten-digit number for homeowners. There is a relatively simple solution to this immediate challenge. By adding one or more zeroes to the beginning of a policy number, the web service can utilize one single SOAP message design and conform to any existing numbering system. The question is, what will happen if Titan decides to acquire more insurance companies that have incompatible policy-numbering protocols? We don't have a ready answer, and for the time being we choose not to create a contingency for this, but the discussion itself is very educational for everyone involved.

Table 17.3 Factors Contributing to the Granularity of the "Get Premium Due" Web Service

Factor	Impact on Granularity	Decision Made by the Training Groups
Variations in policy numbering	Should the web service be designed to accommodate the existing policy-numbering systems, without regard for potential changes in numbering protocols in the future?	The groups decide to limit the policy number aspect of the SOAP message definition to fit Titan's existing numbering protocol.
Different types of "premium due" information that may be required; e.g., monthly payment plan, quarterly, or whole premium	Each different premium definition requires that the web service access a different set of data fields in the policy system.	The groups decide to create three separate "operations" within the web service that correspond to the monthly, quarterly, or whole premium due.
Special cases; e.g., refunds, partial payments, bounced checks, and so on	Many premium inquiries involve special cases. Incorporating special cases into the web service will make it more accurate but will add significant granularity and complexity in development.	The groups decide to defer integration of special cases in the web service until long-term decisions have been reached regarding the state of Titan's finance systems.

The second factor that arises involves the three different types of premium due information that the system might have to supply to consuming applications. Titan allows policies to be paid either in full, by the quarter, or by the month. The groups decide that it is necessary to enable the web service to handle each of these three types of premium requests. As a result, we design the web service with three separate "operations," or subprograms, that can handle each of the three types of premiums.

Finally, we have the issue of special cases. In many situations, the actual premium due on a policy is not simply the monthly payment as reflected on the top page of the policy. Rather, conditions such as overpayments, refunds, bad checks, late fees, and so on complicate the picture. As we discuss the matter, we know that ultimately, in real life, we have to factor these special cases into our web service. However, for the time being, we decide to table the issue for two reasons. First, to extend the web service's functionality all the way to call data out of one of Titan's finance systems will stretch the scope of the pilot project way beyond what is practical in the time given. Second, it is apparent from discussions with upper management that the company is

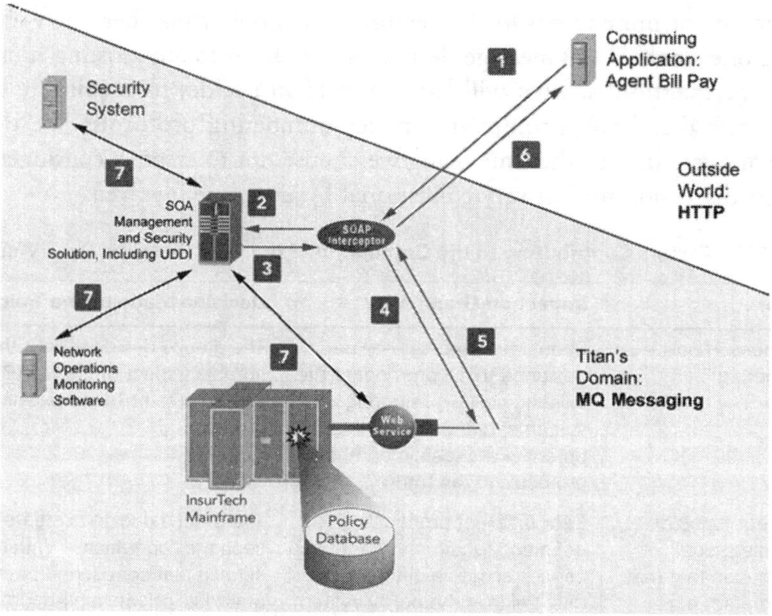

Figure 17.6 The architecture for the "Get premium due" web service in the real world. Using a SOAP interception-based SOA management and security solution, the architecture calls for the interceptor to (1) stop the SOAP request as it enters Titan's domain, (2) send the SOA management solution a request for authentication, authorization, and message protocol transformation, (3) receive a response to permit the SOAP request to go through, (4) pass the message to the web service, (5) receive a SOAP response, (6) transform the SOAP response to the HTTP protocol and forward it to the original consumer, and (7) maintain contact between the web service, the SOA management solution, the security system, and the network operations monitor.

considering a wholesale replacement of the finance systems anyway, so it makes sense to wait until that system is chosen before we worry about it at the web service level. However, in this case, as before, the discussion itself is what mattered most. By talking through these granularity challenges, we all learn a great deal about practical web service design.

As the final part of the pilot project, the groups collaborate on an architecture for the real-world implementation of the "Get premium due" web service. As shown in figure 17.6, the implementation of the service in Titan's real SOA will require the integration of an SOA management and security solution of some kind. We hypothesize that Titan can use a SOAP interception-based SOA management and security solution. With a SOAP interceptor in place, the SOAP request enters Titan's domain, is checked for authentication and authorization, is transformed from HTTP to the MQ message protocol, and then makes its way to the web service. The SOAP interceptor can also arrange for the SOAP response to be transformed back to HTTP and sent to the original consuming application. Meanwhile, the SOA management and security solution can interface with Titan's security system and network operations monitor.

17.5 MEASURING SUCCESS

The conclusion of the pilot project also signals the end of the best practices training period for Titan's IT department. As H.P. Wei, Jay Franklin, Dot Bartlett, and I sit together at a meeting toward the end of the pilot process, we discuss the ways we can measure success for the whole effort. At one basic level, I point out, we have succeeded because the training groups have been able to create a functioning proof of concept and design and architecture for the implementation of the pilot web service in an eventual real-world SOA.

Beyond that, I continue, Titan has achieved some remarkable goals in just three months. The entire team has learned new skills, and even more important, have begun to work together in ways that bode well for the ultimate success of Titan's SOA. Whereas the former Hermes and Apollo people had been two separate, adversarial groups in the past, the training group process has succeeded in lowering many of these barriers to cooperation. Of course, there are still many challenges, but today, once the training period is over, we have a situation where everyone in the whole department is able to communicate openly with each other and discuss enterprise architecture issues with a common set of standards and a new sense of direction and purpose. I consider this achievement to be perhaps the most significant measure of success for the best practices training process. Titan is now ready to begin planning its SOA in earnest.

17.6 SUMMARY

Conducting a web service pilot project is an endeavor that should be viewed with an eye to the educational benefit of each activity involved. The actual web service and end results are, in most ways, less important than what your team learns from the process. In each phase, maximum effort should be exerted to teach the best practices issues to the people involved.

At Titan, the first decision that had to be made concerned the development platform that we will use for the pilot. After lengthy discussions of Java versus .NET, the training groups have decided to use both—by creating both a .NET and Java consuming application for a web service that they'll develop using a Java web services tool.

To select a web service for pilot development, we have returned to our earlier web service inventory and settled on the idea of doing a web service based on the "Get premium due" function that appears in many of Titan's billing and payment business processes. This service has many potential usage scenarios and a great deal of flexibility. In terms of the "report card," the "Get premium due" web service scores very high in all categories.

At the outset, though, the training groups have realized that building the web service and implementing it in a way that is secure and that accommodates Titan's security policies will be a challenge far greater than they have bargained for. The learning experience that has emerged from this discussion has yielded an opinion that Titan will need to install some type of SOA management and security system before it can proceed with the rollout of its first web service. Titan's architects' council is, in fact, looking into these kinds of systems at the same time. The training groups have decided to implement a simpler proof of concept version of the "Get premium due" web service as an alternative to contending with the complexity of a real-world implementation using an SOA management and security system. However, they also recognize that their proof of concept will never scale, having hard-coded security and management considerations into the endpoints, and their efforts to evaluate web services management and security products have intensified after this realization hit home.

We have developed the proof of concept using a process that forces each training group to work "blind." Each group has created a consumer for a web service developed by another group using only the WSDL that is published on the network. During this process the groups were not allowed to speak to each other, because we wanted them to experience true service-oriented development; they had to look up web services specifications and locations using WSDL and UDDI. Though this has proven to be challenging, the groups consider this highly educational.

To design the web service, the groups have also had to figure out how to handle the issue of "granularity"—how many different options and alternative use scenarios should the web service be designed to handle? A web service cannot handle every conceivable scenario, but ideally the service should optimize its reuse potential with the scope of its implementation. The groups have considered such issues as insurance policy number length, multiple premium categories such as monthly versus quarterly, and special cases such as refunds and late charges.

Ultimately, the pilot has been evaluated based on how much everyone learned by doing the work involved and how useful the final result would have been had it been architected in a scalable manner. As the end of the official best practices training period, we pronounced the pilot a success, and not just because the effort has produced software that works as intended. The bigger picture—that Titan's IT people are now working together in a new spirit of cooperation and speaking a common language of standards—has contributed to the sense that the effort has been well worth it.

CHAPTER 18

Plan and proceed

It has been almost six months since Jay and I had the famous "lunch that changed everything," as H.P. Wei likes to call it. Some less charitable employees within the group are known to have other terms of endearment for our path, such as the "lunch that —ed up my life," but they've eventually grown to appreciate the direction we've taken. With the pilot finished, Titan's IT department and leadership has changed most of its fundamental assumptions about application development and enterprise architecture planning. The changes that have taken place have been extraordinary, and most of the department staff members are in shock at how quickly they have all embraced what at first appeared to be a new approach. This "new approach" has eventually revealed itself to be remarkably similar to the previous strategies, only with standardization and reuse now prioritized. The Titan team is anxious to move on to the full-blown SOA planning stage and beyond.

18.1 Forming an SOA plan

You cannot create a successful SOA without a plan. Now, while that may seem obvious, you would be surprised how many large and otherwise well-run organizations approach SOA implementation without a thorough plan. It need not be some gigantic document that no one ever reads. A good SOA plan, regardless of its heft, takes several critical factors into consideration: requirements, existing technology, target architecture, migration plan, financial and resource allocation issues, and timeline.

18.1.1 Heavy lifting

In-depth planning for a real SOA requires a lot of work. As we review the full slate of activities in the planning stage, several of Titan's IT managers quickly realize that we are going to have to bring in some outside consultants to help with the "heavy lifting." Everyone already has a job to do, and we are looking at something like three thousand person-hours of work to complete an effective SOA plan.

H.P. Wei is not happy about this. "Why did they just go through that entire exercise in training if we're now just going to bring in more consultants?" he asks. You might be thinking the same thing. I reply, "It's a fair question, but I don't think one second of the team's time was wasted with the best practices training process. The team is better prepared for an SOA than they had been. If we hadn't done the training, whatever work the consultants did would have almost certainly failed. An organization has to prepare itself for an SOA, even if some of the detail work is done by others. Titan has to be, if nothing else, a highly educated consumer of web services technology and the SOA process." Wei is satisfied by this answer, though I think he's hoping to be able to complete the plan with in-house resources.

Working under the guidance of the architects' council, the consultants, headed by yours truly, begin an exhaustive series of audits in every area of Titan's business operations. Our team interviews dozens of Titan employees and managers in a business process audit that clarifies or restates every single business process that was originally under consideration at the time of the creation of Titan's IT wish list. We map the business processes, and discuss ways to improve their efficiency with Titan's department heads.

As we refine Titan's business process model, we are able to create a full-length requirements analysis. This document, which becomes the basis of Titan's SOA plan, states the functional requirements for each piece of software considered necessary in Titan's current and future IT architectures.

In addition, we conduct a detailed technology audit that maps Titan's complete IT infrastructure and systems. The goal is to develop a total view of the state of Titan's current IT operations, the business requirements for the SOA, and the "gaps" between the two. As we work on the "gap analysis" and other aspects of the SOA plan with the architects' council, it becomes apparent that Titan is going to have to make some big decisions early on about how it wants to proceed.

18.1.2 Making big decisions

Sun Tzu, the Chinese philosopher of war in the fifth century BC, once said, "If you strengthen everywhere, you will be weak everywhere." In addition to being a useful axiom for defeating enemy armies, this attitude is helpful in SOA planning. You cannot implement an SOA everywhere at once. To do so would result in a "weak" implementation overall—in addition to being prohibitively expensive and almost certain to fail technologically. It is far wiser, in my opinion, to proceed in distinct phases.

With this gradual approach in mind, Titan's first big decision is whether to develop the insurance policy section of the new SOA first and then proceed to the claims area, or attempt to do both at once. The answer lies partly in the return-on-investment (ROI) aspects of the decision.

Working closely with the business managers of the policy and claims operations, we are able to calculate basic ROI for each of the two initiatives. As shown in table 18.1, the policy initiative costs substantially more than the claims initiative. Remember that every company is different, and the cost estimates contained herein are theoretical. Your business may experience an SOA process that is a fraction of what I have shown here, or a great multiple thereof, depending on the size and complexity of your organization, as well as your needs. The point of the exercise is to demonstrate the ROI methodology. However, the policy initiative also has the potential to save Titan more money than the claims initiative, both in absolute terms and in relative ROI.

Table 18.1 Comparison of Return on Investment for the Policy SOA Initiative vs. the Claims SOA

Initiative	Hardware Costs	Software Costs	Outside Consultants	Internal Costs	Total Investment	Headcount Savings	Overhead Savings	Return on Investment
Policy SOA	$800,000	$1,250,000	$500,000	$800,000	$3,350,000	$900,000	$300,000	36%
Claims SOA	$600,000	$485,000	$300,000	$500,000	$1,885,000	$200,000	$150,000	18%

Further bolstering the momentum to implement the policy SOA initiative first is the decision by the architects' council to purchase a new policy management system from a new vendor. With the InsurTech mainframe facing obsolescence and the old Apollo systems considered to be inadequate to service Titan's entire policy underwriting operation, the council has spent several months looking at turnkey alternatives. After an exhaustive search, they've decided to go with a solution from PolicyWare, a best-of-breed solution favored by many insurers.

The clincher for PolicyWare was the announcement that its newest release (the one Titan will be purchasing) will offer many of its key functions as web services. PolicyWare, like many enterprise software makers, has realized that the market is heading toward the SOA and has acted accordingly. By buying the new PolicyWare system, Titan is accelerating its SOA implementation plan in one huge step. Luckily, the Titan IT organization is now fully ready to benefit from PolicyWare's newest web service software.

18.1.3 Forming the target architecture

With the PolicyWare purchase decision, Titan's target SOA architecture looks like the one depicted in figure 18.1. As the figure shows, Titan will be able to implement nearly complete SOA in the policy processing area. With the PolicyWare system offering web services for the policy functions needed by Titan's agents, employees, and policyholders, Titan plans to implement its company, agent, and customer portals and IVR systems as the front-end of the policy system. In the claims area, Titan will have to stick with the existing fat clients for the near term, though the company hopes to implement an SOA in claims processing within two years.

The target architecture represents our best guess at what Titan's enterprise architecture will look like when the first phase of the SOA—the policy system—is finished. I encourage Titan's people to keep in mind, however, that this architecture is going to be a work in progress. We need to create the target architecture so we'll know what we're working toward, but at the same time we have to understand that it's going to change over time.

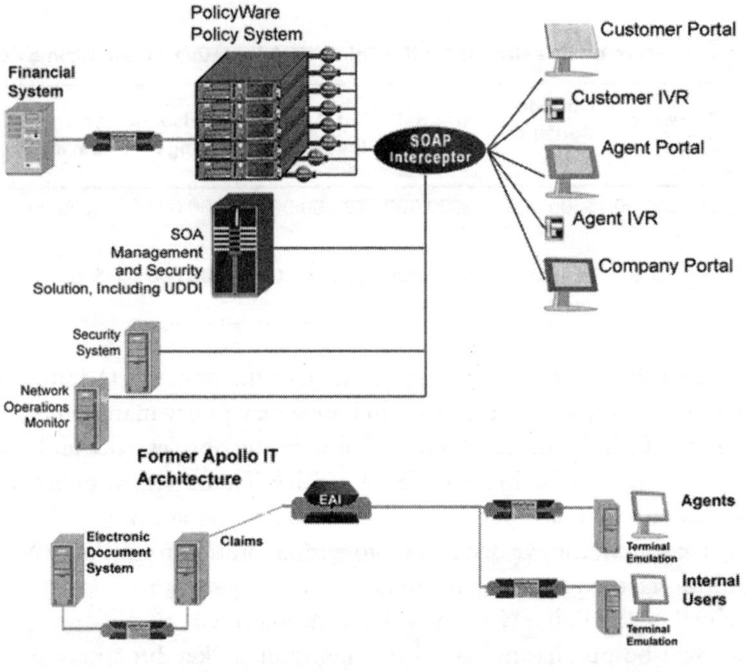

Figure 18.1 The target SOA for Titan Insurance calls for the installation of a new policy system that already features a web service. To ensure security and manageability, Titan plans to acquire a SOAP interception-based security and management solution that will connect with the company's existing security systems. In the near term, Titan has elected not to modify its claims system.

18.1.4 Migration plan

The process of taking Titan from where it currently stands to the first major step of its SOA, the implementation of the PolicyWare system, requires a detailed migration plan. As figure 18.2 shows, the migration calls for the elimination of a number of existing systems and the merging of several others. On the Hermes side, the IVR system, the web server, the agent and internal users' terminal emulation fat clients, the reporting system, and of course the InsurTech mainframe are all to be decommissioned. The Hermes finance system will become Titan's overall finance system, so data from the Apollo system has to be migrated into it.

On the Apollo side, the application server, IVR system, policy system, finance system, and data warehouse are all set to be decommissioned. In the case of the data warehouse, Titan decides to keep the database running "as is" in the near term in case management wants to use it to run research reports. However, it will cease to be a live part of the overall architecture. The EAI system module that connects Apollo's claims and policy systems is also to be eliminated. The old Hermes claims

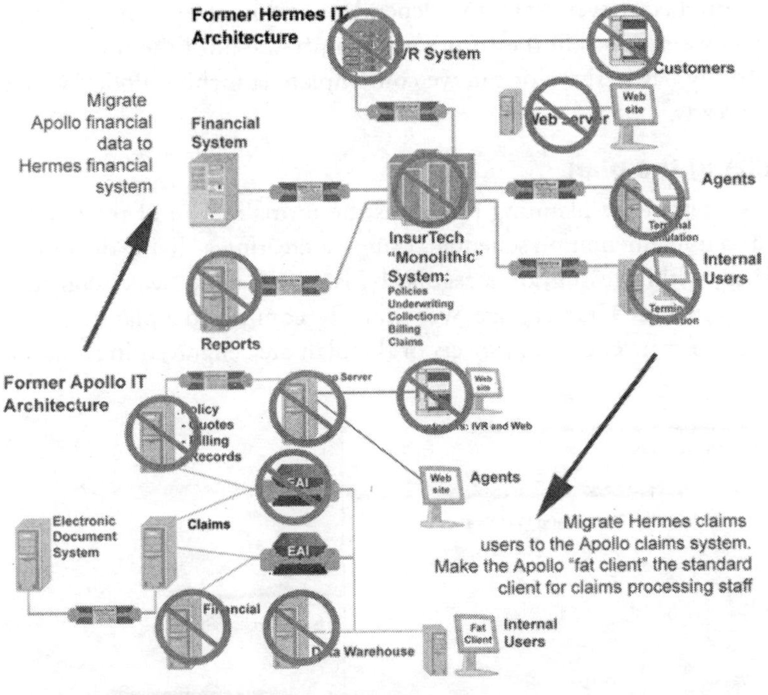

Figure 18.2 The migration plan calls for Titan to decommission many of its existing systems to make way for the new PolicyWare system and its related portals and IVR systems. At the same time, Titan will migrate the old Apollo finance system onto the Hermes finance system and also install the Apollo claims-processing client at the Hermes claims-processing department.

data, which currently resides on the InsurTech mainframe, is to be migrated to the Apollo policy system, which in turn will become Titan's complete claims-processing system, at least until a subsequent phase of SOA development that might replace or change it. The Hermes fat client used in claims processing is to be retired, and Hermes claims-processing staff will have the Apollo claims-processing client installed on their systems.

Now, while it may seem counterintuitive to do the work required to migrate those claims-processing clients from one company to another (remember, there were system incompatibilities that rendered the process fairly costly) the Titan folks have made the decision to do so because they realize they could not create web services in both claims and policies at the same time. Claims will have to wait, and in the meantime, claims processing still has to go on. As a result, even though it's not an ideal situation, Titan will go ahead with the migration of the Hermes claims department to the Apollo claims-processing client.

Ultimately, what we end up with is a highly detailed plan of action based on a "critical path" approach to project implementation (see figure 18.3). In the migration, a number of events are interdependent and have to be managed in parallel. For example, we cannot kill the InsurTech mainframe until the portals and IVR systems are working flawlessly. Nor can we contemplate launching PolicyWare until the portals are ready.

18.1.5 Finalizing the plan

The last step in the planning process is the formalization of the budget, staff allocation, and implementation schedule. I suggest creating a "living document" that can be modified, within reason, on a regular basis. As we all know, circumstances at a large company such as Titan change over time. To commit to a plan that's overly rigid is a mistake. Of course, certain aspects of the plan are "engraved in stone" and cannot be

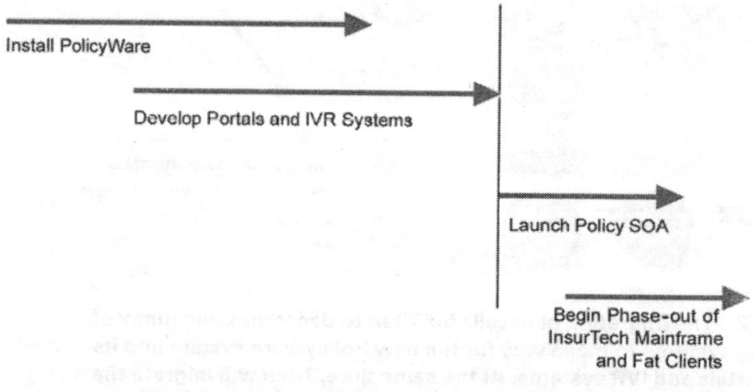

Figure 18.3 The migration plan for the policy system SOA has to follow a "critical path," shown here in simplified terms. The SOA cannot launch until the PolicyWare system is installed and the portals and IVR systems that will connect to it are working properly.

changed, such as the choice of PolicyWare for the policy system. Once that decision has been made, changing it mid-course would be complete folly. On other matters, though, such as portal design, we all agree to make the effort to design it right the first time around, but also to be open to changes as requirements may change in the course of business at Titan.

18.2 THE FOURTH P: PROCEED

With the SOA plan taking its final form and the migration plan ready to roll, Titan is ready to begin the fourth step in the SOA best practices: the fourth P—"proceed." Before we get started, though, I make a recommendation regarding organizational change to H.P. Wei. With Dot Bartlett having taken the lead early on in the whole SOA development process, I suggest that H.P. appoint her as Titan's chief enterprise architect. He agrees.

Proceeding with Titan's SOA is going to be, at the very least, a two-year project. In reality, though, it will be a permanent, ongoing effort of continual improvement. A jury-rigged SOA development team, with staff borrowed from other departments, won't work well at all. Titan needs a dedicated staff for the duration of the PolicyWare installation, at a minimum. After that, the IT department can begin to rotate people in and out as project scope dictates.

The project staff should consist of people from each of the major working groups in the former Apollo and Hermes IT departments. That way, there can be a consensus of views about how to proceed with the complex, interdependent, and multiphased migration plan and SOA development. We don't want to have a situation where old rivalries and affiliations will harm the progress of the SOA. Of course, we're taking a chance assuming that a heterogeneous group of IT staffers will work well together, but we feel that, given the success of the pilot experience, most of the people will get along fine. The bottom line is that the SOA needs a permanent organizational structure to make the implementation a success.

Dot Bartlett's most pressing order of business upon assuming her new role as Titan's chief enterprise architect is to decide on the development platform for the SOA. As we have discussed earlier, there are essentially two choices: Java or .NET. After extensive discussions with her team, as well as vendors, she elects to go with Java. Now, as you reading this you might be thinking, "Aha! The author is expressing a clear preference for Java over Microsoft." Not so. What I am saying is that, in Titan's case, there are some clear reasons why Java is the right choice. For one thing, it's likely that Titan is going to have to continue to be open to integrating various application servers and other pieces of software from IBM, BEA, and others. Java gives the Titan team more flexibility to do that, in their opinion.

Dot also has to choose an SOA management solution. In addition to needing such a solution to manage the web service traffic in her new SOA, Dot believes that the SOA management solution will be critical for measuring the performance of the SOA on an ongoing basis. Like many savvy corporate executives, she understands that, despite Titan's present commitment to the SOA, it is possible that the whole endeavor will be undermined subsequently if it is perceived that the SOA is not performing as promised. Thinking ahead, she wants to have a mechanism for measuring progress and performance so she can be confident that her SOA is delivering on its promises. After an exhaustive lab test, the Titan team elects to go with a web service management solution that functions on a SOAP interceptor model. They do this because, like the Java decision, it gives Titan the most flexibility moving forward to modify and expand the SOA without undue concern for management issues. The SOAP interceptor solution will scale and change with the SOA over time. While these solutions exist for both .NET and J2EE, the most widely deployed case studies to date favor the J2EE direction, with compatibility and support of .NET, over choosing a native .NET solution and having it manage J2EE application servers as well.

The implementation has begun according to plan, but Dot has the foresight to establish a structured review process to track the progress of the SOA initiative. At regular intervals—at first every two weeks and eventually once a month—the architects' council meets to review the progress being made on the SOA. They discuss problems and find resolutions that, in most cases, solve the issue at hand without offending anyone too badly. The meetings also serve as a forum for people to express opinions, both positive and negative, about the way things are going on the SOA. It has not always been an easy process, but the reviews create an environment where almost everyone feels that they are participating and receiving feedback. Dot has expressed to me that any stress stemming from the reviews is vastly preferable to the possibility that the SOA might suffer from internal sabotage or apathy.

I attend the review meetings regularly, and observe with pride that Titan's SOA is developing according to plan, and more or less without major problems. However, that all changes one day when I get a frantic phone call from Jay. At first I think he has suffered some immense personal tragedy, but as I manage to calm him down, I learn that the Titan SOA is in danger of being struck a death blow before it can even get up on its feet.

18.3 FACING DISASTER

The cause of Jay's panic is the announcement, made earlier in the day, that Titan is about to merge with Dominion Casualty, a giant insurance company located in the eastern United States. Dominion is a well-known "mainframe shop" with an IBM culture dating back to the 1960s. Jay and the others are convinced that their beloved SOA, in which they have now invested over a year, is going to be scrapped. However, as it turns out, their panic has been premature.

As the merger plans begin to solidify, it becomes increasingly clear that all of Titan's hard work on the SOA will pay off in unexpected ways. Instead of Dominion charging in to take over the Titan IT department and destroy the SOA, it is actually the Titan team that is viewed as having the superior plan to move forward.

It turns out that the Dominion people have been eager to begin exposing their mainframe legacy systems to web services, but they had not yet begun the process of SOA design and implementation. The Titan team, with its now vast knowledge of SOAs, is able to take the lead in forming a reasonable integration plan that will connect Dominion's legacy systems to the emerging Titan SOA. As this reality sinks in, we all breathe a great sigh of relief and continue with our work of building a truly great SOA for Titan. Disaster has been averted, and the value of everyone's hard work is now being recognized throughout the organization. In fact, had it not been for the SOA initiative it is quite possible that Dominion's IT staff would have emerged as the surviving team rather than Titan's.

18.4 SUMMARY

The two final steps of the "four P's" best practices approach to SOA development, plan and proceed, involve extensive, detailed work. To help with the "heavy lifting" of building a full SOA requirements document for the whole organization, Titan had to bring in some outside consultants. Although this may seem counterintuitive given the amount of time that the company has just invested in training its people, it actually makes perfect sense. If the consultants had come in to help develop the SOA, and the Titan people had not been trained, the effort would surely have failed. This way, the Titan people know what they want from the consultants and the planning project has been a success.

Once the consultants created the requirements document, the planning stage involved several steps. The most critical has been a decision to purchase a completely new policy system from a company called PolicyWare. The great appeal of the newest version of PolicyWare is that it exposes almost all of its software functionality as web services. PolicyWare creates a huge chunk of Titan's SOA right out of the box. The Titan team will only have to build the portals and IVR systems that connect to it.

At the same time, Titan has had to make a choice about what to do with its claims-processing systems in the short term. It made little sense to try to migrate both the policy and claims systems to an SOA at the same time. An ROI analysis revealed the policy system migration to be a better bet financially in terms of both absolute dollars saved and ROI.

Before formalizing its SOA implementation plan, Titan has had to form a migration plan and target architecture. Using a multiphased "critical path" approach, the Titan team has laid out how they will gradually phase out existing systems in the policy area as the new PolicyWare-based SOA comes online. The migration plan also calls for the claims and finance systems of the company to be migrated so that only one system remains for each function.

Before proceeding with the SOA implementation, Titan has decided to make some permanent organizational changes in its IT department. Dot Bartlett, who had led most of the SOA development work, has been appointed chief enterprise architect, a position that enables her to manage the SOA implementation as the effective boss of the entire endeavor. Her first major decision has been to move forward with a Java-based SOA development environment and a SOAP interceptor-based SOA management solution that can both manage the SOA and monitor its performance as a way to ensure that the initiative is delivering on its promises. This solution also helps Titan establish basic SLAs around services and ensure quality of service to consumers that promote reuse. Lastly, the solution allows Titan to leverage its existing identity systems to ensure proper authentication and authorization of the applications attempting to access the services once deployed. In addition, Titan's IT leadership has established a formal review process for the SOA so they can monitor its progress and resolve any conflicts that emerge.

Looking ahead

This is a very exciting time to be involved in enterprise information technology. The service-oriented architecture, long a dream of many in the IT field, is becoming a reality at a pace that few anticipated just a few years ago. Even in the time that it has taken to write this book, striking changes have taken place in the SOA landscape. When I first contemplated writing this book, I was confident that I would have to explain what an SOA was to most IT executives I met. Now, I can be confident that they already know.

Seventy percent of Fortune 500 companies are conducting web services pilots, or even rolling web services out into production. Thousands of other businesses and Internet-based organizations are using web services as a standard way of designing software applications. The progress made in just one or two years has been staggering. In a few years' time, any companies not actively using web services to improve their business efficiency will be in the minority.

To be sure, many challenges loom ahead. The standards bodies continue to grapple with conflicts over standards, and the subtle creep of "proprietary standards" always seems to be lurking in the shadows, threatening to spoil the truly revolutionary nature of what we are trying to accomplish. I have much faith, though, that true open standards will prevail. The stakes are too high, and the promise—which we have all seen now with our own eyes—is too great to compromise. The shift is too significant now to be thwarted by any one company, even the global players. Those companies that consider themselves entitled to step out of the standards process may find themselves penalized by doing so.

The exercise of writing this book has also given me a lot of insight into a number of issues that I once took for granted in my software development and entrepreneurial background. Most significantly, perhaps, is the confirmation that web services and SOA development are integral to an overall business design process. There can be no effective SOA without a solid business management vision to back it up. Unlike most other IT innovations, the SOA forces business management and IT to work together in true partnership.

The years ahead in the SOA field promise to be exciting and challenging. I hope that this book has helped you attain a solid, pragmatic perspective on the technological and managerial issues that must be addressed to develop a successful SOA. If I have succeeded, then you will likely have many more questions than you did when you started reading. The SOA is a new opportunity but an old concept—as old as software itself: build once and reuse across the enterprise and among partners. It has been a great pleasure sharing my experiences, knowledge, and insights with you. I wish you the best of luck in all of your IT and business management endeavors.

index

Numerics

A

B

C